Governmental Accounting

Steven M. Bragg

For more information about AccountingTools® products, visit our Web site at www.accountingtools.com.

ISBN-13: 978-1-938910-83-8

Printed in the United States of America

Table of Contents

Preface

Governmental accounting differs significantly from the accounting used by other organizations, since the focus is on the provision of services, rather than earning a profit. Because of this change in focus, governments use funds to maintain better control of costs, while also formatting their financial statements differently and using a different basis of accounting. *Governmental Accounting* explains the intricacies of these differences, covering fund accounting, budgetary accounting, the comprehensive annual financial report, and much more.

The book is divided into three sections. In Chapters 1 through 7, we cover the underpinnings of governmental accounting, including such topics as funds, the basis of accounting, the measurement focus, and common accounting transactions. In Chapters 8 through 17, we address every aspect of financial reporting, including the comprehensive annual financial report, budgetary reporting, and the statistical section. In Chapters 18 through 21, we address more specific accounting issues, including claims accounting, landfill closure and postclosure costs, and nonexchange transactions.

You can find the answers to many questions about governmental accounting in the following chapters, including:

- Who formulates governmental accounting standards?
- What are the different types of funds and how are they used?
- How does the measurement focus impact financial reporting?
- How do I depreciate capital assets?
- How do I account for debt service activity?
- How do I account for encumbrances?
- How do I report the results and financial position of a component unit?
- What are the contents of a comprehensive annual financial report?
- What information must be included in the notes to the financial statements?
- How should a budgetary comparison schedule be structured?
- What are the four types of nonexchange transactions and how do I account for each one?

Governmental Accounting is designed for professionals and students, who can use it as a reference tool for recording governmental accounting transactions and generating financial statements.

Centennial, Colorado
March 2017

About the Author

Steven Bragg, CPA, has been the chief financial officer or controller of four companies, as well as a consulting manager at Ernst & Young. He received a master's degree in finance from Bentley College, an MBA from Babson College, and a Bachelor's degree in Economics from the University of Maine. He has been a two-time president of the Colorado Mountain Club and is an avid alpine skier, mountain biker, and certified master diver. Mr. Bragg resides in Centennial, Colorado. He has written the following books and courses:

7 Habits of Effective CFOs
7 Habits of Effective Controllers
Accountant Ethics [for multiple states]
Accountants' Guidebook
Accounting Changes and Error Corrections
Accounting Controls Guidebook
Accounting for Casinos and Gaming
Accounting for Derivatives and Hedges
Accounting for Earnings per Share
Accounting for Inventory
Accounting for Investments
Accounting for Intangible Assets
Accounting for Leases
Accounting for Managers
Accounting for Stock-Based Compensation
Accounting Procedures Guidebook
Agricultural Accounting
Behavioral Ethics
Bookkeeping Guidebook
Budgeting
Business Combinations and Consolidations
Business Insurance Fundamentals
Business Ratios
Business Valuation
Capital Budgeting
CFO Guidebook
Change Management
Closing the Books
Coaching and Mentoring
Constraint Management
Construction Accounting
Corporate Cash Management
Corporate Finance
Cost Accounting (college textbook)
Cost Accounting Fundamentals
Cost Management Guidebook
Credit & Collection Guidebook
Developing and Managing Teams
Employee Onboarding

Enterprise Risk Management
Fair Value Accounting
Financial Analysis
Financial Forecasting and Modeling
Fixed Asset Accounting
Foreign Currency Accounting
Fraud Examination
GAAP Guidebook
Governmental Accounting
Hospitality Accounting
How to Run a Meeting
Human Resources Guidebook
IFRS Guidebook
Interpretation of Financial Statements
Inventory Management
Investor Relations Guidebook
Lean Accounting Guidebook
Mergers & Acquisitions
Negotiation
New Controller Guidebook
Nonprofit Accounting
Partnership Accounting
Payables Management
Payroll Management
Project Accounting
Project Management
Public Company Accounting
Purchasing Guidebook
Real Estate Accounting
Records Management
Recruiting and Hiring
Revenue Recognition
Sales and Use Tax Accounting
The MBA Guidebook
The Soft Close
The Statement of Cash Flows
The Year-End Close
Treasurer's Guidebook
Working Capital Management

On-Line Resources by Steven Bragg

Steven maintains the accountingtools.com web site, which contains continuing professional education courses, the Accounting Best Practices podcast, and hundreds of articles on accounting subjects.

Governmental Accounting is also available as a continuing professional education (CPE) course. You can purchase the course (and many other courses) and take an on-line exam at:

www.accountingtools.com/cpe

Chapter 1
Governmental Accounting Overview

Introduction

Governmental accounting differs significantly from the accounting used by business-oriented organizations, because governments are structured to have different priorities than earning a profit. Instead, they are supposed to provide services to their citizens in a cost-effective manner. Also, the amount of cash that governments can use to provide those services is strictly limited by legislative mandate. Consequently, the governmental accounting system is structured to maintain tight control over resources, while also compartmentalizing activities into different funds in order to clarify how resources are being directed at various programs.

In this chapter, we give an overview of governmental accounting by focusing on the sources and applicability of governmental accounting standards, as well as the types of funds, accounts, and reporting requirements that are associated with a governmental accounting system.

Sources of Governmental Accounting Standards

Given the unique needs of governments, a different set of accounting standards has been developed for these organizations. The primary organization that is responsible for creating and updating these standards is the Governmental Accounting Standards Board (GASB), which is the successor of the National Council on Governmental Accounting (NCGA). The GASB is tasked with the development of accounting and financial reporting standards for state and local governments, while the Financial Accounting Standards Board (FASB) has the same responsibility, but for all other entities not related to governmental activities.

In this book, we summarize the accounting and financial reporting standards for governments. These standards are considered to be generally accepted accounting principles, but only in regard to their use by governmental entities. Thus, the contents of this book can be referred to as "GAAP for Governments." Generally Accepted Accounting Principles (GAAP) are a cluster of accounting standards and common industry usage that have been developed over many years. It is used by organizations to:

- Properly organize their financial information into accounting records;
- Summarize the accounting records into financial statements; and
- Disclose certain supporting information.

By adhering to GAAP, all government entities are able to issue financial statements that are formatted the same and which contain the same types of disclosures. Without GAAP, these financial statements would not be comparable. Consequently, every government entity must be in compliance with GAAP.

Information Sources

The accounting and reporting standards that are used by state and local governments come from the following sources:

- Statements of the GASB
- Interpretations of the GASB
- Technical Bulletins of the GASB
- Implementation Guides of the GASB
- Concept Statements of the GASB
- Statements of the National Council on Governmental Accounting (NCGA)
- Interpretations of the NCGA
- Industry Audit Guide of the American Institute of Certified Public Accountants, Audits of State and Local Governmental Units
- Additional AICPA[1] literature that has been cleared by the GASB

The aggregated accounting and reporting standards have been organized by the GASB into a centralized codification, which is organized into the following five parts:

1. General Principles
2. Financial Reporting
3. Measurement
4. Specific Balance Sheet and Operating Statement Items
5. Stand-Alone Reporting – Specialized Units and Activities

These accounting and reporting standards are summarized into many of the following chapters. The layout and chapter titles of the following chapters have been structured to roughly match the table of contents of the official codification of the governmental accounting and financial reporting standards. By organizing the book in this way, it is easier for the reader to refer back to the original codification for additional information.

Application of Governmental Accounting Standards

Entities that are subject to governmental accounting standards are those that have at least one of the following characteristics:

- The officers are appointed by popular election.

---

[1] The American Institute of Certified Public Accountants

- A controlling majority of the governing body is appointed by state or local governments.
- A government can unilaterally dissolve the entity, with its net assets reverting to the government.
- The entity has the power to both enact and enforce a tax levy.
- The entity can issue debt that pays interest that is exempt from federal taxation, plus at least one of the preceding characteristics.

Examples of these entities are school districts, public hospitals, public employee retirement systems, water and sewer authorities, airport authorities, and public-sector universities.

The federal government and nonprofit organizations are not considered to be within the scope of governmental accounting. For more information about the accounting for nonprofits, see the author's *Nonprofit Accounting* book.

Legal Provisions

In addition to GAAP, the financial operations of a government entity may be governed by a number of legal provisions. For example, statutes may specify methods of collection, delinquency dates, and tax rate limits. A key legal document is the approved operating budget, which sets not-to-exceed limits on expenditures. These legal provisions may mandate that the accounting system be altered to ensure that the provisions are complied with, and that the system reports the information required by the law.

EXAMPLE

The legislature of a state passes a law, requiring that all gasoline taxes be separately accounted for in a highway construction fund, and that these funds be used solely for capital expenditures on highways. The state's accounting system must be able to store the tax proceeds in this manner and report on how the funds were subsequently used.

Some legal provisions to which a government is subjected may conflict with GAAP. For example, there may be a statutory requirement that a specific fund be accounted for using the cash basis of accounting, even though GAAP requires that the accrual basis be used. When these conflicts exist, it is not necessary to maintain two entirely separate sets of books to be in compliance with both GAAP and the law. Instead, maintain the baseline system so that it complies with the law, and layer on additional reports to bring the entity's reporting into compliance with GAAP.

In order to be in compliance with GAAP, a government entity should disclose any significant violations by the entity of any legal or contractual provisions, as well as any actions taken to address those violations. In those cases in which adherence to GAAP does not result in sufficient compliance with legal requirements, additional reporting should be made by the entity to bring it into compliance.

Goals of a Governmental Accounting System

A governmental accounting system must be able to meet the following goals:

- To present fairly the funds and activities of the entity in conformity with GAAP, with full disclosure; and
- To ascertain and show compliance with legal and contractual provisions that are finance-related.

Fund Accounting Systems

A governmental accounting system should be organized on a fund basis. Fund accounting is usually required by law as a method for controlling the use of resources. The fund is the most important element of a governmental system. It is defined as follows:

> A fund is an entity with its own set of accounts, which are segregated in order to carry on specific activities or attain certain objectives.

The financial statements of a number of funds can be included in the reporting for a primary government, of which the funds are a constituent part.

There are several types of funds that may be operated and reported on by a government entity. The key types are as follows:

- Governmental funds

  - General fund
  - Capital projects funds
  - Debt service funds
  - Permanent funds
  - Special revenue funds

- Proprietary funds

  - Enterprise funds
  - Internal service funds

- Fiduciary funds

  - Agency funds
  - Investment trust funds
  - Pension trust funds
  - Private-purpose trust funds

We cover funds in much more detail in the next chapter, Fund Accounting.

Note: A government should attempt to minimize the number of funds it uses, since each incremental addition increases the level of complexity that the accountant must deal with.

Types of Assets

Within each fund, governmental accounting focuses on assets and liabilities. Assets are defined as resources controlled by a government. The most common classifications within which assets are reported are as follows:

- *Cash.* This is the funds currently stored in a government's bank accounts, as well as any cash stored by the government. This usually means that cash includes the amounts in all demand deposit accounts, as well as all petty cash balances. It does not include cash that has been restricted for any reason.
- *Cash equivalents.* This is short-term, highly liquid investments that are easily convertible into known amounts of cash, and which are so close to their maturities that there is a minimal risk of a change in value due to variations in interest rates. Examples of cash equivalents are money market funds and commercial paper.
- *Investments.* Investments are payments made to acquire the securities of other entities in order to gain a return. For a government, investments are likely to be debt or equity securities, as well as mutual funds and money market investments.
- *Taxes receivable.* This includes any type of tax owed to a government, such as property taxes and sales taxes.
- *Accounts receivable.* This includes funds owed to a government by third parties because of goods sold or services provided to these parties. For example, a water utility bills its customers; all unpaid bills are classified as accounts receivable.
- *Prepaid expenses.* This includes payments for services that will be received in the future, such as insurance payments that cover future periods.
- *Inventory.* This includes all goods being offered for sale. For example, a government-run medical dispensary maintains an inventory of medications.
- *Capital assets.* This includes all long-lived assets owned by a government. Examples of capital assets are buildings, land, office equipment, and vehicles.
- *Intangible assets.* This includes all non-tangible assets that have useful lives extending over more than one reporting period. Examples of these assets are easements, trademarks, and water rights.

Types of Liabilities

A liability is defined as a legally binding obligation payable to another entity. The most common classifications within which liabilities are reported are as follows:

- *Accounts payable.* This includes all bills received by a government that have not yet been paid. For example, a utility bill is received near month-end but is not due for payment until the following month, so it is classified as an account payable until it is paid.

- *Accrued expenses.* This includes all expenses that have been incurred, but for which no supplier invoice has yet been received. For example, a government receives supplies near month-end, but has not yet received the related supplier invoice, so the expense is accrued for the purpose of preparing month-end financial statements, after which the accrual is replaced by recording the actual supplier invoice.
- *Debt.* This includes all types of obligations that a government has entered into in order to borrow money. For example, there may have been a bond issuance to pay for a capital asset construction project.

Budget Issues

Every governmental unit should adopt an annual budget. A budget is a type of control that has the force of law, since it is subject to the approval of the legislative branch of the applicable government. The individuals managing a governmental unit conduct their activities based on the expenditure levels authorized in the budget.

This budget is incorporated into the accounting system. The accounting system then provides the basis for an appropriate level of budgetary control, which includes budgetary comparisons that are presented for the general fund as well as for each major special revenue fund for which there is a legally adopted annual budget (the types of funds are covered in the next chapter). The ability of the management team to adhere to the budget can then be used as a component of their ongoing performance evaluations.

Financial Reports

A government should follow these guidelines in regard to its financial statement reporting:

- *Interim reports.* A government should prepare interim financial statements and reports to assist management in its control of financial operations, as well as for legislative oversight purposes and external reporting.
- *Annual report.* A government should prepare a comprehensive annual financial report, covering all funds and activities of the primary government, including an overview of all separately-presented component units of the reporting entity. This overview should include an introduction, management's discussion and analysis (MD&A), basic financial statements, required supplementary information, fund statements, schedules, narrative explanations, and a statistics section.
- *Minimum requirements.* The minimum requirements for the annual report are the MD&A, required supplementary materials other than MD&A, and the financial statements, which include the following:
  - Government-wide financial statements
  - Fund financial statements
  - Notes to the financial statements

- *Organizational inclusions.* Management can include an organization in the financial reporting of a primary government, even if the inclusion does not meet the financial accountability criteria for doing so, if the inclusion prevents the reporting entity's financial statements from being misleading.

Summary

In this chapter, we provided an overview of the reasons why governmental accounting varies from other types of accounting, the sources of governmental accounting standards, and the types of funds, accounts, and reports that are used in an accounting system. In the following chapters, we delve into governmental accounting in much greater detail. The most essential chapters needed for a basic understanding of governmental accounting are the next two chapters. In the following Fund Accounting chapter, we address the different types of funds and how they are used. The Basis of Accounting and Measurement Focus chapter covers the modified accrual basis of accounting and the measurement focus, which are concepts unique to governmental accounting. The reader should have a thorough understanding of the information in these next two chapters before delving into the more specific accounting and reporting topics addressed in later chapters.

Chapter 2
Fund Accounting

Introduction

A governmental accounting system is organized on a fund basis; doing so makes it easier to maintain control over resources while also compartmentalizing activities to clarify how resources are being directed at various programs. This chapter discusses the nature of a fund and summarizes the different types of funds, along with several related topics.

Fund Accounting Overview

It is essential for many government entities to track funding sources and uses for specific activities, rather than for the entity as a whole. To do so, a fund is created for each of these activities, containing its own assets and liabilities. These funds can then be combined to arrive at the financial statements for the government entity as a whole. There are several types of funds that a government can use; they are noted in the following sub-sections. A government should report these funds to the extent that there are activities that meet the criteria for the funds.

Definition of a Fund

A *fund* is an accounting entity with a self-balancing set of accounts that is used to record financial resources and liabilities, as well as operating activities, and which is segregated in order to carry on certain activities or attain targeted objectives. A fund is not a separate legal entity.

Funds are used by governments because governments need to maintain very tight control over their resources, and funds are designed to monitor resource inflows and outflows, with particular attention to the remaining amount of funds available. By segregating resources into multiple funds, a government can more closely monitor resource usage, thereby minimizing the risk of overspending or of spending in areas not authorized by a government budget.

Governmental Funds

The governmental fund is the default fund to be used to account for all activities of a government, except for those required to be accounted for in a different fund. Thus, the governmental fund is a government's primary operating fund.

The governmental fund has a budgetary orientation, with a particular emphasis on the sources, uses, and remaining balances of funds. Financial resources are segregated into separate funds for tracking purposes. The residual fund balance in a governmental fund is the difference between fund assets and deferred resource outflows, and liabilities and deferred resource inflows.

When financial statements are prepared for governmental funds, they are presented using the current financial resources measurement and the modified accrual basis of accounting (as discussed in the next chapter). The main consideration when accounting for governmental funds is to measure the financial position of the fund and its changes in financial position. The required financial statements for a governmental fund are as follows:

- Balance sheet
- Statement of revenues, expenditures, and changes in fund balances
- Supplemental reporting schedules as needed

The governmental fund category includes the following funds:

- *Capital projects funds*. Used to account for financial resources that have been set aside for capital outlays (usually major outlays). There is no requirement to use this type of fund. If a government decides to do so, another decision is whether to use a single capital projects fund for all capital projects, or to use a separate fund for each one. Capital projects funds should not be used when accounting for assets held in trust for individuals, other governments, or private organizations.
- *Debt service funds*. Used to account for financial resources that have been set aside to pay for principal and interest. The use of this fund may be required by a government's bond indentures. When there are debt service transactions associated with a special assessment for which there is no government obligation, the resources are instead accounted for in an agency fund.
- *General fund*. Used to account for all financial resources not being reported in any other fund. This is the chief operating fund of a government; a government is only allowed to use one general fund.
- *Permanent funds*. Used to account for financial resources for which only the earnings can be used for the support of government programs. This type of fund would typically be used when a government receives an endowment. Permanent funds should not be used in place of private-purpose trust funds, where resources are being used for the benefit of individuals, other governments, or private organizations.
- *Special revenue funds*. Used to account for the proceeds from targeted revenue sources for which there is a commitment for expenditures other than capital projects or debt service. A common application is the proceeds from grants, since these revenues must be used for specific types of expenditures. The targeted revenue sources could be assigned directly to a special revenue fund, or are allocated to it from another fund. The revenue sources are recognized as special revenue when they arrive in the special revenue fund from which they will be expended. The use of this type of fund is not required unless there is a legal mandate for it. Special revenue funds should

not be used when accounting for assets held in trust for individuals, other governments, or private organizations.

EXAMPLE

The City of Abalone charges a per-event landing fee at its municipal airport. The fee is restricted by legislation to be used for airport activities. Airport activities, as defined in the legislation, include capital projects and operational expenditures. Airport costs are not expected to be fully recovered through the fee, because about 30% of the costs will be supported by a general fund transfer. A special revenue fund can be used to account for these fees, rather than a capital projects fund, since use of the funds is not restricted to capital outlays.

EXAMPLE

The legislature of a state government passes legislation that mandates the creation of a fund to track financial resources for which a portion is to be maintained as a minimum fund balance. Since a portion of the fund balance is considered to be permanently invested while the remaining funds are to be spent, the fund type can be either a permanent fund or a special revenue fund.

EXAMPLE

A state government has a revenue-sharing arrangement for the use of state-owned land, where the government receives a usage royalty. Of the amount received, 75% is directed toward the funding of affordable housing initiatives, while 25% is held in trust for a third party land conservation fund. In this situation, two separate funds may be used to store the incoming funds, or the entire amount can be stored in a single special revenue fund. In the latter case, the government should report a liability for those royalties held in trust for the land conservation fund. The remainder of the fund should be designated as restricted, because it is reserved for the funding of affordable housing.

EXAMPLE

A state government passes legislation that allows for the periodic transfer of funds from the general fund to a different fund that is designed for a specific purpose. The receiving fund should not be designated as a special revenue fund, since the transfer of funds is not considered revenue. However, if there are also substantial restricted or committed revenues in the fund, it can be designated as a special revenue fund.

EXAMPLE

Shell City levies several types of property taxes, each of which can only be used in a certain way. All property taxes are received into Shell's general fund, where they are recognized as "payable to other funds," rather than as general fund revenue. The funds are then distributed to other funds, where they will be expended in accordance with the operating instructions for each fund. These distributions are classified as restricted revenues by the receiving funds, since they were not recognized as revenue by the general fund.

Proprietary Funds

Proprietary funds are used to account for the business-type activities of a government. These funds emphasize operating income, financial position, changes in net position, and cash flows. When financial statements are prepared for proprietary funds, they are presented using the economic resources measurement focus and the accrual basis of accounting (as discussed in the next chapter). This is the same approach used by commercial organizations, so revenues are recognized when earned and expenses are recognized when a liability is incurred. This means that depreciation expense is charged to expense in the financial statements of a proprietary fund, as are expenses related to longer-term liabilities, such as landfill liabilities and accrued interest expense. Also, a proprietary fund records and reports long-term debt, such as bonds payable. The required financial statements are as follows:

- Statement of net position
- Statement of revenues, expenses, and changes in fund net position

The proprietary funds category includes the following funds:

- *Enterprise funds.* These funds are used to account for any activity for which external users are charged a fee for goods and services, even when the government subsidizes a portion of the activity's costs. An enterprise fund may be used to issue bonds, so that the revenue stream of user fees being collected by the fund can be pledged to the associated debt service. A government may want to set up an enterprise fund just so that it will have information about the total cost of providing a service. State unemployment compensation funds and public entity risk pools must be reported in enterprise funds. An activity must be reported in an enterprise fund under any of the following circumstances:

  - The activity is funded with debt that is only secured by a pledge of the net proceeds from the activity.
  - The activity's service provision costs must be recovered with fees, as stipulated by laws and regulations.
  - The activity's pricing policy is designed to recover its costs.

- *Internal service funds.* These funds are used to account for activities that provide goods or services to other funds, as well as departments or agencies of the primary government, or to other government entities on a cost-reimbursement basis. This fund should only be used when the reporting government is the primary participant in the activity. When this is not the case, set up an enterprise fund instead. There is no GAAP requirement to use internal service funds. If internal service funds are to be used, it is easier to track information about the services being provided if a separate internal service fund is maintained for each one. For example, there could be separate internal service funds for data processing, printing services, and purchasing. These funds are generally assumed to operate on a breakeven basis, so any ongoing fund surpluses or deficits might indicate the need to adjust the internal prices being charged to recipients.

> **Note:** there is no clear definition of a "primary participant" in an internal service fund. When the situation is not clear, consider whether the fund's primary purpose is to serve the government or to provide goods and services (and charge a fee for doing so).

EXAMPLE

A state government operates an enterprise fund for its lottery operations. The fund is used to account for the ongoing operation of the lottery, including the distribution of net lottery proceeds to other state funds, as mandated by existing legislation. The lottery fund recognizes revenue and reports distributions to other funds as transfers. The receiving funds cannot report revenue, since revenue has already been recognized by the lottery fund.

EXAMPLE

Helix City's water and sewer operation is governed by an annual operating budget in which fees are set at a level sufficient to fully recover all budgeted costs, as well as the depreciation on related assets. Since the costs of the water and sewer operations are recovered with fees, the related accounting should be for an enterprise fund.

EXAMPLE

Mollusk City manages its own utilities, with separate operations for the provision of electricity and water and sewer services. Each of these operations has separately issued bonds that are to be repaid solely from their revenues. It is not necessary to create and manage separate enterprise funds for each of these operations, only that an enterprise fund must be used to report the activities of the operations.

EXAMPLE

A state government issues revenue bonds for a highways fund. The operating revenues of the fund are pledged as security for the bonds. However, the effective interest rate investors are willing to pay under this arrangement is relatively high, so the legislature elects to reduce the risk of the bonds by backing them with its full faith and credit. There is little chance that the government will be required to use its general funds to service the debt. In this situation, the highways fund can be structured as an enterprise fund, but there is no requirement to do so, since the bonds are not secured solely by the revenues of the highways fund.

A few other accounting issues related to proprietary funds are noted in the following bullet points:

- *Capital contributions.* A proprietary fund may receive capital contributions. These contributions appear on the statement of revenues, expenses, and changes in net position, after operating revenues and expenses.
- *Debt.* When debt is issued by a proprietary fund or is issued by the general government for the purposes of the proprietary fund, and the debt will be repaid by the fund, the associated long-term liability is also recorded within the fund.
- *Deposits.* Customers of an enterprise fund may be required to pay a deposit when they first sign up for service. These deposits are to be classified as a current liability of the fund.
- *Duplicate transactions.* An internal services fund records revenue when it charges other funds for its services, while the receiving funds record an expenditure or expense. This means that additional revenue and expense (or expenditure) is being recorded internally by a government. When the accountant creates government-wide financial statements, these duplicate transactions must be removed.

Fiduciary Funds

Fiduciary funds are used to report on assets held in trust for others. In this type of fund, the reporting emphasis is on net position and changes in net position. When financial statements are prepared for fiduciary funds, they are presented using the economic resources measurement focus and the accrual basis of accounting (as discussed in the next chapter). The required financial statements for a fiduciary fund are as follows:

- Statement of fiduciary net position
- Statement of changes in fiduciary net position

The fiduciary funds category includes the following funds:

- *Agency funds.* Used to report on resources held in a custodial capacity, where funds are received, temporarily invested, and remitted to other parties. For example, an agency fund may be used when a government collects taxes on behalf of another government.
- *Investment trust funds.* Used to report the external portion of an investment pool that is reported by the sponsoring government.
- *Pension and employee benefit trust funds.* Used to report on assets held in trust for pension plans, other postemployment benefit plans, and employee benefit plans.
- *Private-purpose trust funds.* Used to report on trust arrangements where individuals, private organizations, and other governments are the beneficiaries. This type of fund should not be used to account for any grant programs that support a government's own activities.

The following best practices apply to the administration of funds:

- There should only be one general fund, which is the main operating fund of the reporting entity.
- Favor using the general fund over other funds where possible.
- A smaller entity may not require any internal service funds.
- Avoid the use of special revenue funds unless there is a legal mandate to do so.

EXAMPLE

A state government collects escheat property. Escheat involves the transfer of title or property to the government when an individual dies with no heirs. Escheat is typically on a revocable basis, so that ownership will revert to any rightful heirs that may eventually appear. If the intent is to hold these amounts for claimants, a private-purpose trust fund is used. Or, a governmental or proprietary fund can be used to account for this property, incorporating liabilities for those amounts expected to be paid to claimants or other government entities. Yet a third option is to use an agency fund, which is appropriate when the amounts are to be held for other governments.

Fund Contents

Each fund must include a set of self-balancing accounts that addresses the needs for which the fund was created. The accounts included in a fund should address all of the following:

- Assets
- Liabilities
- Net assets
- Revenues
- Expenditures or expenses
- Transfers

The requirement to have a complete set of accounts in a fund does not mean that the identified assets and liabilities must be physically segregated.

Note: It is not necessary to have a separate bank account for each fund, unless required by law or a bond indenture.

Interfund Loans

Loans may be used to transfer funds from one fund to another. When such a loan occurs, the amounts loaned to or received from other funds should be stated in the fund accounts as receivables or payables. In cases where there are offsetting loans between funds, they are not to be netted for reporting purposes. Instead, they should be reported separately as payables and receivables. However, it is acceptable to net offsetting loans for reporting purposes when they are current amounts.

Evaluation Periods

The typical fund is planned for and evaluated on an annual basis, especially if it is funded by an annual appropriation. This means that all proprietary and fiduciary funds, as well as most governmental funds, are classified as period-oriented funds. However, capital projects funds are typically planned and evaluated over the term of the associated projects, which may extend over several years. This means that capital projects funds should be structured to report on total resources and expenditures to date, even if the term extends through several fiscal years. When dealing with these project-oriented funds, the accountant should also report on fund transactions within the current fiscal year and the financial position of the fund at the end of the current fiscal year.

Special Questions Related to Funds

In this section, we make note of several special situations related to how financial resources are accounted for in various types of funds. They are as follows:

- *Administration costs.* The administration costs for a state's unemployment compensation enterprise fund should be included in the general fund, unless there is a legal requirement to do otherwise. The reasoning is that unemployment charges are not designed to recover administrative costs.
- *Debt service fund usage.* It is not necessary to create a debt service fund whenever there is debt service activity, especially when the debt service is only in the current fiscal year. The use of such a fund is only necessary when legally mandated, or when funds are being accumulated for principal and interest payments occurring in later years.
- *Expenditures for small capital items.* When a government wants to expend funds for items that are capital in nature but which are too small to be accounted for as capital assets, the expenditures can still be made from a capital projects fund.
- *Unused appropriations.* A parks district is allowed to store unused appropriations in a separate fund at year-end, which must then be used for capital improvement projects. This fund cannot be reported as a special revenue fund, because the funds transferred into it are not committed or restricted revenues, and legislation mandates that the funds be used for capital projects. An option is to report the fund as a capital projects fund.

Summary

The number of funds established by a government can vary considerably. Some funds are required by law or by contracts (such as bond indentures). Other funds are established if management wants to exert a higher level of control over a particular area of a government's operations, or to separately monitor certain activities.

Taken to an extreme, a government could have hundreds of funds. Though this many funds could give management a fine-grained level of control, it also reduces the efficiency of the accounting function and makes it more difficult to roll up the fund information into a coherent set of financial statements.

A more efficient approach is to minimize the number of funds. There should always be just one general fund, along with perhaps a special revenue fund, a capital projects fund, and a debt service fund – which is a total of four funds. The legal environment and management decisions could result in substantially more funds, but the basic rule should be to use the minimum number of funds required by law and in accordance with the sound administration of funds.

Chapter 3
Basis of Accounting and Measurement Focus

Introduction

Governmental accounting is complicated by the presence of what may be a large number of funds. To make matters even more complex, some types of funds use a different basis of accounting and measurement focus. To clarify the difference between these concepts, the basis of accounting governs *when* transactions will be recorded, while the measurement focus governs *what* transactions will be recorded. This chapter covers both the basis of accounting and the measurement focus.

Basis of Accounting

As just noted, the basis of accounting governs *when* transactions will be recorded. This concept applies to the recognition and reporting of revenues, expenditures, expenses, and transfers. For governmental accounting purposes, the cash basis, accrual basis, and modified accrual basis may apply. The cash basis and accrual basis are discussed in the following sub-sections. The modified accrual basis is addressed in the next section.

Cash Basis

Under the cash basis of accounting, the receipt of cash triggers the recognition of revenue and expenses, while the disbursement of cash triggers the recognition of expenditures, expenses, and transfers out. For example, a government receives an invoice from a supplier for supplies. The terms of the invoice state that the government does not have to pay the invoice for 60 days. Under the cash basis, the government does not recognize the expense related to the supplies until payment is made, which is 60 days after the supplies were received.

Accrual Basis

Under the accrual basis of accounting, the occurrence of a business event triggers the recognition of most transactions, irrespective of the underlying movement of cash. This basis of accounting is generally better than the cash basis, since transactions are recorded immediately, without the time delay associated with cash-basis transactions.

> **Note:** When it is not practical to measure an item until the related cash is received or disbursed, either the cash or accrual basis of accounting may be used. The same treatment can be applied to immaterial transactions.

The cash basis and accrual basis are the two theoretical extremes of how transactions can be recognized and reported. Governments use a variation on the accrual basis of accounting, which is called the modified accrual basis. The modified basis has characteristics of both the cash basis and the accrual basis. It is covered in the next section.

Modified Accrual Basis in Governmental Fund Statements

The accrual basis of accounting is adjusted when dealing with governmental funds. The sum total of these adjustments is referred to as the modified accrual basis. The following sub-sections address various aspects of the modified accrual basis.

Revenue Recognition

Revenue and governmental fund resources (such as the proceeds from a debt issuance) are recognized when they become *susceptible to accrual*. This means that these items are not only available to finance the expenditures of the period, but are also measurable. The "available" concept means that the revenue and other fund resources are collectible within the current period or sufficiently soon thereafter to be available to pay for the current period's liabilities. The "measurable" concept allows a government to not know the exact amount of revenue in order to accrue it. For example, an accrued revenue figure could be based on actual cash collections subsequent to the fiscal year end, or on historical collection patterns. Another possibility would be to accrue the revenue associated with a cost-reimbursement grant based on the amount of costs incurred to date.

Examples of revenues and deferred inflows of resources that typically should be recorded on the modified accrual basis include:

- Grants from other governments
- Interfund transfers and similar transactions
- Property taxes
- Regularly billed charges for routinely provided services
- Sales and income taxes where taxpayer liability is established and collectability is assured or losses can be estimated

Additional points pertaining to the treatment of revenue items under the modified accrual basis are:

- *Interest and dividends.* Recognize interest and dividends on the modified accrual basis. Further, recognize changes in the fair value of investments as revenue at the end of each annual reporting period.
- *Miscellaneous revenue.* As a matter of practicality, it may be easier to recognize miscellaneous revenue items when cash is received. Examples of these items are inspection charges, parking fees, and golf fees.

- *Prior receipt.* When revenues in material amounts are received prior to the normal receipt date, initially recognize them as liabilities and later recognize them as revenues in the periods to which they apply.

Expenditure Recognition

The key measurement focus in a government fund's financial statements is on expenditures, which are decreases in the net financial resources of a fund. Most expenditures should be reported when a related liability is incurred. This means that a governmental fund liability and expenditure is accrued in the period in which the fund incurs the liability. This requirement is most commonly applicable for those liabilities that are normally paid in full and in a timely manner from current financial resources. Examples of these liabilities are employee compensation, professional services, supplies, and utilities.

Governmental fund liabilities and expenditures related to claims and judgments, compensated absences, termination benefits, receipts of goods and services for pollution control, and landfill closure and post-closure care costs should be recognized to the extent that the liabilities are normally expected to be liquidated with expendable available financial resources.

A government may choose to accumulate and earmark net assets for eventual use as payments for incurred but unmatured liabilities. If so, this does not constitute an outflow of current financial resources and therefore should not result in the recognition of a governmental fund liability or expenditure.

In most cases, a government should accrue a governmental fund liability and expenditure in the period in which the entity incurs the liability. An exception is unmatured long-term indebtedness, which is reported as a general long-term liability of the government and not as a liability of a governmental fund. This exception is dealt with in more detail in the Reporting Liabilities chapter.

For any type of expenditure to which the modified accrual basis applies, the essential concern is whether and to what extent a liability has matured.

EXAMPLE

Mr. Smithson is an employee of Qanix City. He has accrued sick time for the past 15 years and not used it. The accrued amount of this sick time is $3,500. According to Qanix policy, unused sick time is payable to employees when they leave the employment of the city. Thus, the liability associated with the sick time does not become due until Mr. Smithson leaves the city, nor does the related expenditure. The fiscal year-end of Qanix is on June 30. If Mr. Smithson were to leave his position the next day, on July 1, Qanix would not record a liability or expenditure for its June 30 financial statements. Conversely, if Mr. Smithson were to leave his position one day sooner, on June 30, Qanix would have to record the $3,500 liability and expenditure in its June 30 financial statements, since the amount is due within the fiscal year.

We deal with additional expenditure-related topics in the following sub-sections.

Inventory Items

An inventory item can be considered an expenditure either when it has been purchased or when it has been consumed. When there are significant amounts of inventory, it should be reported on the balance sheet.

Insurance Items

When an expenditure related to insurance extends over more than one accounting period, it is permissible to account for it as an expenditure in the period of acquisition, rather than allocating it among several reporting periods.

Encumbrances

An encumbrance is a commitment related to an unperformed contract to buy goods or services. It is frequently recorded in the accounting records in order to maintain budgetary control. If an encumbrance is still outstanding at year-end, it does not constitute a liability or an expenditure. The encumbrance concept is addressed in more detail in the following Budget and Budgetary Accounting chapter.

Claims, Judgments, and Compensated Absences

The amount of claims, judgments, and compensated absences that are recorded as expenditures should be the amount accrued during the year that would normally be offset by and liquidated with available financial resources. Only the current portion of these liabilities should be reported in a fund. Any remaining portion of these liabilities should be reported in the governmental activities column in the government-wide statement of net position.

Measurement Focus

As noted in the introduction to this chapter, measurement focus governs *what* transactions will be recorded. The focus used by governmental funds is the *current financial resources measurement focus*. In essence, the operating statement of a governmental fund shows changes in the amount of financial resources that will be available in the near future because of transactions occurring within the fiscal period being reported. This has two effects on the operating statement, which are:

Change in Spendable Resources	Reported as
Increase	Revenues or other financing sources
Decrease	Expenditures or other financing uses

In short, the focus of governmental funds is on current financial resources, which means assets that can be converted into cash and liabilities that will be paid for with that cash. Stated differently, the balance sheets of governmental funds do not include long-term assets or any assets that will not be converted into cash in order to settle current liabilities. Similarly, these balance sheets will not contain any long-term liabilities, since they do not require the use of current financial resources for their settlement. This measurement focus is only used in governmental accounting.

The focus used by proprietary funds is the *economic resources measurement focus.* This approach focuses on whether a proprietary fund is economically better off because of transactions occurring within the fiscal period being reported; there is no consideration of whether there are current financial resources. This has two effects on the operating statement, which are:

Impact on Economic Position	Reported as
Improve	Revenues or gains
Diminish	Expenses or losses

The time period addressed by the economic resources measurement focus extends beyond the short-term, so a proprietary fund will include long-term assets and liabilities on its balance sheet. This approach is quite similar to what is used by commercial organizations.

As a general statement of principle, government-wide financial statements are to be prepared using the economic resources measurement focus and the accrual basis of accounting. Fund financial statements are to be prepared using the modified accrual or accrual basis of accounting when measuring financial position and operating results. More specifically:

- *Governmental funds.* Prepare financial statements using the current financial resources measurement focus and the modified accrual basis of accounting. Recognize revenues when they become available and measurable. Recognize expenditures when the fund liability is incurred if it is measurable, except for unmatured interest on general long-term liabilities (which is recognized when due).
- *Proprietary funds.* Prepare the statements of net position and revenues, expenses, and changes in fund net position using the economic resources measurement focus and the accrual basis of accounting.
- *Fiduciary funds.* Prepare financial statements using the economic resources measurement focus and the accrual basis of accounting.
- *Transfers.* Report transfers between funds in the accounting period in which the interfund receivable and payable arise.

In the following table, we note the accounting basis and measurement focus to be used by each type of fund.

Accounting Basis and Measurement Focus by Fund

Fund Type	Accounting Basis	Measurement Focus
Governmental	Modified accrual	Current financial resources
Capital projects fund	Modified accrual	Current financial resources
Debt service fund	Modified accrual	Current financial resources
General fund	Modified accrual	Current financial resources
Permanent fund	Modified accrual	Current financial resources
Special revenue fund	Modified accrual	Current financial resources
Proprietary	Accrual	Economic resources
Enterprise funds	Accrual	Economic resources
Internal service funds	Accrual	Economic resources
Fiduciary	Accrual	Economic resources
Investment trust fund	Accrual	Economic resources
Pension and employee benefit trust fund	Accrual	Economic resources
Private-purpose trust fund	Accrual	Economic resources

Accrual Basis Reporting in Government-Wide Financial Statements

The general guidance for the preparation of government-wide financial statements is that the statement of net position and the statement of activities should be prepared using the economic resources measurement focus and the accrual basis of accounting. This means that one should recognize revenues, expenses, gains, losses, assets, deferred outflows of resources, liabilities, and deferred inflows of resources resulting from exchange and exchange-like transactions when the exchange takes place. Such a transaction is considered to have taken place when an exchange has been completed in the ordinary course of operations, unless the circumstances indicate that collection of the price cannot be reasonably assured. Thus, revenues from exchange transactions should usually be accounted for as of the completion of a transaction; it may be necessary to create a provision for uncollectible accounts at that time.

Note: A *deferred inflow of resources* occurs when there is an acquisition of net assets that applies to a future reporting period. A *deferred outflow of resources* occurs when there is consumption of net assets that applies to a future reporting period. A *resource* is an item that can be drawn down to provide services to citizens.

A useful distinction to be aware of is that long-term assets and liabilities *are* recorded in the government-wide financial statements, but they are *not* recorded in the general fund or any of the special-revenue funds.

Accrual Basis in Proprietary Fund Statements

When accounting for a proprietary fund, the general guidance is to prepare the statements of net position and revenues, expenses, and changes in fund net position using the economic resources measurement focus and the accrual basis of accounting.

When accounting for an exchange transaction, the related revenue should be recognized when the exchange occurs, unless collection of the price cannot be reasonably assured. If a provision for uncollectible accounts can be included, revenues from exchange transactions can generally be accounted for when they are completed.

Revenue Recognition When Right of Return Exists

There may be situations applicable to business-type activities and proprietary funds where a product may be returned, either for a refund, an exchange, or a credit toward other purchases. When there is a right of return, revenue can be recognized at the time of sale, but only if *all* of the following conditions have been met:

- The price is fixed or readily determinable at the date of exchange.
- The government has been paid by the buyer, or the buyer is obligated to do so; payment is not contingent on the buyer's subsequent resale of the product.
- The buyer's payment obligation to the government would not be changed if the product were to be damaged, destroyed, or stolen.
- The buyer has economic substance separate from what has been provided by the government.
- The government does not have a significant obligation to assist the buyer in reselling the product.
- The amount of product returns can be reasonably estimated.

When the preceding conditions can be met and revenue is recognized, it is also necessary to accrue for the cost of any estimated returns.

When the accountant elects to not recognize revenue because of the failure to meet one or more of the preceding conditions, recognition can occur later when the return privilege has expired or if the conditions are subsequently met.

Disclosures

The following disclosures related to the basis of accounting may need to be included in the notes accompanying the financial statements:

- *Available criterion.* Disclose the period of time used to define the term "available" for purposes of recognizing revenue in the governmental fund financial statements. This disclosure should be contained within the summary of significant accounting policies.

- *Revenue recognition.* Disclose the government's revenue recognition policies in the summary of significant accounting policies.

Summary

The modified accrual basis of accounting contains several significant departures from the accrual basis of accounting that are tailored to the governmental accounting environment. These differences can have a particular impact on the timing and amount of many types of revenue that are specific to government entities, such as grants, interfund transfers and property taxes. The modified accrual basis also departs from the accrual basis in the area of expenditure recognition, where the focus is on decreases in the net financial resources of a fund and on differing treatments of matured and unmatured liabilities.

The inclusion of the current financial resources measurement focus and the economic measurement resources focus into the accounting for funds certainly makes it more difficult to ascertain how accounting transactions are to be recorded. To improve the reader's comprehension, we have included a number of sample transactions in the Common Accounting Transactions chapter, noting how the entries differ, depending on which measurement focus is being used.

Chapter 4
Reporting Capital Assets

Introduction

Capital assets are higher-cost tangible and intangible assets that are used in operations and which are expected to have useful lives longer than one reporting period. Special accounting rules apply to these assets, which are covered in this chapter. Examples of capital assets are noted in the following table.

Capital Asset Examples

Buildings	Land
Building improvements	Land improvements
Easements	Machinery
Equipment	Vehicles
Infrastructure	Works of art and historical treasures

The land improvement asset in the preceding table may be subject to some interpretation. This asset is supposed to include betterments that ready land for its intended use. Examples of land improvements are excavation, fill, grading, and the installation of utilities. Land improvements can also involve the removal of existing buildings and landscaping.

A further classification of capital assets is infrastructure assets, which are stationary assets that typically have substantially longer useful lives than most types of capital assets. Examples of infrastructure assets are noted in the following table.

Infrastructure Asset Examples

Bridges	Drainage systems	Tunnels
Dams	Lighting systems	Water and sewer systems
	Roads	

Valuation of Capital Assets

Capital assets are to be reported at their historical cost. This historical cost includes any charges incurred to position an asset in its intended location and condition for use. Examples of these costs are:

- Freight charges
- Professional fees
- Site preparation costs

Donated assets are to be reported at their acquisition value, plus any charges incurred to position these assets at their intended location and condition for use. Acquisition value is the price that an entity would have paid to acquire an asset having similar service potential in an orderly market transaction at the acquisition date. Acquisition value can be calculated from price quotes in periodicals, manufacturers' catalogs, recent sales of comparable items, and so forth.

EXAMPLE

A museum received a sculpture as a donation five years ago. The accounting staff mistakenly never recognized the asset at that time. This issue has now been discovered. In the five years since the sculpture was donated, its value has increased from $80,000 to $120,000. The asset should be recognized at its original $80,000 valuation, since donations should be valued as of their acquisition date.

Note: A transfer price of $1, or some similarly inconsequential amount, is not considered the true acquisition value of a capital asset, so a market-based acquisition value must be derived instead.

EXAMPLE

Qanix City mandates that the developer of a new industrial park build the water, sewage, and utility infrastructure for the park and then donate it to the city once the park has been completed. Qanix can then report the donated asset at the cost incurred by the developer, or by asking the city's department of public works to derive an estimate of cost.

EXAMPLE

The same developer constructs a street next to the industrial park and donates it to the city. The acquisition value of the street to the city includes both the infrastructure asset and a right-of-way easement on the land on which the road was constructed. The value of the easement is essentially equivalent to the ownership of the underlying land, since the grantor of the easement retains no right of use. Consequently, the estimated purchase price of the land could be used as a basis for determining the acquisition value of the easement.

Note: The arbitrary assignment of a nominal value to a right-of-way easement is considered inappropriate.

Capitalization Thresholds

A government can set a capitalization threshold, below which expenditures are charged to expense and above which capital assets are recorded. There is no requirement for a capitalization threshold, but a government typically sets one in order to keep the accounting staff from being overly burdened with tracking capital assets that have very low values.

When setting a capitalization threshold, consider whether a single threshold should be set for all capital assets, or whether a different threshold should be used for different types of assets. Issues that may impact this decision include any applicable laws and regulations, or management's interest in tracking certain kinds of assets in more detail. For example, a city manager might want to have detailed records kept on laptops being used by city employees, and so sets a lower capitalization threshold for computer equipment than for other classes of assets.

Networks and Subsystems

Capital assets may be aggregated for various purposes within networks and subsystems, so it is useful to understand the meanings of these terms. A *network* is the sum total of all assets that, as a group, provide a particular service for a government. For example, an electricity generation and distribution system can be considered a network. A *subsystem* is the sum total of all assets that, as a group, make up a portion of a network. Thus, a dam, power station, and electricity lines could be considered subsystems of an electricity generation and distribution network.

For recordkeeping purposes, a network or subsystem can consist of dissimilar items. For example, a set of roads could be designated as a network, which is comprised of such varied assets as pavement, signage, and traffic metering systems.

Capitalization of Interest Costs

The related cost of interest can be capitalized into the acquisition cost of some assets related to business-type activities and enterprise funds. This interest cost is for the amount of interest incurred during the period required to bring an asset to its intended location and condition for use. Interest can only be capitalized for certain types of assets, which are:

- Assets constructed for the government's own use
- Assets designated for sale or lease that have been produced as discrete projects
- Investments accounted for using the equity method, while the investee is conducting activities to begin its planned principal operations, provided that those activities include resources used to acquire qualifying assets for its operations
- Assets that are donated or granted to other organizations

Further, interest costs should not be capitalized for the following assets:

- Inventories
- Assets already in use or ready for their intended use
- Assets not being prepared for their intended use

- Assets not included in the financial statements
- Investments accounted for using the equity method, after the principal operations of the investee have begun
- Investments made in regulated investees that are capitalizing the cost of their debt and equity capital
- Assets that have been acquired with gifts and grants, where the donor or grantor restricts asset purchases to the extent that resources are available to do so
- Land that is not being prepared for its intended use

EXAMPLE

Sunflower City is building a parking structure next to its municipal stadium. The underlying land required significant grading and other preparatory work for several months prior to the start of construction on the parking structure. The interest outlay on the land preparation is capitalized into the acquisition cost of the parking structure.

Capitalization Rate

The amount of interest cost that can be capitalized for a qualifying asset is that amount of interest incurred during the asset acquisition period that could have been avoided if the asset had not been acquired or built. The amount of this capitalized interest is calculated by applying an interest rate (also known as the *capitalization rate*) to the average amount of accumulated expenditures for the asset during the reporting period. The capitalization rate is derived from the rates associated with those government borrowings outstanding during the period. If there is a plan to borrow funds specifically for the acquisition of an asset, then use the interest rate on that borrowing transaction as the capitalization rate, up to the maximum amount of the borrowing. If the average outlay in the period exceeds the borrowing specifically targeted at the asset, the capitalization rate to be applied to the rest of the outlay is the weighted average of the interest rates associated with the government's other borrowings.

Note: The total interest cost capitalized in a reporting period cannot exceed the total amount of interest cost incurred in the period.

Capitalization Period

It is permissible to capitalize the cost of interest when all three of the following conditions have been met and are continuing:

- Outlays have been made for the asset
- Activities needed to prepare the asset for its intended use are in progress
- Interest costs are being incurred

There can be quite a range of permissible activities needed to prepare an asset for its intended use. For example, there may be administrative activities to secure permits, design building plans prior to construction, and deal with litigation. However, if there is a general suspension of activities, interest capitalization stops until activities resume.

> **Note:** Brief interruptions in activities will not halt interest capitalization, nor will interruptions that are externally imposed or which are an inherent part of the asset acquisition process.

The capitalization period has ended when the asset is substantially complete and ready for its intended use. When an asset can be completed in segments, where each segment can be used independently of the other segments, interest capitalization should cease for each completed segment. In other cases where all segments must be completed before an asset is ready for use, interest capitalization should continue until the entire asset has been completed.

Impact of Tax-Exempt Borrowings

When a tax-exempt borrowing is used to finance the acquisition of an asset, the amount of interest cost capitalized should be net of any interest earned on the funds obtained from the borrowing transaction.

When to Capitalize Expenditures

There are a number of situations that a government may encounter in which it is not clear whether an outlay should be charged to expense as incurred, or whether it should be capitalized. In the following bullet points, we note the correct treatment of several common scenarios:

- *Road maintenance.* A government is incurring costs to resurface a road. This cost is normally capitalized, since it extends the road's original useful life. However, if the government is only filling potholes, doing so is considered maintenance that does not extend the useful life of the road, so this cost should be charged to expense. In another scenario, an existing road is being widened; since the road's capacity is being expanded, this cost can be capitalized. When an existing road has been entirely replaced, its original cost and accumulated depreciation should be removed from the accounting records.
- *Land and easements.* Land and easements should be classified as land and right-of-way easements, respectively. They should never be classified as part of an infrastructure asset.
- *Parks.* Parks as a whole are not classified as infrastructure. Instead, a park is likely comprised of land (which is not depreciable), buildings and stadiums (which are depreciable) and networks of roads and related facilities that may

be classified as infrastructure assets and which can be accounted for using the modified approach (as described later in this chapter).

Depreciation of Capital Assets

Capital assets are to be depreciated over their useful lives. The only exceptions to this rule are as follows:

- The assets are inexhaustible
- The assets are intangible assets with indefinite useful lives
- The assets are infrastructure assets using the modified approach (as noted later in this chapter)

An inexhaustible asset has an economic benefit that is used up at so slow a rate that its estimated useful life is considered to be extraordinarily long. Land and land improvements are classified as inexhaustible assets. However, improvements that are considered part of a structure or which deteriorate over time (such as fencing) can be depreciated.

Depreciation Methods

The periodic depreciation expense is measured by using a systematic and rational method to allocate the net cost of an asset over its estimated useful life, not including its estimated salvage value. Any established depreciation method may be used. We describe several in the following sub-sections. Depreciation may be calculated for any of the following:

- A class of assets
- A network of assets
- A subsystem of a network
- Individual assets

Useful Life

Any depreciation calculation employs the useful life concept, which is the estimated lifespan of a capital asset. The useful life of an asset may be determined based on internal information, from general guidelines obtained from industry or professional organizations, or from comparable assets held by other governments. The determination of an asset's useful life also involves consideration of its current condition, how it will be used, and the period over which it is expected to meet service demands.

The useful life of an asset can be reviewed and adjusted later in its life. If there is a change in useful life, it is applied prospectively to all remaining depreciation that has not yet been charged against the asset. If there are a number of factors that could impact the useful life of an asset, it may be useful to conduct a periodic reassessment. For example, if a government does not have sufficient funds to provide periodic maintenance to its truck fleet, the trucks may have a shorter useful life than would normally be the case. Or, if a government has a right to extend existing water rights for five extra years for no additional cost, the useful life of the water rights can be extended by the five year period.

EXAMPLE

A city government purchases broadcast rights for a public service station from the federal government for $80,000. The rights cover a 10-year period, so the useful life of the broadcast rights asset is assumed to be 10 years. If the city could renew the rights for 10 more years for a nominal fee, the useful life could be extended to 20 years. However, if the city must pay an additional $80,000 to renew the broadcast rights, then this constitutes a new asset purchase, so the useful life of the original asset is assumed to encompass only 10 years.

Additional information about useful life for intangible assets is provided later in the Intangible Assets section.

Composite Depreciation

A composite method is being used when depreciating a group of similar assets, or dissimilar assets of the same class. For example, a library could use the composite method to depreciate its books. Under this approach, a depreciation rate is computed for the composite group, after which this rate is multiplied by the cost of the entire asset group to arrive at depreciation expense. The relevant depreciation rate can be calculated based on a weighted or unweighted average of the estimated useful lives of the assets in the composite group. Another possibility is to derive a depreciation rate based on an assessment of the remaining useful lives of the assets in the group. However it was derived, the depreciation rate is then multiplied by the cost of the assets in the group to arrive at the depreciation expense related to the assets.

EXAMPLE

A state government elects to use composite depreciation for a group of similar assets when it decides to use the same depreciation rate for all interstate highways within the state. The state contains three interstate highways. An accountant working in the comptroller's office then derives an unweighted average of the useful lives of these three interstates, which are 12 years, 17 years, and 22 years. This results in the following depreciation rate:

$$\frac{1}{(12 + 17 + 22) \div 3} = .05882 \text{ depreciation per year}$$

The aggregate historical cost of the three interstate highways is $180 million. In the current year, the related depreciation expense is $10,587,600, which is calculated as $180,000,000 × .05882.

The initially-derived composite depreciation rate should be maintained over the life of a group of assets. However, the rate can be altered if there is a significant change in the composition of the assets in a group.

> **Note:** Composite depreciation should not be applied across different classes of assets.

When a government uses composite depreciation for a group of assets and then retires an asset from the group, no gain or loss is recorded. Instead, the asset cost is removed from the capital assets account and charged to the accumulated depreciation account. A sample of the entry that could be used for the removal of several miles of arterial roads is:

	Debit	Credit
Accumulated depreciation	8,500,000	
Infrastructure – arterial roads		8,500,000

A government might then add an asset to the group of assets. If so, its calculation of depreciation is to subtract the book value of the removed assets, add the book value of the new assets, and multiply the result by the existing annual depreciation rate.

EXAMPLE

A government begins with a group of road assets having a book value of $10,000,000. It then removes $500,000 of road assets and adds $750,000 of road assets. Its original depreciation rate was 5% per year. Based on this information, the calculation of the entity's composite depreciation is:

Beginning balance of asset group	$10,000,000
- Retirements	-500,000
+ Additions	+750,000
= Ending balance of asset group	$10,250,000
× Depreciation rate	× 5%
= Depreciation expense	$512,500

Straight-Line Depreciation

Under the straight-line method of depreciation, depreciation expense is recognized evenly over the estimated useful life of an asset. The straight-line calculation steps are:

1. Subtract the estimated salvage value of the asset from the amount at which it is recorded on the books.

2. Determine the estimated useful life of the asset. It is easiest to use a standard useful life for each class of assets.
3. Divide the estimated useful life (in years) into 1 to arrive at the straight-line depreciation rate.
4. Multiply the depreciation rate by the asset cost (less salvage value).

EXAMPLE

The government of Montana City purchases a snowplow for $60,000. It has an estimated salvage value of $10,000 and a useful life of five years. The City calculates the annual straight-line depreciation for the vehicle as:

1. Purchase cost of $60,000 – Estimated salvage value of $10,000 = Depreciable asset cost of $50,000

2. 1 ÷ 5-Year useful life = 20% Depreciation rate per year

3. 20% Depreciation rate × $50,000 Depreciable asset cost = $10,000 Annual depreciation

---

Sum-of-the-Years' Digits Method

The sum of the years' digits (SYD) method is more appropriate than straight-line depreciation if the asset depreciates more quickly or has greater production capacity in earlier years than it does as it ages. Use the following formula to calculate it:

$$\text{Depreciation percentage} = \frac{\text{Number of estimated years of life as of beginning of the year}}{\text{Sum of the years' digits}}$$

The following table contains examples of the sum of the years' digits noted in the denominator of the preceding formula:

Total Depreciation Period	Initial Sum of the Years' Digits	Calculation
2 years	3	1 + 2
3 years	6	1 + 2 + 3
4 years	10	1 + 2 + 3 + 4
5 years	15	1 + 2 + 3 + 4 + 5

The concept is most easily illustrated with the following example.

EXAMPLE

Montana City buys a computer system for $100,000. The system has no estimated salvage value and a useful life of five years. The City calculates the annual sum of the years' digits depreciation for this machine as:

Year	Number of estimated years of life as of beginning of the year	SYD Calculation	Depreciation Percentage	Annual Depreciation
1	5	5/15	33.33%	$33,333
2	4	4/15	26.67%	26,667
3	3	3/15	20.00%	20,000
4	2	2/15	13.33%	13,333
5	1	1/15	6.67%	6,667
Totals	15		100.00%	$100,000

The sum of the years' digits method is clearly more complex than the straight-line method, which tends to limit its use unless software is employed to automatically track the calculations for each asset.

Double Declining Balance Method

The double declining balance (DDB) method is a form of accelerated depreciation. It may be more appropriate than the straight-line method if an asset experiences an inordinately high level of usage during the first few years of its useful life.

To calculate the double-declining balance depreciation rate, divide the number of years of useful life of an asset into 100 percent and multiply the result by two. The formula is:

$$(100\% \div \text{Years of useful life}) \times 2$$

The DDB calculation proceeds until the asset's salvage value is reached, after which depreciation ends.

EXAMPLE

Montana City purchases an additional snowplow for $50,000. It has an estimated salvage value of $5,000 and a useful life of five years. The calculation of the double declining balance depreciation rate is:

$$(100\% \div \text{Years of useful life}) \times 2 = 40\%$$

By applying the 40% rate, the City arrives at the following table of depreciation charges per year:

Year	Book Value at Beginning of Year	Depreciation Percentage	DDB Depreciation	Book Value Net of Depreciation
1	$50,000	40%	$20,000	$30,000
2	30,000	40%	12,000	18,000
3	18,000	40%	7,200	10,800
4	10,800	40%	4,320	6,480
5	6,480	40%	1,480	5,000
Total			$45,000	

Note that the depreciation in the fifth and final year is only for $1,480, rather than the $3,240 that would be indicated by the 40% depreciation rate. The reason for the smaller depreciation charge is that the City stops any further depreciation once the remaining book value declines to the amount of the estimated salvage value.

Units of Production Method

Under the units of production method, the amount of depreciation charged to expense varies in direct proportion to the amount of asset usage. Thus, more depreciation is charged in periods when there is more asset usage, and less depreciation in periods when there is less asset usage. It is the most accurate method for charging depreciation, since it links closely to the wear and tear on assets. However, it also requires the tracking of asset usage, which means that its use is generally limited to more expensive assets. Also, total usage must be estimated over the life of the asset.

Tip: Do not use the units of production method unless there is a significant difference in asset usage from period to period. Otherwise, a great deal of time will be spent tracking asset usage, with a resulting depreciation expense that varies little from the results that would have been calculated with the straight-line method (which is far easier to calculate).

Follow these steps to calculate depreciation under the units of production method:

1. Estimate the total number of hours of usage of the asset, or the total number of units to be produced by it over its useful life.
2. Subtract any estimated salvage value from the capitalized cost of the asset, and divide the total estimated usage or production from this net depreciable cost. This yields the depreciation cost per hour of usage or unit of production.

3. Multiply the number of hours of usage or units of actual production by the depreciation cost per hour or unit, which results in the total depreciation expense for the accounting period.

If the estimated number of hours of usage or units of production changes over time, incorporate these changes into the calculation of the depreciation cost per hour or unit of production. This will alter the depreciation expense on a go-forward basis.

EXAMPLE

Montana City's gravel pit operation builds a conveyor system to extract sand from a sand pit at a cost of $400,000. The sand is then spread on local roads. The City expects to use the conveyor to extract 1,000,000 tons of sand, which results in a depreciation rate of $0.40 per ton (1,000,000 tons ÷ $400,000 cost). During the first quarter of activity, the City extracts 10,000 tons of sand, which results in the following depreciation expense:

= $0.40 depreciation cost per ton × 10,000 tons of sand

= $4,000 depreciation expense

Modified Approach

The modified approach allows a government to avoid incurring depreciation charges. Under this approach, it is not necessary to depreciate infrastructure assets that are part of a network, as long as both of the following requirements are met:

- The government manages the assets with an asset management system; and
- The government documents that the assets are being preserved at a level of condition that it has established and disclosed.

To meet the first requirement, the asset management system should do the following:

- Contain a current inventory of eligible assets.
- Perform condition assessments of the assets and summarize the results of these assessments using a measurement scale.
- Estimate the annual amount required to maintain and preserve the eligible assets at the level of condition established and disclosed by the government.

The documentation requirement for the modified approach includes the following:

- Condition assessments are performed at least once every three years. Condition assessments can be conducted based on a statistical sampling plan, where every asset has an equal chance of being selected for testing during a three-year period.

- The results of the three most recent condition assessments provide reasonable assurance that assets are being preserved at or above the condition level established and documented by the government.

Earlier, we referred to a network of assets. An example of a network is a highway that has a series of rest area facilities built alongside it, as well as road maintenance sheds.

Note: It may be more efficient to conduct condition assessments on a cyclical basis, so that one third of all eligible infrastructure assets are reviewed each year.

When eligible assets meet the preceding requirements and therefore are not depreciated, all subsequent expenditures made for these assets must be charged to expense as incurred. This charge to expense is not a requirement for asset additions and improvements, which are instead capitalized. An expenditure is considered to have added to or improved an infrastructure asset when it has increased the capacity or efficiency of the asset.

EXAMPLE

A county government is engaged in a major reconstruction of a county road. The government has used the modified approach to account for this asset. The reconstruction effort includes both the preservation of the existing road and widening it to accommodate more vehicular traffic. That portion of the costs devoted to preservation should be charged to expense, while the cost incurred to widen the road should be capitalized.

EXAMPLE

The county is also engaged in a major rehabilitation project for a bridge, which is accounted for using the modified approach. The county's standard practice is to construct a comparable new bridge next to the old bridge and then tear down the old bridge. Since this is a preservation activity, the cost incurred to build the replacement bridge and tear down the old bridge is charged to expense as incurred. If the new bridge had instead had a larger service capacity, that portion of the cost incurred to increase the capacity level could have been capitalized.

In those cases where the preceding requirements can no longer be met for an asset, the asset should be depreciated in subsequent periods. At that time, an appropriate useful life and salvage estimate is made for the asset, and depreciation is calculated from this information.

Note: A change from depreciation to the modified approach is considered a change in accounting estimate.

It is allowable for one agency or department of a government to account for infrastructure assets using the modified approach, while another agency or department does not. However, when agencies or departments are reporting on different segments of the same network, a consistent approach should be applied by all of these entities.

Intangible Assets

An intangible asset lacks physical substance, is a nonfinancial asset, and has a useful life extending over more than one reporting period. An example of an intangible asset is commercially available computer software that has been purchased or licensed by a government. Intangible assets are treated like other capital assets, except that the related depreciation is renamed amortization. The following additional points regarding intangible assets may apply:

- *Recognition in the financial statements.* Recognize the asset in the statement of net position only if it is identifiable. This is the case when the asset can be separated from the government and sold or transferred, or the asset arises from legal rights, even if those rights are not separable from the government or transferable.
- *Recognition of internally developed assets.* When an intangible asset has been internally generated, outlays related to the development of that asset can only be capitalized when all of the following apply:
  - An objective has been stated for the project, as well as the nature of the service capacity expected when the project has been completed;
  - The feasibility of the project has been demonstrated; and
  - The government can demonstrate that it has the intention, ability, and presence of effort to complete the project.

EXAMPLE

A government agency wants to allocate funds toward the development of a patent that can spot underground heat related to burning coal seams, using drones equipped with highly sensitive thermal emission scanners. The preceding sentence is a clearly-stated objective for the project.

To continue with the example, the nature of the service capacity is to improve the allocation of firefighting teams to areas where a forest fire is most likely to be triggered by a burning coal seam.

The agency has made a budgetary commitment to fund the project and entered into contracts with several producers of thermal imaging devices to construct a demonstration unit. The agency has also assigned a manager and support team to the project, and contacted its legal department in regard to securing patent protection for the scanning system.

- *Recognition of new computer software.* When a government internally develops computer software or uses a third-party contractor to do so, it can capitalize the costs of the software based on the following stages of project completion:
  - o *Preliminary project stage.* This stage includes conducting a user needs analysis, determining system requirements, evaluating alternatives and the existence of required technologies, supplier selection, and consultant selection. Outlays for this stage should be charged to expense as incurred.
  - o *Application development stage.* This stage includes software coding, installation and testing. Outlays for this stage should be capitalized. The training of employees involved with developing internally generated software is not considered part of the application development stage.
  - o *Post-implementation/operation stage.* This stage includes application training and software maintenance. Data conversion is part of this stage, but can be classified as part of the application development stage if doing so is necessary for making the software operational. Outlays for this stage should be charged to expense as incurred.
  - o *Recognition of software updates.* Outlays for the modification of computer software that is already operating can be capitalized if the result is an increase in software functionality, an increase in software efficiency, or an extension of the useful life of the software. If none of these improvements occur, the outlays are instead charged to expense.

> **Note:** A government's website is considered computer software, and so can be capitalized as an intangible asset.

- *Useful life.* The useful life of an intangible asset should not exceed any legal or contractual limitations. The renewal period of an intangible asset should be considered when determining its useful life, since the useful life can encompass several renewal periods. An intangible asset can have an indefinite useful life when there are no legal, regulatory, technological, or other factors that might otherwise limit its useful life. An example of an asset having an indefinite life is a permanent right-of-way easement. When an intangible asset is deemed to have an indefinite life, it is not amortized. If an asset with an indefinite life is later reclassified as having a definite lifespan, it should be amortized from the reclassification date.

> **Note:** Interest can be capitalized on the development of internally generated intangible assets by business-type activities and enterprise funds.

- *Business process reengineering.* A common occurrence is for business process reengineering to occur as part of a software development project, since processes can be altered to fit changes in the new software. Even though these activities may be closely intertwined, the accounting for reengineering work is to charge these costs to expense as incurred. The reason for the differing treatment is that process reengineering involves the redeployment of existing resources, rather than the creation of a new resource.
- *Interface costs.* A government may incur costs to modify existing software so that it can interface with a new computer system. If this outlay increases the functionality or efficiency of the existing software or extends its estimated useful life, then this cost can be capitalized. If not, the costs are assumed to have been incurred for standard maintenance activities, and are charged to expense as incurred.
- *Legal defense outlays.* A government may need to expend funds for assistance to defend its legal rights pertaining to an intangible asset. A legal defense of rights does not extend the useful life of the asset, nor does it add any capacity. Therefore, this cost is charged to expense as incurred. However, a different type of legal cost *can* be capitalized – when outlays are incurred to initially register an intangible asset, as would be the case with a patent filing.
- *Maintenance contract.* Governments routinely enter into annual software maintenance agreements with suppliers, where they pay a fee in exchange for maintenance services and upgrades. Theoretically, the portion of these agreements associated with software upgrades that increase the functionality or efficiency of the software can be capitalized. However, it is generally easier to establish a policy under which maintenance fees are charged to expense as incurred.

Works of Art and Historical Treasures

Works of art and historical treasures are commonly housed by museums, libraries, art galleries, zoos, and similar institutions. These assets are to be capitalized at their historical cost or acquisition value. A government is encouraged, but not required, to capitalize a collection when all of the following conditions have been met:

- The collection is not held for financial gain, but rather for public exhibition, education, or research for public service; and
- The collection is protected, cared for and preserved, and kept unencumbered; and
- There is a policy covering the collection, stating that the proceeds from the sales of collection items be used to acquire other items for collections.

A capitalized collection may contain exhaustible individual items, where their useful lives are reduced by their display or other applications. If so, the collection should be depreciated over its estimated useful life. When a collection or individual item is deemed to be inexhaustible, depreciation is not required.

Asset Transfers

When a capital asset is transferred within the same reporting entity, the receiving fund should continue to report the asset's original cost and the related amount of accumulated depreciation. Thus, the accumulated depreciation for a capital asset follows the asset, no matter where it goes within a government entity.

When a capital asset is shifted to an entirely different entity, the asset is removed from the accounting records of the entity that is losing the asset and added to the records of the entity that is gaining the asset.

EXAMPLE

The town of North Aldan is shifting the ownership of a border road to the town of South Aldan. North Aldan's accountant should write off the road's book value in the period of the transfer, recording a functional expense in the amount of the road's book value.

Impairment of Capital Assets

Capital assets should be evaluated for impairment when there are events or changes in circumstances indicating that the service utility of an asset may have significantly and unexpectedly declined. These events or changes were not expected to occur when the asset was initially acquired. The *service utility* of an asset is the usable capacity that it was expected to provide when it was acquired. The current usable capacity of an asset may be less than its original usable capacity due to a variety of impairment events, which include physical damage or obsolescence, as well as the enactment of laws that limit its use. The impairment concept also applies to capital assets being accounted for using the modified approach.

The process for determining whether a capital asset is impaired follows these steps:

1. *Identify potential impairments.* A potential impairment should be conspicuous or known to the government, so there is no need to perform additional steps to identify additional potential impairment events. When an impairment is considered to be temporary, the asset should not be written down. Some of the more common indicators of impairment are:

   o Physical damage to the asset
   o Enactment of laws that impact asset usage
   o Evidence of obsolescence
   o A change in the manner of use of an asset
   o Construction stoppage

EXAMPLE

Due to a funding shortfall, Helix City has stopped using an elementary school, which is a change in the manner of use of the school building asset. This can be considered impairment of the asset. Helix has also stopped the development of software for resource management, which can be considered a construction stoppage, and is therefore also an asset impairment. Further, a new law mandates upgrades to Helix's backup water treatment facility, for which it has no available funding. This last item can be considered asset impairment due to the enactment of a law.

Helix's middle school has also been shut down due to declining enrollment, but there is no need to take an impairment charge, since a projected increase in future enrollments indicates that the asset impairment will be temporary.

EXAMPLE

A state government runs a data processing center that is currently operating near its maximum capacity. A user at a local university is about to conclude a special project for weather modeling that will cut the usage rate of the data processing center in half. This decline in demand should not be considered evidence of asset obsolescence, since the user was a one-time project.

2. *Test for impairment.* If the first step indicates that there are one or more potential impairment conditions present, the accountant should proceed with a test for impairment, where both of the following factors must be present:

   o There is a significant decline in service utility, where expenses are now too high in relation to the benefit obtained from the asset.
   o The decline in service utility was unexpected, where the circumstances of the impairment are not part of the normal life cycle of the asset.

When there is no expectation that an impaired asset will continue to be used by the government, it should be reported at the lower of its carrying value or fair value. When an asset is impaired because construction on it has stopped, the asset should also be reported at the lower of its carrying value or fair value.

Note: When an impairment test indicates that asset impairment has not occurred, the accountant should still reevaluate the remaining estimated useful life and salvage value of the asset, which may result in a change in the remaining periodic depreciation charges against the asset.

For illustrative purposes, the preceding discussion is summarized into the following flowchart.

Decision Process for an Asset Impairment Situation

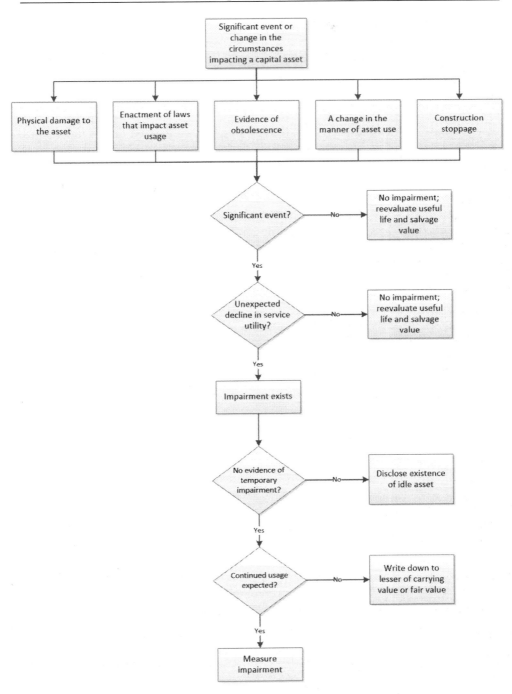

If it is decided that impairment is present, the next issue is determining how much of the asset's historical cost should be written off. The following three methods are available for doing so, where the method chosen should best reflect the decline in service utility of the asset:

- *Restoration cost approach.* This is the cost that would be incurred to restore the utility of the asset. Impairments resulting from physical damage should use this approach.
- *Service units approach.* This is the cost associated with the decline in utility of the asset, which is derived by evaluating the change in maximum estimated service units for the asset, both before and after the impairment event. Impairments resulting from changes in laws, environmental factors, or obsolescence should use this approach.
- *Deflated depreciated replacement cost approach.* This is a derivation of the cost of an asset needed to replace the current level of service, which is then depreciated to reflect its presumed usage and then deflated to convert the asset to its historical cost. Impairments resulting from a change in the manner or duration of use should use this approach.

EXAMPLE

Okie City's library has been heavily damaged by a tornado. The building was constructed 10 years ago for $3 million, including $200,000 to purchase the underlying land. The library has an expected useful life of 50 years. Fixing the tornado damage will cost $800,000. The capitalization policy of the city states that 25% of the rebuilding cost is allocated to demolition and scrap removal, and 75% to rebuilding the structure. The estimated replacement cost of the library is $4.5 million.

The calculation of the impairment loss, using the **restoration cost approach**, is:

	Historical Cost	Estimated Useful Life	Accumulated Depreciation	Current Carrying Amount
Land	$200,000			
Building construction	2,800,000	50 years	$560,000	$2,240,000
Total reconstruction cost	800,000			
Percentage rebuilding cost	× 75%			
Restoration cost (current $)	600,000			
Replacement cost (current $)	4,500,000			
Restoration cost ratio	× 13.333%			
Current carrying amount	2,240,000			
Impairment loss	$298,666			

44

EXAMPLE

A state government built a canal system five years ago, spending $14 million on the canal locks. The locks were originally expected to have a useful life of 50 years. A new federal regulation mandates that these locks be replaced with more robust locks to guard against storm surges, with additional security to protect them from terrorist attacks. The new regulation goes into effect in five years. The existing canal locks are impaired due to the adoption of a new regulation, which has altered the service potential of the asset from 50 years to 10 years.

The calculation of the impairment loss, employing the **service units approach**, is:

Historical cost	$14,000,000
Total service units in years	50
Cost per service unit	$280,000
Number of service units made unusable by regulation	× 40
Impairment loss	$11,200,000

EXAMPLE

The Minnow City Government built offices for its administrative staff five years ago, at a cost of $4 million. Since then, the City has suffered a catastrophic and permanent decline in tax revenues, resulting in 80% of its staff being laid off. As a result, the offices have been converted into a storage facility for the City. The offices were originally planned to have a life of 40 years. The current replacement cost for a warehouse of the same dimensions is $1.2 million. A commercial construction index was at 100 when the offices were constructed, and is now at 112.

The calculation of the impairment loss, using the **deflated depreciated replacement cost approach**, is:

Historical cost	$4,000,000
Accumulated depreciation (5 ÷ 40 years)	-500,000
Carrying amount	$3,500,000
Replacement cost of warehouse	$1,200,000
Accumulated depreciation (5 ÷ 40 years)	-150,000
Depreciated replacement cost	$1,050,000
Original commercial construction index	100
Current period commercial construction index	112
Deflation factor	0.89286
Deflated depreciated replacement cost	$937,503
Impairment loss	$2,562,497

There are two possible ways to include the effects of an asset impairment in a capital asset account. These approaches are:

- Increase the accumulated depreciation account by the amount of the loss. This approach treats the impairment as though additional years of useful life have been used up.
- Proportionally reduce the capital asset account and the accumulated depreciation account so that the net decrease in the two accounts equals the impairment loss. This approach treats the impairment as though a portion of the asset has been disposed of.

Once an asset impairment has been recognized, it should not be reversed at a later date, even if the circumstances have changed and there is no ongoing evidence of asset impairment.

Impairment Losses under the Modified Approach

A capital asset accounted for under the modified approach may incur physical damage. Such damage would normally trigger an impairment review. However, this is not the case when the modified approach is used. Since the government has committed to maintain the asset at a certain condition level, management is obligated to restore the asset to its predetermined condition level. Because of this commitment, physical damage is treated as temporary.

Capital Asset Disposal

When a government disposes of a capital asset, a gain or loss is calculated as the difference between the net book value of the asset and its sale price (if any). If the asset was being depreciated, then the net book value is likely to be substantially lower than the original acquisition cost of the asset. If the asset was instead an infrastructure asset that was being accounted for under the modified approach, then the net book value would be its original acquisition cost.

> **Note:** A capital asset is not written off when it is fully depreciated, only when it has been dispositioned (that is, sold, donated, or scrapped).

Infrastructure Asset Recordkeeping

There is no specific requirement for maintaining certain levels of record detail for infrastructure assets. At a minimum, however, records should be maintained that allow the accountant to meet the disclosure requirements for infrastructure assets. Here are several scenarios that could drive the level of recordkeeping used:

- All roads could be aggregated into a single road network for an entire state.
- Roads could be recorded as geographic subsystems, such as by county.

- Roads could be capitalized individually.
- Individual segments of roads could be separately capitalized.

Reporting of Capital Assets

There is a distinction between the reporting requirements for capital assets, depending upon whether they are associated with a fund. The following guidelines apply:

- Capital assets associated with a proprietary fund are reported in the financial statements of both the fund and the government.
- Capital assets associated with fiduciary funds are only reported in the statement of fiduciary net position.
- All other capital assets of the government entity are only reported in the entity's statement of net position.

There are several situations relating to capital assets that call for special reporting in the financial statements. A selection of these situations follows:

- *Construction in progress.* Construction in progress is comprised of those costs accumulated to date against an unfinished construction project. These costs should be included in the capital assets line item in the statement of net position, even though the project is not yet complete and depreciation is not yet being charged against it. Construction in progress should be reported with other assets that are not being depreciated, such as land, land improvements, and infrastructure assets being accounted for with the modified approach.
- *Impairment losses.* If an impairment loss is associated with a program, it should be reported as a direct expense of the program that uses the asset.
- *Intangible assets.* If the types of intangible assets being reported by a government differ in their nature and usage, do not report them together in a single major class of capital assets. For example, software and right-of-way easements should not be reported within the same asset class. However, intangible assets having a similar nature and usage, and so should be classified together. For example, there could be a class of assets for land use rights that combines timber rights, water rights, and mineral rights.
- *Joint funding.* When two or more government entities jointly fund a capital asset, the government with primary responsibility for maintaining the asset should report it.
- *Land use rights.* Land use rights assets associated with existing government property should be bundled together with the associated property asset, since this group of assets collectively represents the government's ownership of the property. However, if the land use rights were acquired separately from the underlying property, the rights should be recognized as a separate asset.
- *Reversionary interests in assets.* The federal government may retain a reversionary interest in capital assets that were purchased by a state or local

government with federally-awarded funds. The entity acquiring these assets should report them, since this is the party that both uses the assets and makes decisions regarding how they are to be employed. These assets are recorded at their historical costs.

- *Unclear ownership.* A government should report an infrastructure asset if it has primary responsibility for maintaining the asset. This concept applies to situations in which outright ownership of an asset is unclear, such as in regard to sewers and water lines. For example, a city government is not responsible for sidewalks if homeowners are financially responsible for their repair.

Disclosure of Capital Assets

A number of disclosures are required for capital assets. In addition, there should be a clear distinction between the reporting of general capital assets and the capital assets of proprietary and fiduciary funds. These disclosures are noted in the following subsections.

General Disclosures

Depreciable capital assets should be reported net of their associated accumulated depreciation in the statement of net position. When capital assets are not being depreciated, these assets should be reported separately if the government has a significant amount of these assets. A government may opt to report capital assets in greater detail, such as by major asset class.

Depreciation is to be reported in the statement of activities.

Disclosure of General Capital Assets

General capital assets are not specifically related to activities reported in proprietary or fiduciary funds. Instead, they are associated with governmental activities. These assets are not reported as assets in governmental funds. Instead, they are reported in the governmental activities column in the government-wide statement of net position.

Disclosure of Capital Assets of Proprietary Funds

Capital assets reported within a proprietary fund should be reported in both the government-wide statement of net position and the proprietary fund statement of net position.

Disclosure of Capital Assets of Fiduciary Funds

Capital assets reported within a fiduciary fund should only be reported in the statement of fiduciary net position.

Disclosure of Depreciation

Depreciation should be stated in the following reports:

- The government-wide statement of activities
- The proprietary fund statement of revenues, expenses, and changes in fund net position
- The statement of changes in fiduciary net position

When a government is using the modified approach to limit the use of depreciation, it should present the following schedules with its financial statements:

- The last three condition assessments, noting the assessment dates
- The estimated amount required to maintain the required condition level. This amount is calculated at the beginning of the fiscal year and is compared to the amounts actually expensed for each of the past five reporting periods. The amounts actually expensed should be reported on the accrual basis of accounting.

SAMPLE DISCLOSURE OF LAST THREE CONDITION ASSESSMENTS

	Percentage of Lane-Miles in Good or Better Condition		
	20X4	20X3	20X2
Main arterial	89.4%	88.8%	87.6%
Arterial	87.0%	86.5%	86.0%
Secondary	84.7%	84.6%	84.4%
Overall system	87.2%	87.0%	86.8%

	Percentage of Lane-Miles in Substandard Condition		
	20X4	20X3	20X2
Main arterial	1.2%	1.5%	1.9%
Arterial	4.0%	3.8%	3.6%
Secondary	4.3%	4.3%	4.5%
Overall system	3.9%	3.9%	4.1%

The condition of road pavement is determined using the Achilles pavement measurement system, which is derived from a weighted average of five distress factors contained in pavement surfaces. The system is used to classify roads in good or better condition (75-100), fair condition (50-74), and substandard condition (less than 50). The County's policy is to maintain at least 80% of its street system at the good or better condition level. The County does not allow more than 5% to be in substandard condition. The County conducts condition assessments every year.

SAMPLE DISCLOSURE OF AMOUNTS REQUIRED TO MAINTAIN REQUIRED CONDITION

(000s)	20X4	20X3	20X2	20X1	20X0
Main arterial:					
Needed	$8,049	$8,070	$7,998	$6,450	$6,080
Actual	8,101	8,002	8,014	6,238	6,071
Arterial:					
Needed	4,825	4,705	4,625	4,400	4,150
Actual	4,831	4,699	4,637	4,384	4,129
Secondary:					
Needed	2,005	1,990	1,985	2,250	2,175
Actual	2,013	1,978	2,001	2,219	2,184
Overall system:					
Needed	14,879	14,765	14,608	13,100	12,405
Actual	14,945	14,679	14,652	12,841	12,384
Difference	-$66	$86	-$44	$259	$21

If a government is just beginning to report depreciation for assets under the modified approach, it may be necessary to report as little as one condition assessment, if that is the only assessment that has yet been prepared. The same limited reporting may be used for the disclosure of expenses related to the maintenance of qualifying assets in prior years.

The following information can also be supplied when using the modified approach:

- The basis used for the condition measurement and the measurement scale being used to assess and report asset condition.
- The condition level at which the government wants to preserve those of its infrastructure assets being reported using the modified approach.
- Those factors significantly affecting trends in the information reported in the required schedules. This can include changes in the measurement scale, the basis used for the condition measurement, or the condition assessment methods used. Further, provide an estimate of the effect that a change in the condition level needed to preserve assets will have on estimated maintenance costs for these assets.

SAMPLE DISCLOSURE

The County oversees its network of bridges using its Bridge Oversight Program. The County accounts for all of the bridges in this network using the modified approach.

The County employs a bridge condition rating system that ranges from 1 (impaired) to 10 (new). A bridge is considered to be in need of maintenance or preservation when its condition drops below a rating of 6, and is considered unsafe when its condition drops below a rating of 2.

The County's policy is to keep the number of unsafe bridges at or below 1% of the total number of bridges. The most recent annual assessment of bridge condition confirms that the policy is being met.

Actual maintenance and preservation costs exceeded estimates by 9% in the past year, due to an unusually cold winter that negatively impacted the condition of the bridges.

	Condition Rating	20X4		20X3		20X2	
		Nbr of Bridges	% of Bridges	Nbr of Bridges	% of Bridges	Nbr of Bridges	% of Bridges
Acceptable	6.5-10	182	87.5%	180	88.7%	174	87.4%
Marginally deficient	4.0-6.4	18	8.7%	16	7.9%	17	8.5%
Moderately deficient	2.0-3.9	6	2.8%	5	2.4%	7	3.6%
Severely deficient	1.0-1.9	2	1.0%	2	1.0%	1	0.5%
Total		208	100.0%	203	100.0%	199	100.0%

Disclosure of Accumulated Depreciation

Accumulated depreciation can be reported on the statement of net position as a separate line item, or it may be netted against capital assets. The notes accompanying the financial statements should include the amount of accumulated depreciation separately, as well as changes in accumulated depreciation.

Disclosure of Capitalized Interest

The following information related to capitalized interest should be disclosed:

- When there is a reporting period in which no interest cost is capitalized, state the amount of interest cost charged to expense in the period.
- When there is a reporting period in which some interest cost is capitalized, state the total interest cost incurred in the period and the amount of it that has been capitalized.

Disclosure of Assets Not Being Depreciated

When assets are not being depreciated, they should be reported separately in the statement of net position. However, this rule only applies if the aggregate total of these assets is considered significant.

Disclosure of Impairment

When an impairment loss is recognized, disclose in the notes accompanying the financial statements a general description of the loss, as well as the amount and the financial statement classification of the loss. Further, disclose the carrying amount of any impaired capital assets that are idle as of the end of the reporting year; this disclosure should be made even if the asset impairment is considered to be temporary.

Summary

The baseline level of reporting for capital assets is not especially difficult. A government could standardize its approach for recording the cost of its capital assets and apply straight-line depreciation to those assets. However, the accounting can be substantially more complex when accelerated depreciation is used, and especially when interest capitalization and/or the modified approach are added to the mix. The accountant should evaluate the impact of these additional layers of complexity on the reported results of the entity, as well as the incremental amount of additional work involved to ensure that they are applied correctly. In many cases, a more streamlined and basic approach to reporting capital assets should be sufficient.

Chapter 5
Reporting Liabilities

Introduction

The liabilities reported by a government must be properly classified as short-term or long-term, and there are also instances in which a liability may not be reported at all, or is only disclosed in the accompanying footnotes. These issues are discussed in the following sections.

Reporting Long-Term Liabilities

The reporting of liabilities should include a clear distinction between fund long-term liabilities and general long-term liabilities. The particulars are:

- *Proprietary fund liabilities.* Long-term liabilities that are directly related to proprietary funds and which are expected to be paid from them should be reported in the proprietary fund statement of net position, as well as in the government-wide statement of net position.
- *Fiduciary fund liabilities.* Long-term liabilities that are directly related to fiduciary funds and which are expected to be paid from them should be reported in the statement of fiduciary net position.
- *All other liabilities.* Any other unmatured general long-term liabilities should only be reported in the governmental activities column of the government-wide statement of net position. These liabilities are not reported as liabilities in governmental funds, since doing so would be misleading from the perspective of current period management control. General long-term debt includes the following:

Notes	Unmatured bond principle
Special assessment debt with a government obligation	Warrants
Other forms of long-term general obligation debt	

The general long-term debt classification may include much more than liabilities from debt issuances; it may also include a number of liabilities that can also be assigned to a specific fund, depending on the circumstances. Examples of liabilities that may be either government-wide or fund-specific are:

Bonds	Notes
Claims and judgments	Pensions
Compensated absences	Pollution remediation obligations
Landfill closure and post-closure care	Termination benefits

These liabilities are fund-specific, even though a governmental unit may have pledged its full faith and credit as assurance that they will be paid.

Any liability arising from inter-fund activities is not a general long-term liability, and so should not be reported in governmental funds.

Current Liabilities

A current liability is an obligation that is expected to be settled with current assets or by the creation of new current liabilities. A current liability is typically an obligation for an item in the operating cycle of a government, such as:

- Collections received prior to the performance of services, such as a deposit in advance of providing cable service
- Payables incurred to buy supplies used in the provision of services
- Rentals
- Royalties
- Wage accruals

Other liabilities are classified as current liabilities, even though they are not strictly part of the operating cycle. Instead, they are expected to be settled within one year. Examples of these liabilities are:

- Agency obligations triggered by the collection of cash for third parties
- Amounts that must be spent under sinking fund provisions
- Serial maturities of long-term obligations
- Short-term debts caused by capital asset purchases

There are yet more liabilities that can be classified as current liabilities, because they are either due on demand or within one year of the date of the financial statements, even if actual liquidation is not expected within that period. Further, an obligation is to be classified as a current liability if it is callable by the creditor for either of the following reasons:

- Because the debtor violated a provision of the debt agreement; or
- If a debt agreement violation is not cured within a designated grace period, the debt will be callable.

A callable debt obligation must be classified as a current liability unless the entity meets either of these conditions:

- The creditor has either waived or lost the right to call the debt within one year of the date of the financial statements.
- The government entity has the option to cure the violation and it is probable that the violation will be cured within the required time period.

The reported amount of current liabilities should also include accrued amounts for which settlement is expected within the next year. An accrual for a current liability should only be recorded when the following conditions are present:

- It is only possible to approximate the amount; or
- The person(s) to be paid cannot yet be designated

Short-Term Obligations

Short-term obligations are obligations expected to mature within one year of the date of the current financial statements. Long-term obligations are expected to mature beyond this period. When a short-term obligation is refinanced on a long-term basis, it is either extended or replaced with a long-term obligation. This refinancing arrangement means that it will not be necessary to consume working capital to settle the obligation. If the government intends to refinance the obligation on a long-term basis and has the ability to do so, then the short-term obligation can be excluded from current liabilities.

When a government wants to refinance a short-term obligation on a long-term basis, it can do so in one of these ways:

- Issue a long-term obligation in order to refinance the short-term obligation after the date of the financial statements, but before they have been issued.
- Enter into a financing agreement that allows the government to refinance the obligation on a long-term basis on readily determinable terms, and where the following conditions are present:
  o The agreement does not expire within one year of the date of the financial statements and cannot be cancelled by the lender, barring the violation of a provision of the agreement; and
  o There has been no violation of the financing agreement, or a waiver has been obtained; and
  o The lender is expected to be financially able to honor the agreement.

The amount of a short-term obligation being reclassified away from current liabilities is capped at the proceeds from the new long-term obligation. Or, if a refinancing is to be addressed by a financing agreement, the amount that can be reclassified away from current liabilities is capped at the amount available for refinancing under the agreement. It may be necessary to reduce the amount of the reclassification further if there is information indicating that the monetary resources made available under the financing agreement will be restricted in any way. Further, if the amount available under the agreement fluctuates (such as when the value of underlying collateral varies), the amount of the reclassification should be reduced to a reasonable estimate of the minimum amount expected to be available.

There may be a situation in which a short-term obligation is repaid before the offsetting funds are obtained from a long-term refinancing arrangement. If so, the government is likely using current assets to settle the obligation. For example, a short-term obligation of $100,000 is settled after the date of the financial statements, after which the government enters into a long-term financing arrangement where the proceeds are to be used to replenish current assets. Since one event clearly occurs before the other, the short-term obligation must be reported as a current liability.

Modified Accrual Recognition of Liabilities and Expenditures

Under most circumstances, a government must accrue a governmental fund liability and related expenditure in the period when the liability is incurred. A key exception is unmatured long-term indebtedness, which is reported as a general long-term liability of the government, not as a liability within a governmental fund. Unmatured long-term indebtedness is that portion of the entity's general long-term indebtedness that has not yet come due for payment. This exception also applies to other types of long-term indebtedness, such as:

- Capital leases
- Compensated absences
- Claims and judgments
- Landfill closure and post-closure obligations
- Pensions
- Pollution remediation obligations
- Termination benefits

Note: If debt service fund resources have been provided in the current year for loan payments due early in the next year, it is allowable to recognize the expenditure and related liability in the debt service fund. Resources have been provided when cash has been transferred to the fund.

Conversely, a matured liability should be reported as a governmental fund liability. This type of liability includes items that are payable in full when incurred, as well as that portion of general long-term indebtedness that has come due for payment.

In addition to these general guidelines, several additional accrual modifications may apply, depending on the circumstances. These modifications are:

- *Debt service.* Debt service on bonds and other formal debt issuances should be recognized when due as a governmental fund liability and expenditure.
- *Other liabilities.* Other types of liabilities should be recognized to the extent that they are normally expected to be liquidated with expendable available financial resources. Recognition will be as governmental fund liabilities and expenditures. Examples of these other liabilities are:
  - Claims and judgments
  - Compensated absences
  - Landfill closure and post-closure care costs
  - Receipts of goods and services for pollution remediation
  - Termination benefits

There may be cases in which debt has been issued that is intended to finance projects that will be repaid from assessments made against the owners of the benefited property. This debt should be reported under the following guidelines:

- *General obligation debt*. When general obligation debt will be partially repaid from special assessments, report the debt only as a general long-term liability in the governmental activities column in the government-wide statement of net position.
- *Special assessment debt with obligation*. When debt is issued for which the government has some type of obligation, report it as a general long-term liability in the governmental activities column in the government-wide statement of net position. The only part of this liability not so reported is that portion that is a direct obligation of an enterprise fund, or which is expected to be repaid from the operating revenues of the enterprise fund. The following additional reporting rules may apply:
  - Any portion of the debt that is to be repaid from property owner assessments is to be reported as "special assessment debt with governmental commitment".
  - Any portion of the debt that will be repaid from general government resources is to be reported the same as other general long-term liabilities.
  - Any portion of the debt that is a direct obligation of an enterprise fund or is expected to be repaid from the fund's revenues is to be reported as a liability of that fund in the proprietary fund statement of net position, as well as in the government-wide statement of net position.
- *Special assessment debt with no obligation*. When debt is issued for which the government has no obligation, do not report it in the government's financial statements.

The proceeds of a long-term debt issuance that are not recorded as fund liabilities are usually described as "other financing sources" in the operating statement of the recipient fund. When reported, possible captions can include "long-term notes issued" or "bonds issued". When there is a debt issuance for which the government is not obligated, it should not be identified as (for example) "bond proceeds," but rather as "contribution from property owners" or some similar caption.

Debt Service Funds

A debt service fund accounts for financial resources that are committed to the payment of principal and interest. The fund is usually employed for the payment of principal and interest in the current year, but can also include funds intended for principal and interest payment activities in later years. This type of fund should be used to report financial resources.

Contingent Liabilities

When a government has a contingent liability for which an accrual is not required, it should still disclose the existence of the liability in the notes accompanying the financial statements. This disclosure requirement includes situations in which the entity is contingently liable for the indebtedness of a trust fund or proprietary fund. If such a fund is in default or default is imminent, the contingent liability should be reported separately from the other liabilities in the fund balance sheet, as well as in the government-wide statement of net position.

Additional Liability Reporting Topics

This section addresses two additional topics related to the reporting of liabilities. They are:

- *Separate liability reporting.* A government should separately report those portions of its liabilities that relate to governmental fund liabilities and general long-term liabilities. Governmental fund liabilities are claims against current financial resources.
- *Timing of debt reporting.* Generally, a government records the issuance of debt when the debt instruments are issued, which is on their closing date. However, in situations where the closing date precedes year-end but the related funds are not received until early the next year, the entity should record the related funds receivable and debt obligation as of the closing date.

Disclosure of Liabilities

A government must disclose information about the long-term liabilities of the primary government that are presented in the government-wide statement of net position. See the Notes to Financial Statements chapter for more information. Further, a government must disclose segment information when it reports enterprise funds or uses enterprise fund accounting and when revenue bonds or similar instruments are outstanding. See the Segment Information chapter for more information.

When a government is engaged in debt service, it should disclose the following information:

- Separately state the principal and interest requirements to maturity for each of the next five fiscal years, as well as in five-year increments thereafter. If the entity uses variable-rate debt, it should disclose interest using the interest rate in effect as of the date of the financial statements.
- State the terms that can cause the interest rate associated with variable-rate debt to change.

When a government is contingently liable for the indebtedness of a trust fund or proprietary fund and the fund is in default or default is imminent, disclose all significant facts related to the situation.

Summary

A government routinely enters into long-term financing arrangements to fund its infrastructure projects. In order to present financial statements that are not misleading in regard to the extent and timing of these obligations, the accountant must be fully aware of the applicable rules. It is also relatively common for a government to act as a guarantor of debt, in which case it may be necessary to include disclosures with the financial statements that describe the situation. The reporting of current liabilities is considerably more routine, though the accountant must be aware of the situations in which short-term obligations must be classified as current liabilities.

Chapter 6
The Budget and Budgetary Accounting

Introduction

Governments use budgeting as one of their key financial planning and control tools. Ideally, every government should prepare an annual budget for each of its governmental, proprietary, and fiduciary funds.

The governments of states and larger municipalities require their various departments and agencies to submit budget requests, which are then used by the applicable legislative body as the basis for appropriation bills or ordinances. These appropriations state the maximum expenditures allowed for the budget year. The government cannot exceed these expenditure levels, unless the legislative body subsequently amends its appropriation bill to accommodate more expenditures.

Depending on the applicable legal provisions, any unexpended or unencumbered appropriations may lapse at the end of the fiscal year, or they can continue forward as authorizations for future expenditures.

In this chapter, we provide an overview of budgetary periods, budget types, budgetary control, and encumbrances.

Budgetary Period

A budget is a financial plan that covers a specific period of time. There are two types of governmental budgets, which are the annual and long-term budgets. As the name implies, an annual budget authorizes all financial operations for one fiscal year. A long-term budget provides financial estimates for a longer period, usually in the range of from four to six years, along with possible financing options. Annual budgets are usually required, since they form the basis for a governmental system of control. Long-term budgets are less likely to be required, since they are not control documents. Instead, they are used to plan for major programs or capital outlays.

Budget Types

A budget is structured to be either fixed or flexible. A fixed budget contains fixed dollar amounts for all stated line items. This document is based on a single activity level for the government entity to which it is related. A flexible budget contains formulas that will alter the stated amount of a line item, depending on the related activity level.

Most government budgets are fixed, on the assumption that revenue levels are relatively fixed. The control system that underlies these budgets is targeted at keeping expenditure levels from surpassing projected revenue levels.

A proprietary fund is more likely to have a flexible budget associated with it, since this type of fund tends to have a variable revenue level, depending on the amount of demand for the fund's goods and services. Since revenues fluctuate, the expenditure budget must be flexible enough to change in accordance with revenue levels.

A budget should be prepared using the same basis of accounting on which it will be reported, so there will be no confusion about the amount of revenues received or expenses incurred. Governmental fund annual budgets should be prepared on the modified accrual basis of accounting, since this is the basis of accounting most likely to be used to report fund performance. In those cases where there is a legal requirement to prepare a budget using a different basis of accounting (such as the cash basis), the accountant should maintain sufficient supplemental records to allow for the presentation of financial statements in accordance with the most applicable basis of accounting.

Budgetary Control

The planning process requires planners to determine the types and amounts of services to be provided, and to allocate resources among the various departments and programs. There are three possible levels of control that can be assigned to departments and programs. They are:

1. An appropriated budget
2. A legally authorized non-appropriated budget
3. Non-budgeted activities that are not subject to an appropriated budget or a legally authorized non-appropriated budget

The following types of budgets are used in a governmental environment:

- *Executive budget.* This budget includes all budgetary information submitted by the chief executive to the legislative body.
- *Appropriated budget.* This budget has been created by an appropriation bill and signed into law. The creation of an appropriated budget begins with the original budget, which is then adjusted for reserves, transfers, allocations, and supplemental appropriations to arrive at the final budget.
- *Non-appropriated budget.* This budget is not subject to appropriation, since it is authorized by a constitution, charter, or statute.
- *Budgetary execution and management.* This budget includes all other budgetary transactions that do not require formal legislative enactment. These transactions can include sub-allocations, contingency reserves, transfers, deferrals, and so forth.

Budgetary accounting is a control technique that can be used to assist in controlling expenditures. Budgetary accounting involves the initial inclusion of budgetary accounts in fund ledgers. Once they have been used as a control during the fiscal year, these accounts are reversed as part of the year-end closing process. Since budgetary accounts are eventually removed from the accounting records, they have no effect on a governmental fund's financial position or its fund balance.

Budgetary accounts should be included in general funds, special revenue funds, and other funds that are budgeted on an annual basis and which have multiple types of revenues, expenditures, and transfers. These accounts are most useful for controlling funds through which complex transactions flow. Conversely, budgetary accounts may not be needed when there is already an adequate level of control or where there are few transactions (such as a debt service fund).

When a flexible budget is applied to a fund, the expense estimates in the budget are considered to be approved plans, rather than appropriations, since the expense levels can change in accordance with fluctuations in revenue. Budgetary control is achieved by comparing actual expense levels to the expense amounts indicated in the budget, once the effects of revenue changes on the budgeted expenses have been considered.

Encumbrances

An encumbrance is a commitment related to an unperformed contract for goods or services. An encumbrance should be recorded in the accounting records in order to maintain a higher level of budgetary control over expenditures and cash planning. This is especially important for general and special revenue funds. The following additional points may apply when encumbrances are used in an accounting system:

- There may still be some encumbrances outstanding at year-end, reflecting the extent to which contracts have not yet been completed. These year-end balances are not treated as expenditures or liabilities.
- When a contract has been completed, there is no longer a need for an associated encumbrance, so the encumbrance should be removed from the accounting records.
- When there is a significant encumbrance, disclose it in the notes to the financial statements, disclosing this information for each major fund and in aggregate for all non-major funds.

Summary

The budget is an essential component of the governmental control system, since it states the amounts and sources of revenues and transfers in, as well as how these funds are to be used or directed elsewhere. In situations where transaction volumes are high or unusually complex, it makes sense to use budgetary accounting to keep tight control over expenditure levels. When this is not the case, there may be a reduced need for budgetary accounting.

Chapter 7
Common Accounting Transactions

Introduction

In this chapter, we cover a number of common accounting transactions, showing the format of each journal entry and noting how the entry may change, depending on the type of fund in which a transaction is being recorded. There is no underlying case study from which the information in the journal entries is drawn; instead, the numbers in each journal entry are simply placeholders used to show how a journal entry could be constructed. The following sections are sorted in alphabetical order by the general classification of accounting transaction. The sequence of these classifications is as follows:

- Capital asset transactions
- Debt transactions
- Encumbrance transactions
- Interfund transactions
- Inventory usage
- Reimbursement transactions

Capital Asset Transactions

A government usually invests heavily in capital assets, and so will require many journal entries to record the related purchasing, capitalization, depreciation, and other transactions. In this section, we cover the journal entries for the purchase, depreciation, and sale of a capital asset.

Asset Purchase Transaction

When a governmental fund is used to record the acquisition of a capital asset, the transaction is considered to be a decrease of the fund's current financial resources. This results in the following entry:

	Debit	Credit
Expenditures – capital assets	50,000	
Cash		50,000
To record the acquisition of a capital asset		

If the acquisition is instead recorded in a proprietary fund, the transaction is considered to be a substitute of one resource (cash) for another resource (the capital asset). The entry is:

	Debit	Credit
Capital assets - vehicles	50,000	
Cash		50,000
To record the acquisition of a capital asset (vehicle)		

Depreciation Transaction

The treatment of depreciation varies by the type of fund in which a capital asset is recorded. If the initial asset acquisition was recorded in a governmental fund, then no depreciation is recorded, since there is no reduction in the current financial resources of the fund. If the asset had instead been recorded in a proprietary fund, the focus would have been on the economic depletion caused by the use of the asset. The following journal entry would be used to record the depreciation:

	Debit	Credit
Depreciation expense	2,000	
Accumulated depreciation - vehicles		2,000
To record periodic vehicle depreciation		

Asset Sale Transaction

When a governmental fund is used to record the sale of a capital asset, the resulting inflow of cash from the sale is considered an increase in its current financial resources, which triggers the following entry:

	Debit	Credit
Cash	12,000	
Miscellaneous revenues		12,000
To record the sale of a capital asset (vehicle)		

If the sale is instead recorded in a proprietary fund, there may be a gain or loss on the sale. In addition, all accumulated depreciation that had previously been recorded against the asset is now reversed. We provide two sample journal entries for an asset sale, with the first version recording a gain and the second recording a loss.

	Debit	Credit
Cash	8,000	
Accumulated depreciation	45,000	
Capital assets - vehicles		50,000
Gain on sale of asset		3,000
To record the sale of a capital asset (vehicle) with gain		

	Debit	Credit
Cash	1,000	
Accumulated depreciation	45,000	
Loss on sale of asset	4,000	
Capital assets - vehicles		50,000
To record the sale of a capital asset (vehicle) with loss		

Debt Transactions

A government may incur a substantial amount of debt in order to fund its operations and pay for capital assets. In this section, we cover the journal entries for the initial acquisition of debt, debt payments, and interest accruals.

Initial Debt Transaction

A government may record the issuance of debt within a governmental fund or a proprietary fund. The more likely case is that the issuance is recorded in a governmental fund, since proprietary funds are limited to business-type activities. When the debt is recorded in a governmental fund, the transaction is treated as an increase in its current financial resources. A typical initial entry to record the debt in a governmental fund is as follows:

	Debit	Credit
Cash	975,000	
Expenditures – bond issuance costs	25,000	
Other financing source		1,000,000
To record the receipt of cash from the sale of bonds		

If the issuance of debt is instead recorded in a proprietary fund, the inflow of resources is considered to be offset by the eventual need to repay the debt, so there is no change in the economic resources of the fund. This results in a different initial journal entry than was used for a governmental fund, which is:

	Debit	Credit
Cash	975,000	
Bond issuance expense	25,000	
Bonds payable		1,000,000
To record the receipt of cash from the sale of bonds		

Debt Payments

A government will periodically make payments for the interest on its outstanding debt, which may include a principal repayment. When such a payment is recorded in a governmental fund, there is a decrease in the current financial resources of the fund. In this case, the principal and interest components are combined into a single line item as an expenditure. A typical entry is:

	Debit	Credit
Expenditures – debt service	6,000	
Cash		6,000
To record debt service payment on debt		

The entry is different when the transaction is recorded in a proprietary fund. In this case, the economic resources of the fund are only being reduced by the amount of the interest expense. The principal portion of the debt is offset by a reduction in the original debt liability. A typical entry is:

	Debit	Credit
Bonds payable	5,000	
Interest expense	1,000	
Cash		6,000
To record principal and interest payment on debt		

Interest Accrual

If a debt service payment is not made within a reporting period, some amount of interest expense will have accrued during the period. A proprietary fund accrues this interest as an expense. A typical entry follows.

	Debit	Credit
Interest expense	1,500	
Interest payable		1,500
To accrue interest expense on debt		

If accrued interest were to then be paid by a proprietary fund, the entry would reverse the amount of the interest payable that had previously been accrued. For example:

	Debit	Credit
Interest payable	1,500	
Cash		1,500
To record interest payment on debt		

Debt Service Fund Transactions

A government might set up a debt service fund to accumulate resources from which debt obligations are paid. Since a debt service fund is a governmental fund, it uses the modified accrual basis of accounting and the current financial resources measurement focus, where the intent is on current financial resources. Consequently, the initial transfer of funds from the general fund into a debt service fund would be dealt with in the following manner:

	Debit	Credit
Cash	110,000	
Other financing sources – operating transfers in (general fund)		110,000
To record the transfer of funds from the general fund		

The fund manager invests excess cash in the debt service fund that will not be needed until the next debt service payment, as noted in the following journal entry:

	Debit	Credit
Investment	42,000	
Cash		42,000
To record the investment of excess cash		

Based on its investments, the fund then accrues interest on its invested funds, using the following entry:

	Debit	Credit
Interest receivable on investments	400	
Revenues - interest		400
To record accrued interest on invested funds		

The fund manager pays out cash to meet the government's principal and interest obligations to investors and lenders, using the following entry:

	Debit	Credit
Expenditures – debt service	16,000	
Cash		16,000
To record debt service payments made to bond holders		

Encumbrance Transactions

A government can choose to enter encumbrances into the accounting system to indicate that there are open commitments related to unfilled purchase orders and contracts. The following journal entry shows how an encumbrance could be entered into the system for an issued purchase order.

	Debit	Credit
Encumbrances	9,000	
Budgetary fund balance – reserved for encumbrances		9,000
To record an encumbrance related to purchase order A1097		

When the items bought with the purchase order are received, the encumbrance is reversed and replaced with the liability related to the purchase order. The reversing journal entry needed to make the first change is:

	Debit	Credit
Budgetary fund balance – reserved for encumbrances	9,000	
Encumbrances		9,000
To reverse the encumbrance associated with purchase order A1097		

We assume that the actual supplier invoice differs somewhat from the original encumbrance, so the replacing entry for the purchase order contains slightly different amounts, as noted next:

	Debit	Credit
Expenditures	8,850	
Accounts payable		8,850
To reverse the payable related to purchase order A1097		

Interfund Transactions

A government's general fund may loan funds to other funds for various reasons, perhaps to avoid cash shortfalls in the other funds. The initial entry to reflect such a loan, as issued by the general fund, could be set up as follows:

	Debit	Credit
Due from capital projects fund	25,000	
Cash		25,000
To record the loan of funds to the capital projects fund		

The receiving fund records the offsetting part of this obligation, such as:

	Debit	Credit
Cash	25,000	
Due to general fund		25,000
To record the receipt of a loan from the general fund		

Inventory Usage

A government may routinely purchase significant amounts of inventory, which it consumes over a period of time. If these purchases are recorded in a governmental fund, there is a decrease in the current financial resources of the fund, which are set up as a reserved portion of the fund balance. The initial entry to reflect the acquisition of inventory is:

	Debit	Credit
Inventory	24,000	
Cash		24,000
To record the purchase of inventory items		

As these inventory items are consumed, they are identified within the governmental fund as expenditures. For example:

	Debit	Credit
Expenditures - inventory	9,000	
Inventory		9,000
To record the consumption of inventory items		

Some of the inventory items may not be consumed by the end of the fiscal year. When this is the case, a portion of the fund balance is set aside (reserved) for the residual inventory amount. For example:

	Debit	Credit
Fund balance	16,000	
Fund balance – reserved for inventory		16,000
To reserve the fund balance for inventory on hand at year-end		

This residual amount of inventory is then consumed in the following year, as noted in the following example:

	Debit	Credit
Expenditures - inventory	16,000	
Inventory		16,000
To record the consumption of beginning-year inventory on hand		

Once the inventory has been consumed, the related reserve of the fund balance can be reversed, since it is no longer needed. A sample entry is:

	Debit	Credit
Fund balance – reserved for inventory	16,000	
Fund balance		16,000
To reserve the fund balance for inventory on hand at year-end		

The preceding series of entries were used to record the initial purchase of $25,000 of inventory, of which $9,000 was consumed within the purchase year and $16,000 was consumed in the following year.

Reimbursement Transactions

A payment may be made by one fund but is attributable to a different fund, which calls for the reimbursement of the paying fund by the benefiting fund. Proper recordation of a reimbursement transaction involves recording an expenditure or expense in the reimbursing fund, and an expenditure or expense reduction in the fund that is reimbursed for its initial payment. A sample entry for the general fund (which in the example is assumed to be making the initial payment) is:

	Debit	Credit
Expenditures - supplies	2,000	
Cash		2,000
To record payment for supplies		

A portion of this purchase is attributable to a different fund (in this case, the electrical utility), so the general utility needs another entry to indicate a receivable, as indicated in the following entry:

	Debit	Credit
Due from electrical utility	500	
Expenditures - supplies		500
To record receivable for reimbursement of the supplies payment		

The reimbursing fund then records a journal entry to indicate its subsequent payment of the general fund, as noted in the following entry:

	Debit	Credit
Expenses - supplies	500	
Cash		500
To record reimbursement payment to general fund		

Summary

The sample journal entries noted in this chapter were focused on those transactions that might actually require a manual journal entry. Very common transactions are usually handled automatically by the data entry forms set up in a government's accounting software, so that the entries associated with such matters as the recordation of supplier invoices, payments to suppliers, and taxpayer billings do not require the separate creation of a journal entry. Instead, the accounts associated with these data entry forms are assigned when the software is initially configured, and will not need to be changed again unless the underlying accounts are subsequently altered.

Chapter 8
Classification and Terminology

Introduction

A government has a reasonable amount of leeway in structuring its financial statements. Nonetheless, it should adhere to some presentation standards, so that its financials are comparable to those of other governments, while also being comparable from period to period. In general, the following principles should be followed in structuring financial statements:

Governmental Funds

- The statement of activities should present the activities accounted for in governmental funds by their function, coinciding with the level of detail required in the fund statement of revenues, expenditures, and changes in fund balances.
- The statement of activities should include activities accounted for in enterprise funds by different identifiable activities.
- Classify governmental fund revenues by fund and source.
- Classify governmental fund expenditures by fund, function or program, organization unit, activity, character, and principal classes of objects.
- Classify the proceeds of general long-term debt issues separately from revenues and expenditures within governmental fund financial statements.
- Report contributions and transfers separately from general revenues in the government-wide statement of activities.

Proprietary Funds

- Report proprietary fund revenues by major sources, and distinguish them as being operating and non-operating.
- Classify proprietary fund expenses in the same manner as those of similar business organizations or activities, and distinguish them as being operating and non-operating.
- Report contributions and transfers separately after non-operating revenues and expenses in a proprietary fund's statement of revenues, expenses, and changes in fund net position.

We will expand upon these principles and other related matters throughout the chapter.

Interfund Activity

Interfund activity within and among the governmental, proprietary, and fiduciary funds should be classified in the following manner:

- *Reciprocal interfund activity.* This type of activity involves the transfer of funds that are expected to be paid back. Such a loan should be reported as an inter-fund receivable by the lending fund and as an inter-fund payable by the borrowing fund. In situations where repayment is not expected within a reasonable time frame, reduce the amount not expected to be paid as a transfer from the lending fund to the receiving fund. An alternative situation is when there is a sale and purchase of goods and services between funds at prices approximating the market rate. These transactions should be reported by the selling fund as revenue and as an expense or expenditure by the purchasing fund. Any of these amounts that are unpaid are recorded as inter-fund receivables by the seller and as interfund payables by the purchaser.
- *Non-reciprocal interfund activity.* A non-reciprocal interfund transfer occurs when there is a one-way flow of assets between funds (that is, there is no repayment requirement). This type of transfer is to be reported as other financing uses by the fund issuing the transfer and as other financing sources by the receiving fund. There may also be interfund reimbursements, where a fund responsible for an expenditure or expense transfers a payment to the fund that initially paid for the item in question.

EXAMPLE

The Department of Administration of Qanix City pays the utility bill for the entire city government, and is then reimbursed by the various city departments via inter-departmental billings. In this situation, the utility expense initially recorded by the Department of Administration is reduced by the amount of the internal charges. The Department should not record these inter-departmental billings as revenue, since it does not provide utilities to the rest of the city's departments.

Reporting of Internal Activities and Balances

When there are internal activities between the funds of a government, these activities should be eliminated in the government-wide entity's statement of net position. Otherwise, interfund receivables and payables will appear in the statement of net position when the government-wide entity does not have these assets and obligations. Similarly, internal service fund transactions should be eliminated from the statement of activities, since these transactions net to zero from the perspective of the government as a whole.

Only the net amount transferred between governmental and business-type activities should be reported on the statement of activities. This net amount can be determined by combining the transfers in and out within each category to arrive at a single net amount of transfers figure.

When there are receivables from or payables to fiduciary funds, these amounts should be included in the statement of net position as being receivable from or payable to external parties – which is actually the case, since the nature of a fiduciary account is to collect and disburse cash on behalf of a third party.

Reporting of Internal Service Fund Balances

When the asset and liability balances of an internal service fund have not been eliminated in the statement of net position, report these balances in the governmental activities column. The only exception is when enterprise funds are the main participants in an internal service fund, in which case the government should report the residual assets, liabilities, deferred outflows of resources, and deferred inflows of resources in the business-type activities column within the statement of net position.

Classifications within the Statement of Net Position

There are several classifications of line items to consider when constructing a statement of net position. The following sub-topics address each one.

Current Assets

The term *current assets* refers to a group of line items on the statement of net position that are either cash already or which can be converted into cash, sold, or consumed within one year. Given this definition, the following line items are usually considered to be current assets:

- Cash available for current operations
- Cash equivalents
- Marketable securities
- Inventories of merchandise, raw materials, work-in-process, and finished goods
- Operating supplies and maintenance materials and parts
- Trade accounts and notes receivable
- Receivables from taxpayers, customers, employees, and other governments
- Notes receivable if they conform to normal trade practices
- Prepayments

Note: Prepayments are considered to be current assets, since the lack of these payments would otherwise require the use of current assets within a year.

Cash for which there are withdrawal restrictions should not be classified as current assets, nor should cash that has been designated for disbursement in the purchasing or construction of non-current assets or for the settlement of long-term debts.

Similarly, receivables should not be classified as current assets if they are not expected to be collected within the next year.

The total amount of current assets should be stated in the statement of net position.

Allowances

A government may recognize an allowance against a decline in the value of an asset. For example, an allowance for doubtful accounts may be created to recognize possible losses on receivables outstanding. These allowances should be deducted from the assets with which they are paired on the statement of net position.

Current Liabilities

The term *current liability* refers to a group of obligation line items on the statement of net position that are expected to be liquidated with existing assets that are classified as current assets, or through the creation of other current liabilities. These liabilities should be involved in the operating cycle of a business, or they are expected to be settled within one year. Given this definition, the following line items are usually considered to be current liabilities:

- Trade payables
- Wages payable
- Royalties payable
- Short-term debts
- Serial maturities of long-term obligations
- Amounts to be expended under required sinking fund provisions
- Payments collected on behalf of and reimbursable to third parties
- Obligations that are due on demand or within the next year
- Long-term obligations that are callable due to the debtor's violation of a loan provision

> **Note:** Callable obligations are not classified as current liabilities when the creditor has waived the right to demand repayment, or when the debtor will probably cure the prior violation of a loan provision within a designated grace period.

When there is an expectation that a short-term obligation will be refinanced, it is not classified as a current liability, as long as there is intent to refinance the obligation on a long-term basis and the government is able to do so. The ability to refinance has not been demonstrated when a short-term obligation has been replaced by another short-term obligation.

The total amount of current liabilities should be stated in the statement of net position.

Classifications within Governmental Fund Financial Statements

There are several classifications of line items to consider when constructing governmental fund financial statements. The following sub-topics address each one.

Other Long-Term Debt Transactions

There are a number of debt issuance costs that may be incurred when a government issues debt. These costs can include:

- Bond insurance
- Legal fees
- Rating agency fees
- Underwriting fees

When the cost of a debt issuance is paid out of the proceeds of a debt issuance, the costs are reported as expenditures. When the costs are paid from existing resources, they are reported as expenditures as soon as the related liability has been incurred.

Capital Asset Sales

The proceeds from the sale of a capital asset should be reported as other financial sources in governmental funds.

Revenues

Revenues occur when there are increases in fund financial resources, not including interfund transfers and proceeds from the issuance of debt. Governmental fund revenues are classified by fund and source. Examples of fund sources are:

- Charges for services
- Fines and forfeits
- Intergovernmental revenues
- Licenses and permits
- Taxes

Revenues are frequently reported at the level of organizational units, which can be useful for increasing the amount of management control over the revenue-generation process.

Expenditures

Expenditures are the reduction of fund financial resources, not including interfund transfers. Expenditures may be reported in several ways, in order to enhance the amount of management control over the organization. The accounting classifications that may be used are:

- *Fund*. An accounting entity with a self-balancing set of accounts that are used to record financial resources and liabilities, which are segregated in order to carry on certain activities or attain targeted objectives.
- *Function or program*. Groups together related activities that are intended to accomplish a major service or fulfill a regulatory responsibility.
- *Organization unit*. Corresponds to the government's organizational structure.
- *Activity*. Used to calculate expenditures per unit of activity, which can then be used to evaluate current performance and set future performance standards.
- *Character*. Classifies expenditures by the fiscal periods they are intended to benefit. The classification options are:
    - Current expenditures, where the benefit is solely in the current period
    - Capital outlays, where the benefit should be across multiple periods, extending into the future
    - Debt service, where the benefit could span several periods, including historical periods
    - Intergovernmental, where the benefit is transferred between governmental units
- *Object class*. Classifies expenditures by the types of goods or services obtained.

Tip: The number of object classifications should be minimized, since the control emphasis is more likely to be at the level of functions, organization units, or activities.

Classifications within the Government-Wide Statement of Activities

There are several classifications of line items to consider when constructing a government-wide statement of activities. The following sub-topics address each one.

General

A government should include a sufficient level of detail in its government-wide statement of activities if doing so provides useful information without making it more difficult for a reader to understand the statement. There is no ideal level of detail, since there is a broad range in the number of programs that a government may support.

Okie City manages two separate water districts, one on each side of the Okefenokee River. The city uses two separate enterprise funds to account for the activities in each of these districts. The city can report each of these districts separately in its statement of activities, but does not have to do so, since the activities that the two districts engage in is the same.

Okie City also has an electric utility and a fiber optic cable utility, both of which are accounted for in a single enterprise fund. Okie cannot report a single utilities function in the statement of activities, because the provision of electricity and Internet access are different activities. Possible labeling for separate line items could be "Electric Utility" and "Internet Access Utility."

Expenses

Expenses should be reported by function, except in cases where an expense is classified as special or extraordinary (which are explained in a later section).

Three categories of revenue should be reported in the statement of activities, which are as follows:

- Program-specific capital grants and contributions
- Program-specific operating grants and contributions
- Charges for services

In cases where government-wide expenditures are accounted for in the general fund, the expenses associated with specific functions or programs should be reported as direct expenses of the various functions or programs in the statement of activities. When expenses cannot be specifically identified with functions or programs, they should be classified for reporting purposes as general government or some similar type of cost center.

EXAMPLE

Okie City charges its employee pension costs to a general administration account in the general fund. Pension costs are directly associated with specific employees, and so should be charged to the city functions where the employees work, such as the city power plant and the wastewater treatment facility. This can be accomplished by reclassifying pension costs out of the general administration account and into the various city functions.

Revenues

When determining the function to which program revenue should be assigned, the key factors are:

- For charges to services, the determining factor is which function generates the revenue.
- For grants and contributions, the determining factor is whether the revenue is restricted to a certain function.

EXAMPLE

A state government manages a permanent fund in its fish and wildlife function, but a portion of the earnings generated by this fund is restricted for the use of the state parks function. These earnings should be reported as revenue of the state parks function, since the revenue is restricted to that function.

When there is no program to which revenues can be assigned, report them as general revenues. All taxes are considered to be general revenues, even when they have been levied for a specific purpose. Tax revenues should be reported by type of tax, such as:

- Franchise taxes
- Income taxes
- Property taxes
- Sales taxes

General revenues should be reported in the statement of activities after the total net expense of the government's functions. Certain transactions should be reported separately from general revenues (though in the same area of the statement of activities) in order to clarify the sources of financing the net cost of government programs. These transactions include:

- Contributions to permanent endowments
- Contributions to permanent fund principal
- Contributions to term endowments
- Special and extraordinary items (see the next section)
- Transfers between governmental and business-type activities

Operating special assessments are classified as program revenues, because only those property owners who benefit from a special assessment benefit from the arrangement. This means that the assessments are essentially charges for services, and so would qualify as program revenues.

EXAMPLE

A light rail from a nearby major city has just been built through the Hillside neighborhood of Helix City. The residents of Hillside experience an immediate upsurge in the crime rate, as gangs from the major city take the light rail out to Hillside. Accordingly, the property owners in the Hillside neighborhood agree to pay for additional police protection in their area, which is paid for with a special assessment. Only those property owners in this specific neighborhood benefit from the change, rather than the entire real estate tax base. Thus, the assessment constitutes a charge for services.

A government may levy a tax, for which the proceeds will be restricted for use within a specific program or function. In this case, the tax is applied to a general group, while the proceeds are narrowly defined (which was not the case for operating special assessments, where only those who benefit from the proceeds are taxed). In this case, the tax is classified as general revenue and not program revenue.

Special and Extraordinary Items

An *extraordinary item* is unusual in nature and infrequent in occurrence. Examples of extraordinary items are costs related to the failure of a dam or the destruction caused by an earthquake. A *special item* is one that is within the control of management and is either unusual in nature or infrequent in occurrence. Examples of special items are the termination benefits resulting from the layoffs associated with closing a city's municipal airport, and the losses incurred when a government disposes of its wastewater management operations. The reporting requirements for these items are:

- *Statement of activities.* Extraordinary items are to be reported separately at the bottom of the statement of activities. Special items are also to be reported separately; they should be reported before any extraordinary items.
- *Governmental fund statement of revenues, expenditures, and changes in fund balances.* Special and extraordinary items should be reported separately in a governmental fund statement of revenues, expenditures, and changes in fund balances after the "other financing sources and uses" line item. If both a special and an extraordinary item occur in the same period, report these line items separately in a "special and extraordinary items" classification.
- *Proprietary fund statement of revenues, expenditures, and changes in fund net position.* Report extraordinary and special items separately, after non-operating revenues and expenditures.

The following criteria should be met before classifying something as either extraordinary or special:

- *Unusual.* The event or transaction should be abnormal to a high degree and unrelated to the ordinary activities of the government. Whether something is unusual depends on the characteristics of the government, such as its location, the types of activities in which it engages, and the nature of its regulations.
- *Infrequent.* The event or transaction is one that would not reasonably be expected to recur in the future. The probability of recurrence depends on the nature of the government entity. The prior history of an event or transaction can be used to assess the probability of its recurrence in the future.

Some gains and losses are not considered extraordinary items, because they are relatively common and can be expected to occur again in the future. Examples of these items are:

- Adjustments made to the accruals on long-term contracts
- Exchange gains and losses related to foreign currency
- Gains and losses triggered by the disposition of capital assets
- The effects of a strike
- The write-down of receivables, inventory, intangible assets, and similar items

In addition, if there are any significant transactions or other events that can be considered unusual or infrequent and are not within the control of management, disclose them in the notes accompanying the financial statements.

Right of Offset

The assets and liabilities of a government entity should not be offset against each other in the government-wide statements of net position, except in cases where there is an actual right of offset. The same rule applies for the proprietary fund statement of fund net position. A right of offset exists when (for example) two government entities can net their payables to and receivables from each other, so that only the net difference is transferred between them.

Reporting Net Position

The *net position* is the difference between all other elements in a statement of financial position, so it is a summarization of other line items. Net position should be displayed in three components on the statement, as follows:

- *Net investment in capital assets.* Includes capital assets (net of accumulated depreciation), less the outstanding balances of bonds, mortgages, notes, and other borrowings associated with the acquisition or construction of capital assets. If there are any deferred inflows or outflows of resources related to the acquisition or construction of capital assets, also include them in this summarization. If there is no debt or deferred inflow of resources associated with the capital assets, consider classifying this line item as "investment in capital assets" to avoid misleading readers.

Note: If debt is issued to refund existing debt that is related to capital assets, the replacement debt is also considered to be capital-related.

- *Restricted.* Report a restricted net position component when there are externally-imposed constraints placed on the net position, such as by creditors, grantors, contributors, or laws. It may be necessary to display the restricted component of net position in two components, which are expendable and non-expendable. A non-expendable net position must be reported when amounts are to be retained in perpetuity or there is a minority interest in component units. The restricted component represents restricted assets that have been reduced by any liabilities related to those assets. A liability is considered to be related to an asset when the asset is a direct result of the liability being incurred, or if the liability will be liquidated along with the asset with which it is paired.
- *Unrestricted.* The unrestricted component of net position is the residual amount remaining that was not included in the calculation of the net investment in capital assets or the restricted components of net position.

Note: There may be internal constraints, where resources have been committed to specific activities. These commitments cannot be classified as restricted, since they can be removed or altered.

The same reporting structure for net position should be used when reporting the net position of proprietary funds.

EXAMPLE

A county's job training center has received a $2 million bequest from someone who once benefited from its services. According to the terms of the bequest, the principal amount must be maintained, while any investment earnings can be used to pay for additional job training. As of year-end, the fair value of this endowment has declined to $1.9 million. The restricted non-expendable net position should state the reported amount of $1.9 million. If the market recovers, allowing the $2 million principal amount to be regained, the restricted non-expendable net position would be reported as $2 million. If the market is unusually robust and the principal amount exceeds $2 million, the excess amount over $2 million would be reported as a restricted expendable net position.

Governmental Fund Reporting

A fund balance for a governmental fund should be stated in report classifications so that there is a hierarchy of information, showing the requirements imposed on the government to use resources in accordance with various restrictions. The fund balances that can be reported are as follows:

- *Non-spendable fund balance.* This classification is comprised of amounts the government is not allowed to spend, because there is a legal or contractual requirement to maintain the funds. For example, the principal balance of a permanent fund is considered a non-spendable fund balance. This classification can also include amounts that are not in *spendable form.* Assets are not in spendable form when there no expectation that an asset will be converted into cash (as may be the case with inventory), property that has been acquired for resale, and the long-term amount of loans receivable.
- *Restricted fund balance.* This classification is used for amounts that have been restricted for specific purposes. A restriction is considered to be in place when the constraints placed on the use of resources have been imposed by law or by third parties such as creditors, contributors, or grantors. Investment proceeds may also be classified as restricted if the underlying constraint limits the use of the proceeds. The amount reported as a restricted fund balance should not be greater than the restricted assets in a fund.
- *Committed fund balance.* This classification contains amounts that can only be consumed on specific activities, as directed by the government's highest level of decision-making authority. It is possible that these amounts could be redeployed for other purposes, which is not the case with items classified within the restricted fund balance.
- *Assigned fund balance.* This classification is used when the government's intent is to use resources for a specific purpose. In this situation, no actual restriction or commitment is placed on the resources. The level of intent should be expressed by the governing body or the entity to which resource usage authority has been assigned.
- *Unassigned fund balance.* This classification is the residual classification for the general fund; all funds not reported within one of the preceding classifications are stated here.

> **Note:** Some governments may not find it necessary to have both committed fund balances and assigned fund balances. One or the other report classification may be sufficient.

EXAMPLE

A wealthy citizen passes away and leaves a major bequest to the local county government, stipulating that the interest earned from investment of the funds be used to maintain the trail system in a local park. The bequest stipulates that the principal amount can never be spent. The county government should account for the bequest in a permanent fund. The donation should be reported as revenue in the governmental fund statements and included in the non-spendable fund balance.

EXAMPLE

The following table demonstrates a possible presentation format for a special revenue fund that includes amounts that have been designated as restricted, committed, or assigned. The fund has three specific purposes, which are curb maintenance, road maintenance, and sidewalk repair.

	Restricted	Committed	Assigned	Total
Curb maintenance				
Beginning balances	$12,000	$82,000	$4,000	$98,000
Additions	4,000	--	--	4,000
Expenditures incurred	-16,000	-82,000	-1,000	-99,000
Ending balances	--	--	3,000	3,000
Road maintenance				
Beginning balances	40,000	17,000	--	57,000
Additions	28,000	13,000	100,000	141,000
Expenditures incurred	-68,000	-30,000	-100,000	-198,000
Ending balances	--	--	--	--
Sidewalk repair				
Beginning balances	2,000	--	14,000	16,000
Additions	6,000	31,000	--	37,000
Expenditures incurred	-8,000	-11,000	--	-19,000
Ending balances	--	20,000	14,000	34,000
Fund totals	$--	$20,000	$17,000	$37,000

Classification and Terminology

EXAMPLE

The following table presents a possible presentation format for the fund balance section of a balance sheet. This information is presented at an aggregate level in order to compress the size of the presentation. The specific purpose details related to this table would be disclosed in the footnotes accompanying the financial statements.

	General Fund	Storm Water Management Fund	Road Repair Fund	Debt Service Fund	Capital Projects Fund	Other Funds	Total
		Special Revenue Funds					
Fund balances:							
Non-spendable	$200,000	$14,000	$180,000	$--	$--	$64,000	$458,000
Restricted	325,000	11,000	20,000	260,000	600,000	89,000	1,305,000
Committed	210,000	5,000	61,000	--	120,000	42,000	438,000
Assigned	92,000	--	--	100,000	--	--	192,000
Unassigned	172,000	--	--	--	--	--	172,000
Total fund balances	$999,000	$30,000	$261,000	$360,000	$720,000	$195,000	$2,565,000

A *stabilization arrangement* may be set up where a government sets aside funds for use in emergency situations, or when there are budgetary imbalances. These amounts are only supposed to be spent when certain circumstances exist. Report stabilization amounts in the general fund as restricted or committed, depending on the source of the constraint that limits their use. If the circumstances do not allow for reporting the funds associated with a stabilization agreement as restricted or committed, then report them as unassigned.

Disclosures

There are a number of disclosures associated with the classification of information on a government's financial statements. The following disclosures may apply:

- *Policies and procedures*. Disclose the policies and procedures related to fund balance classifications in the following areas:
  - *Committed fund balance*. Note the highest level of decision-making authority, as well as the action that must be taken to create, change, or eliminate a fund balance commitment.
  - *Assigned fund balance*. Note the position or group that is authorized to assign amounts to a specific purpose, as well as the policy under which that authorization is given.
  - *Usage assumptions*. Describe whether the government considers re-stricted or unrestricted amounts to have been spent when an expenditure is incurred and both restricted and unrestricted funds are

available. Also, describe whether the government considers commit-ted, assigned, or unassigned amounts to have been spent when an expenditure is incurred when the amounts in an unrestricted fund balance could be used.

- *Encumbrances.* Disclose any significant encumbrances by major fund, as well as in aggregate for non-major funds. Encumbrances are not to be dis-played on the face of the governmental funds balance sheet.
- *Non-spendable fund balance.* If a non-spendable fund balance is displayed in aggregate on the balance sheet, disclose in the accompanying notes the amounts for the two non-spendable components.
- *Stabilization arrangements.* When a stabilization arrangement exists, disclose the authority under which the arrangement was established, the conditions under which the stabilization amounts can be spent, and the stabi-lization balance (unless this amount is already stated on the face of the fi-nancial statements). On the same subject, if there is a minimum fund bal-ance policy, disclose the minimum amount set forth by the policy.
- *Restrictions by enabling legislation.* Disclose the amount of the entity's net position that is restricted by enabling legislation. Enabling legislation au-thorizes a government to levy fees and includes a requirement that the col-lected amounts only be used for the purposes stated in the legislation. If the enabling legislation is later judged to no longer be enforceable, then report the resources as unrestricted from that point forward.

Summary

This chapter has been concerned with the general classification and presentation of information to be included in a government's financial statements. It is critical to establish a classification system that is expected to endure for a significant period of time. Otherwise, the accountant will need to make ongoing adjustments to the financial statements that will render them less comparable to the statements issued in prior periods. To improve the odds that a classification system will last, involve an experienced consultant in the process of structuring and classifying financial information, to ensure that terms and classification groupings are properly defined, as well as the procedures for the recordation of transactions. On an ongoing basis, the accountant should be reluctant to make changes to the established system, unless there are material changes in the information underlying the financial statements.

Chapter 9
The Financial Reporting Entity

Introduction

When assembling information for financial statements, a basic question to ask is the nature of the financial reporting entity for which the statements are being prepared. A larger or more complex government could be involved with joint ventures, jointly governed organizations, and other stand-alone entities. For example, there may be a mix of governmental utilities, governmental colleges, public employee retirement systems, and so forth. A government may be comprised of or linked to a number of these organizations so that it can provide a broad range of services, where each individual entity has a separate management structure and staff that is focused on providing a targeted set of services. By breaking down its structure into many separate entities, a government avoids the diffusion of management skill that can occur when one centralized entity tries to oversee a myriad number of services.

The accountant needs to sort through these arrangements to determine the financial reporting entity, which may involve a subset of the full range of organizations involved with a government. In this chapter, we review the rules relating to a financial reporting entity.

Accountability

In governmental reporting, accountability is a key concern, since those people governing public institutions must be held accountable for their use of public funds. Given the importance of accountability, it should be the core element in defining a financial reporting entity. When the reporting focus is on accountability, financial statements should present to a reader a grouping of organizations that are related by accountability to the constituent citizens.

A group of government entities might initially appear to be separate. However, their governing bodies may have been appointed by the elected officials of a single primary government. Those officials are accountable to citizens for their decisions, even in cases where the decisions are actually being made by designated managers who are operating other organizations. Citizens must be able to assess the abilities of their elected officials by reviewing the financial statements of the entities that the officials were elected to govern. Thus, based on the accountability concept, the financial reporting entity should encompass these additional organizations.

Based on the preceding logic, we can define a *financial reporting entity* as a primary government and those organizations for which the primary government is financially accountable. It may also be necessary to include other organizations in a primary government's financial statements even when the financial accountability criterion does not exist, to keep the financial statements from being misleading.

The Financial Reporting Entity

A government entity's financial statements should allow readers to readily distinguish between the primary government and its component units. This is done by providing information about these units and their relationships with the primary government entity. This level of descriptive separation is more accurate than creating the perception that the primary government and all related component units are really just one large legal entity.

In order to present this relationship information, the government-wide financial statements of a reporting entity should reveal information about the reporting government as a whole by employing separate rows and columns to separate the total primary government and those of its component units that have been discretely presented. The reporting entity's fund financial statements should include the governmental, proprietary, and fiduciary funds of the primary government. In this reporting presentation, major funds are reported individually, while non-major funds are clustered together and reported in aggregate.

When there is a component unit that is fiduciary in nature, it should only be reported in the statements of fiduciary net position and changes in fiduciary net position with the primary government's fiduciary funds.

There may be cases in which a government organization other than a primary government must issue separate financial statements. When this is the case, the entity becomes the nucleus for its own reporting entity. Through the remainder of this chapter, the requirements stated for the financial reporting by a primary government also applies to the reporting by one of these governmental component units or similar entities.

Primary Governments

A *primary government* is one that has its own separately elected governing body, where the election was by citizens in a general, popular election. A primary government is the nucleus of a financial reporting entity. The following are examples of primary governments:

- A state government
- A county government
- A city or town government

EXAMPLE

A state's department of transportation has a safety board whose members are elected by the department's employees. The safety board is funded by an allocation of the state's gasoline tax. The safety board is not considered a separately elected governing body, since the election was not by the citizens in a general, popular election.

A primary government is comprised of every organization that makes up its legal entity, which can include funds, agencies, departments, and other entities that are not legally separate.

A special-purpose government can also be designated as a primary government, as long as it meets all of the following criteria:

- It has a separately-elected governing body.
- It is legally separate, which is the case when it has corporate powers. These powers give an organization a name, the right to sue and be sued without recourse to another governmental unit, and the right to buy and sell property in its own name.
- It is fiscally independent of other governments, which is the case when it can determine its budget, levy taxes or set rates, and issue bonded debt – all without the approval of another party.

A primary government may sometimes be placed under the control of another government, usually to correct financial difficulties. A government that is under such control is still considered to be fiscally independent for the purposes of defining a special-purpose government as a primary government.

A special-purpose entity may be statutorily prohibited from incurring debt. If so, and the entity is still fiscally independent in all other respects, the entity can be designated as a primary government.

> **Note:** A government that meets the definition of a primary government cannot be reported as a component unit of another primary government.

Component Units

A *component unit* is a legally separate organization for which the elected officials of the primary government are financially accountable. A component unit can also be an entity that must be included in a reporting entity's financial statements in order to keep them from being misleading. Examples of component units are:

- Economic development corporations
- Mass transit systems
- Port authorities
- Public universities

> **Note:** An organization that is not legally separate from a reporting entity is not a component unit, and so is treated for reporting purposes as a department or agency of the primary government.

A primary government has financial accountability for a component unit under the following circumstances:

- When the primary government appoints a voting majority of the entity's governing board *and* it is able to impose its will on the entity *or* the entity can provide financial benefits to or impose financial burdens on the primary government.
- When the component unit is fiscally dependent on the primary government *and* the entity can provide financial benefits to or impose financial burdens on the primary government. This situation exists even when the entity has a separately-elected governing board, a jointly appointed board, or a board that has been appointed by a higher level of government.

EXAMPLE

Helix City's power generating facility provides free electricity to the city's government offices. The facility is providing a financial benefit to the city.

Helix City provides substantial financial support to its recreation center, since user fees are set too low for the facility to otherwise break even. This arrangement constitutes a financial burden on the city.

A voting majority is present when the actions of a primary government's appointees alone can control the decisions made by an organization.

Note: Not all governmental organizations will be included in a reporting entity that is governed by elected officials. These outlier organizations are treated as stand-alone governments.

A primary government is able to impose its will on an entity when it can influence the day-to-day operations of the entity. A government has the ability to impose its will on an entity if it can significantly influence the programs, projects, activities, or service levels offered or provided by the entity. The following are indicators that a primary government can impose its will on another entity:

- It can remove members of the entity's governing board at will.
- It can alter or approve the entity's budget.
- It can alter the fees or rates charged by the entity.
- It can veto or alter the decisions made by the entity's governing body.
- It can hire, dismiss, or reassign those individuals responsible for the entity's operations.

> **Note:** When a primary government can remove members of an entity's governing board for cause, this is not the same as being able to do so at will. When cause must be proven before a person can be removed, a primary government may not have the ability to impose its will on an entity.

A primary government may provide a financial benefit to or accept a financial burden from another entity in several ways. Here are several examples:

- There is a legal obligation for the primary government to finance the deficits of the component unit.
- A contractual agreement between a primary government and a component unit requires the primary government to provide assistance under certain circumstances.
- A primary government is obligated to pay for the debt of a component unit if the component unit cannot make timely debt payments.
- A primary government must cover the deficiencies of a component unit on a temporary basis, until funds can be made available from another source.
- A primary government is both authorized to provide funding for reserves maintained by a component unit and establishes such a fund.

A simple exchange transaction between a primary government and another entity does not, by itself, indicate that a financial benefit or burden relationship exists between the two parties. An example of an exchange transaction is when one party buys goods or services from the other.

EXAMPLE

The city of East Smithville operates a separately-incorporated race track. The principal purpose of the race track is to generate profits that are accessible to East Smithville. Thus, the race track provides financial benefits to East Smithville. Given this arrangement, the race track entity can be considered a component unit of East Smithville.

EXAMPLE

East Smithville also has a mass transit operation that manages a bus system within the city's boundaries. The rates charged by this mass transit system are deliberately set lower than the cost structure of the enterprise. As a result, the city must periodically provide funding to the mass transit system via an appropriation to keep it operational. Given this arrangement, the race track entity can be considered a component unit of East Smithville.

EXAMPLE

The water utility of East Smithville is prohibited by statute from issuing debt. If the utility needs financing, it requests that the city issue debt on its behalf and then repays the government from the debt service payments. The water utility is fiscally dependent on the primary government, since it is unable to issue bond debt without the approval of another government.

EXAMPLE

The East Smithville city government guarantees payment of the debts of its wastewater treatment facility. It is highly unlikely that the wastewater unit's debt will ever create a financial burden for East Smithville, given the robust state of the unit's finances. In this case, there is still a financial burden on the city, since a burden is judged to exist based on the *potential* for the imposition of a financial burden.

EXAMPLE

East Smithville borders on the ocean, where there is a large natural harbor. The city government establishes a port authority, with the goal of stimulating the import and export of goods through the East Smithville area. The city appoints all members of the port authority's governing board, who may not be removed from their positions unless there is clear evidence of gross negligence in the conduct of their jobs. The governing board has the authority to hire all members of the management team. Based on these facts, the city cannot impose its will on the port authority. The port authority creates its own budget, issues bonds and sets rates without the approval of the city government. This situation indicates that the port authority is not providing a financial benefit to the city, nor is it imposing a financial burden. Under the circumstances, the port authority cannot be considered a component unit of the primary government.

Application of the preceding rules could occasionally result in situations where an organization can be considered a component unit of more than one primary government. For example, a state government appoints a voting majority of the members of a highway planning board, but the board is fiscally dependent on a local government. In this situation, the organization should only be considered a component unit of just one primary government. One must examine all of the applicable facts to determine which primary government is entitled to designate the organization as an organization unit. In some cases, there will be no designated primary government.

EXAMPLE

Twelve cities have formed a municipal electric authority, which is empowered to generate electricity from several hydroelectric dams and distribute the power to the citizens of the founding cities. Each of the founding cities appoints one person to the governing board of the electric authority. Construction of the necessary dams was funded by a bond offering of the electric authority, for which the cities have no liability. There are purchase agreements between the city governments and the electric authority, setting the prices at which the cities will be billed for electricity for the next ten-year period. The prices are designed to match the electric authority's costs and also pay off its bond obligations. Based on these facts, the participating cities do not have an ongoing financial interest in the entity. Thus, the most appropriate reporting is for each of the cities to report the electric authority as a jointly governed organization.

An entity that is a component unit of a financial reporting entity may in turn have its own component units. The component unit financial data appearing in the financial statements of the financial reporting entity should aggregate the data from *all* of its components units, including these additional layers of units.

Summary

The structure of component units that roll up into a financial reporting entity is not static. Changes in the operating agreements of these entities, as well as their financial relationship to the primary government may result in some component units being added to or dropped from the financial reporting of a primary government. Consequently, the accounting implications of these types of changes should be considered before any alterations are made to the existing agreements between entities. The situation is more likely to be in flux for larger primary governments, which may be comprised of dozens or even hundreds of component units. Conversely, a small government, such as that of a smaller city, will likely find that the composition of its financial reporting entity rarely changes over time.

Chapter 10
Comprehensive Annual Financial Report

Introduction

Financial reporting is needed to assist with the management control, legislative oversight, and other external reporting requirements of a government entity. To this end, a comprehensive annual financial report (CAFR) should be prepared that includes all funds and activities of the primary government, while also providing an overview of all separately-presented component units of the entity.

This chapter covers the components of and reporting rules for a CAFR. A condensed sample CAFR is included at the end of this chapter, showing the outlines of what the report would look like for a city government.

Components of the Comprehensive Annual Financial Report

A CAFR is the official annual report of a government entity. It is intended to report a primary government's financial position and results of operations, while also providing an overview of all separately-presented component units. It should be prepared and published as soon as possible after the fiscal year has been completed. It may also have attached to it the report of an independent auditor (if any), as well as a transmittal letter.

The CAFR is comprised of the following sections:

- *Introduction.* Includes at least a table of contents and a letter of transmittal.
- *Management's discussion and analysis.* This section introduces the basic financial statements and provides a summary analytical overview of the government's financial activities.
- *Basic financial statements*, which include:
    - *Government-wide financial statements.* Displays information about the government as a whole, other than any fiduciary activities. There should be separate columns for the primary government's governmental and business-type activities, and for its component units (if any). The statement of net position and the statement of activities are included.

- *Fund financial statements.* Includes the statements for the primary government's governmental, proprietary, and fiduciary funds, covering major funds individually and non-major funds in aggregate. The following reports are included:
  - *Government funds.* Includes a balance sheet and a statement of revenues, expenditures, and changes in fund balances.
  - *Proprietary funds.* Includes a statement of net position, a statement of cash flows, and a statement of revenues, expenses, and changes in fund net position.
  - *Fiduciary funds.* Includes a statement of fiduciary net position and a statement of changes in fiduciary net position.
- *Required supplementary information.* Includes all required information other than the material stated in the management's discussion and analysis section.
- *Combining and individual fund statements.* Includes combining statements, which are by fund type and for discretely presented component units. A combining statement by fund type is presented when a primary government has several internal service funds, fiduciary funds, or fiduciary component units, or several non-major governmental or enterprise funds. A combining statement for discretely presented component units is reported when a reporting entity has more than one non-major component unit. Individual fund statements are presented when the primary government has just one non-major fund of a particular fund type, or to present information not appearing in the supplementary information.
- *Schedules.* The following schedules should accompany the financial statements:
  - Those needed to demonstrate compliance with legal and contractual provisions.
  - Those needed to assemble information scattered throughout the statements, such as for taxes receivable and long-term debt.
  - Those needed to report more detailed information than what appears in the statements, such as additional detail about revenue sources.
- *Narrative explanations.* Includes discussions needed to understand the various statements, as well as schedules that are not included in the financial statement notes.
- *Statistical section.* See the Statistical Section chapter for more information.

> **Note:** The basic financial statements must include both government-wide financial statements and fund financial statements. Omitting one or the other results in an incomplete presentation.

The government-wide financial statements should contain information about the reporting entity as a whole, separately stating the total primary government and its component units. The financial statements should also differentiate between the primary government's governmental and business-type activities. The entity's fund financial statements should state the primary government's major funds individually and its non-major funds in aggregate. If there are any fiduciary funds or component units, only report them in the statements of fiduciary net position and changes in fiduciary net position.

Introduction to the CAFR

The primary component of the introduction to a CAFR is the letter of transmittal. There are no authoritative requirements for the contents of the letter of transmittal, but it should not contain information that duplicates what can be found in the following management's discussion and analysis (MD&A) section. The letter can refer to information found in the MD&A section, and could add insights that go beyond the information found in the MD&A section. The transmittal can be a good place in which to discuss plans and other information that do not meet the criteria for inclusion in the MD&A section.

Management's Discussion and Analysis

The MD&A section should appear in the CAFR prior to the presentation of the financial statements. The MD&A section provides a brief analysis of a government's financial activities, with a focus on the primary government's financial performance and its financial position at the end of the reporting period. The commentary should distinguish between information about the primary government and its component units. The need to discuss issues pertaining to a component unit should be based on that unit's significance in relation to the primary government. Any discussion of component units should be based on an individual component's significance and relationship to the primary government, but it may occasionally be appropriate to discuss component units in aggregate.

The MD&A section should compare the results of the current year to those of the prior year, covering the positive and negative aspects of the comparison. When comparative financial statements are being presented, the MD&A should address all periods covered. Where possible, supplement the discussion with charts, graphs, and tables. The following topics should be discussed:

- *Overview discussion.* Briefly describe the basic financial statements, including the relationships between the statements and significant differences in the information provided by them. The discussion should assist readers in understanding why the results reported in fund financial statements either reinforce what was stated in the government-wide statements, or provides additional information.
- *Condensed information.* Include a comparison of the current year to the prior year for the government-wide financial statements, using condensed information. If relevant, include the following items in this analysis:

- o Total assets, separately noting capital and other assets
- o Total deferred resource outflows
- o Total liabilities, separately noting long-term liabilities and other liabilities
- o Total deferred resource inflows
- o Total net position, separately noting the net investment in capital assets, restricted amounts, and unrestricted amounts
- o Program revenues, noting major sources
- o General revenues, noting major sources
- o Total revenues
- o Program expenses, at least described by function
- o Total expenses
- o The excess or deficiency, before contributions, to term and permanent endowments or permanent fund principal, special and extraordinary items, and transfers
- o Contributions
- o Special and extraordinary items
- o Transfers
- o Change in net position
- o Ending net position

- *Overall assessment.* Provide an analysis of the government's overall financial position and results of operations, with the intent of assessing whether it has improved or deteriorated over the reporting period. The analysis should include both governmental and business-type activities, as well as reasons for significant changes from the prior year. Also note any important economic factors that had a significant impact on operating results for the year.
- *Fund analysis.* Include an analysis of the balances and transactions associated with individual funds, noting the reasons for significant changes in fund balances and fund net position, as well as whether there are any limitations such as restrictions or commitments that may significantly affect the availability of fund resources in the future.
- *Budget variations.* Review any significant differences between the budget and actual results for the general fund, with a particular emphasis on any variations that are expected to have a significant impact on future services or liquidity.
- *Capital asset and debt activity.* Describe significant capital asset and long-term debt activity during the year. The discussion can include commitments made for capital expenditures, credit rating changes, and debt limitations.
- *Modified approach.* If the modified approach is being used to account for capital assets, then note the following information:

  - o Any significant changes in the assessed condition of eligible infrastructure assets from prior assessments.

o How the current condition compares to the condition level set by the government.

o Any significant differences between the estimated yearly amount needed to maintain infrastructure assets and the actual amount spent in the current period.

- *Facts and conditions.* Note any facts, decisions, or conditions that should have a significant impact on the financial position or results of operations.

Only the preceding topics should be included in the MD&A section, though there is no limit to the level of detail that can be provided for the mandated topics. Other information that is outside of the scope of the MD&A section could be included in the letter of transmittal, or as supplementary information.

Basic Financial Statements – Government-Wide

The government-wide financial statements are comprised of the statement of net position and the statement of activities, which measure all assets, deferred outflows of resources, liabilities, deferred inflows of resources, revenues, expenses, gains and losses. The statements are constructed using the economic resources measurement focus and the accrual basis of accounting.

The basic financial statements are intended to report information about the overall government, not breaking out individual funds or fund types. The statements exclude information about any fiduciary activities. The statements should also distinguish between the primary government and any separately-presented component units, where separate rows and columns are used to clearly identify the total primary government and its discretely presented component units. It is allowable, but not required, to include prior-year data in these reports.

The statements should also separately identify the governmental and business-type activities of the primary government. Governmental funds are typically financed through taxes, while business-type activities are financed by fees to outside parties for goods and services.

Prior-year data may be presented in these financial statements, though there is no requirement to do so. If added, the additional information is usually presented in extra columns that are used for side-by-side comparisons. When a government has a complex structure, it may find that the most useful comparison with prior-year data requires the reproduction and inclusion of prior-year statements.

Statement of Net Position

The statement of net position is structured to report all assets, deferred outflows of resources, liabilities, deferred inflows of resources, and net position. The underlying formula on which the statement of net position is based is:

Assets + Deferred outflows of resources – Liabilities – Deferred inflows of resources

= Net position

The rules related to the structuring and presentation of the statement of net position are:

- *Offsetting line items.* Do not offset assets and liabilities on the statement unless there is a right of offset.
- *Deferred outflows of resources.* The line items stating any deferred outflows of resources are reported in a separate section that follows the presentation of assets.
- *Deferred inflows of resources.* The line items stating any deferred inflows of resources are reported in a separate section that follows the presentation of liabilities.
- *Net position.* The residual amount in the statement is designated as the net position, rather than the net assets figure that is found in the financial statements of a nonprofit entity or the equity figure that is used by a for-profit entity.
- *Order of liquidity.* Assets should be presented in their order of relative liquidity. For an asset, this means that an asset that is easily convertible into cash is stated before an asset that will require more time to convert into cash. For a liability, this means that a liability with a shorter maturity is stated before a liability with a longer maturity, or when cash is expected to be used to liquidate it. If the use of an asset is restricted, the asset may still be considered quite liquid if the restriction lapses in the near term (as may be the case when cash is being held in reserve to pay for a liability that will be settled soon). When an asset is restricted for a longer period of time, it should be presented lower down in the statement.
- *Split maturities.* Liabilities that have average maturities of longer than one year are reported in two pieces, which are the amount due within one year and the amount due in more than one year.

The difference between the line items in the statement of net position is its *net position*. There are three reporting components to a government's net position, which are:

- *Net investment in capital assets.* This part of net position includes capital assets, reduced by accumulated depreciation, minus the outstanding balances of all borrowings attributable to the acquisition or construction of these assets. The effects of deferred inflows and outflows of resources attributable to the acquisition or construction of these assets are also included.
- *Restricted.* This part of net position includes restricted assets, minus liabilities and any deferred inflows of resources associated with those assets. Assets are considered to be restricted when constraints have been placed on asset use by outside parties such as creditors, or when imposed by enabling legislation.
- *Unrestricted.* This part of net position is the residual amount that was not included in the reported net investment in capital assets, or in restricted net position.

> **Tip:** Maintain a separate schedule for the calculation of the net investment in capital assets, since its construction can be difficult. Also, maintain a separate schedule for *each* prior reporting period, so that the calculation of the net investment in capital assets can be proven to auditors.

EXAMPLE

A state legislature passes a law to earmark 10% of the state's fuel tax revenues for investments in clean power sources. The earmarking of existing revenue is considered a funding commitment, rather than a restriction of the funds, so this action is not considered a restriction for the purposes of reporting net position.

EXAMPLE

A resident of Thistle City makes a $500,000 donation to the city, under the condition that the government matches the amount of the donation to create a permanent fund for the combined account. Both the donation and the government match should be reported as a restricted net position, since the matching amount is bound by the restriction imposed by the donor.

If there are large amounts of unspent debt proceeds or deferred inflows of resources at the end of the reporting period, the unspent amount should not be included in the calculation of net investment in capital assets. Instead, the amount is included in either the restricted or unrestricted classifications. Unspent debt proceeds and the related debt liability should be reported within the same classification.

EXAMPLE

Qanix City issues $10 million of bonds towards the end of the year in order to purchase capital assets. Qanix receives the proceeds from the bond issuance in that year, but a delay in the purchasing authorization process results in the related capital assets not being ordered until early in the following year. The entire amount of this debt should be included in the calculation of net position restricted for capital projects (which is a restricted classification). Since the debt is classified into the same location where the proceeds from the bond issuance are classified, the reported net amount is zero.

In the preceding example, the accountant is reporting debt proceeds and the debt liability in the same place, thereby preventing one classification from being overstated while another is understated by approximately the same amount.

When debt is issued with an associated premium or discount, the premium or discount is reported within the same classification as the related debt.

EXAMPLE

Thistle City issues $16 million of bonds to pay for its new wastewater treatment facility. The bonds were issued with a relatively high interest rate, so investors pay a premium for the bonds, resulting in $16.2 million of bond receipts, of which $200,000 is recorded as a premium. This premium is included in the calculation of Thistle's net investment in capital assets, located in the statement of net position.

When a government issues debt with the intent of using the proceeds to refund existing capital-related debt, the replacement debt is also considered to be capital-related for the purpose of reporting the net investment in capital assets in the statement of net position.

A government may be required by the terms of a bond indenture agreement to establish a reserve account, into which it places funds from the bond issuance that will be used to pay for interest and buy back matured bonds. The amount in the reserve account should be classified within the restricted component of its net position, rather than the net investment in capital assets, since the funds cannot be attributed to the acquisition or improvement of capital assets.

It is possible that the restricted net position calculation results in a negative figure. If so, move the net negative figure to the calculation of the unrestricted net position. By doing so, the restricted net position never appears as a negative figure.

A sample statement of net position appears near the end of this chapter, in the Sample Comprehensive Annual Financial Report section.

Statement of Activities

The statement of activities is structured to report the net expense or revenue (sometimes referred to as *net cost*) associated with its individual functions. This net cost approach is used to clarify the relative financial burden of each government function on taxpayers. The rules related to the structuring and presentation of the statement of net position are:

- *Activities by function.* Include in the statement those activities accounted for in governmental funds by function. Also include those activities accounted for in enterprise funds by different identifiable activities.
- *Revenue reporting.* General revenues, contributions made to term and permanent endowments, contributions to permanent fund principal, special and extraordinary items, as well as transfers are to be reported separately, and after total net expenses.

Additional topics related to the statement of activities are covered in the following sub-sections. A sample statement of activities appears near the end of this chapter, in the Sample Comprehensive Annual Financial Report section.

Expenses

The expenses reported in the statement of activities should be stated by function, except for special or extraordinary items, which are reported in separate line items. The minimum level of reporting by function is to include all direct expenses, which are those specifically associated with a program, service, or department. If a government chooses to allocate its indirect expenses (such as administration costs) to functions, then present direct and indirect expenses in separate columns within the report. Doing so makes it easier to compare the direct expenses of different governments.

If the decision is made to allocate indirect expenses to functions, do so using a reasonable basis. If there is no reasonable basis, then it makes little sense to allocate these expenses.

When there is a depreciation expense for capital assets that are associated with a specific function, include the depreciation expense in the direct expenses reported for that function. When a capital asset is being shared by several functions, ratably charge the related depreciation expense to each of the functions.

EXAMPLE

A Helix City administration building houses the offices of the public safety, wastewater management, and road maintenance departments. Accordingly, the building's depreciation is apportioned among these departments based on their proportional use of the building, which is measured based on square footage used.

> **Note:** When a government building serves all or many of the functions of the government, it is not necessary to include the related depreciation expense in the direct expenses of each of the functions. Instead, this depreciation can be included in the statement of activities as a separate line item, or as part of the general government function.

If a separate line is used on the statement of activities to report unallocated depreciation expense, indicate on the face of the statement that this amount does not include any direct depreciation expenses that were charged directly to the various government programs.

The depreciation expense related to infrastructure assets is not allocated. Instead, report it as a direct expense of the function with which capital outlays are normally associated, such as the public works department. A valid alternative is to report this expense in a separate line item on the statement of activities.

Any interest expense incurred on general long-term liabilities should be treated as an indirect expense that is separately reported on the statement of activities. However, it is possible to include this interest expense in direct expenses when the borrowing is needed to support a program, and not doing so would be misleading to the readers of the program information.

EXAMPLE

Dalton County has a program to make reduced-rate loans to school districts within its boundaries. Dalton funds the program with a $10 million bond issuance. The interest expense associated with these bonds should be included in the direct expenses of the loan program, since the borrowing was essential to the ongoing existence of the program. Not including this expense in the program would incorrectly imply that the program is without cost.

Revenues

There are four sources of financing for programs, which are noted in the following table, along with how these revenue types are classified within the statement of activities.

Revenue Types and Classifications

Revenue Source	Classification in the Statement of Activities
Taxpayers	Always reported as general revenue, even if the resulting funds are restricted for the use of a specific program
Those who purchase goods or services from the government	Reported as program revenue
Parties located outside of the government's citizenry, such as other governments	Can be restricted to a specific program; if unrestricted, it is reported as general revenue
The government itself, such as by investing funds	Usually reported as general revenue

Program revenues are derived directly from the program's own activities or come from outside parties in support of the program. These revenues are used to defray the cost of the program. There are three categories of program revenues, which are:

- *Charges for services.* This revenue is generated by charges to customers who purchase or use the goods and services provided. Examples of these charges are garbage collection fees, liquor licenses and building permits. Fines and forfeitures are also included in this category, as well as payments from other governments for goods and services provided.
- *Operating grants and contributions.* This revenue arises from non-exchange transactions with third parties that are restricted for the operational use of a specific program.
- *Capital grants and contributions.* This revenue arises from non-exchange transactions with third parties that are restricted for the acquisition or renovation of capital assets associated with a specific program.

EXAMPLE

A state government provides funding to Qanix City for the construction of a nearby hydroelectric facility. This funding is classified by Qanix as capital grants and contributions. The state government also provides funding for an emergency preparedness class for the city's firefighters, which is classified as operating grants and contributions. In addition, the city's parks and recreation department sells annual passes to the city's tennis courts, which is classified as charges for services.

EXAMPLE

Roadway City is built around a major county road, for which the city has established very low speed limits. Passing motorists are routinely fined for breaking the speed limit, resulting in fines being one of the major revenue sources of the city. Even though Roadway relies in large part on these fines to finance its operations, the fines revenue should be reported within the public safety program, since they are generated by that function.

When there is a multi-purpose grant that does not identify a specifically-targeted program, classify the grant amount as general revenues.

EXAMPLE

A state government awards a $5 million grant to Custer County, which is used to finance a number of the county's programs. The grant award includes a list of the programs to be covered, but does not assign (restrict) specific amounts for individual programs. Since no amounts are being restricted to individual programs, the grant should be classified as general revenue.

Note: There may be cases in which revenue can be associated with two or more programs. If so, adopt a policy for assigning the revenue, and follow it consistently.

Any earnings generated from endowments or permanent funds should be reported as program-specific revenues, if the source funds are restricted to specific programs. If there is no such restriction, then do not report the earnings as being program-specific.

Developers may sometimes contribute infrastructure to a government, such as the road network associated with a group of homes that have just been constructed. Contributed infrastructure is usually classified as program revenue, since the infrastructure is restricted by its nature. In cases where the intended use of a contributed asset is not obvious, it can instead be classified as general revenue.

When revenues are not assigned to programs, classify them as general revenues, which are reported after total net expense in the statement of activities.

Estimated uncollectible taxes should be recorded as a reduction of revenue, rather than as a bad debt expense.

The following presentation format could be used to present an inclusive statement of activities.

Special and Extraordinary Items

An extraordinary item is an event that is unusual in nature and infrequent in occurrence. This type of transaction should be reported separately at the bottom of the statement of activities. A special item is an event that is within the control of management and is either unusual in nature or infrequent in occurrence. This type of transaction is also reported separately at the bottom of the statement of activities, before any extraordinary items.

> **Note:** The default assumption is that an event or transaction is an ordinary and usual activity, which is only changed if there is clear evidence supporting classification as a special or extraordinary item.

Basic Financial Statements – Fund Financial Statements

The following sub-sections deal with several topics related to the basic financial statements that should be issued for funds. Sample financial statements for the various fund types can be found near the end of this chapter, in the Sample Comprehensive Annual Financial Report section.

Major Funds

A government should present separate financial statements for the primary government's governmental and proprietary funds. The focus of the statements should be on major funds, with the information for each of these funds stated in a separate column. The information for non-major funds can be presented in a single column. A fund can be considered "major" based on the following criteria:

- The total of all assets and deferred outflows of resources, the total of all liabilities and deferred inflows of resources, revenues, or expenditure/expenses of the individual fund are at least 10% of the corresponding element total for all funds of that type; and
- The same elements that met the 10% criterion are at least 5% of the corresponding element total for all governmental and enterprise funds, when combined.

In addition to the preceding criteria, any other governmental or enterprise fund that is considered particularly important to the users of a government's financial statements can be reported as a major fund.

It is possible that a fund will only be classified as a major fund for a short period of time. This is especially common for capital project funds, which may experience a high level of activity only for the duration of a specific capital project.

Sample Format for a Statement of Activities

| Functions | Expenses | Program Revenues | | | Net (Expense) Revenue and Changes in Net Position | | | |
| | | Charges for Services | Operating Grants and Contributions | Capital Grants and Contributions | Primary Government | | | |
					Governmental Activities	Business-Type Activities	Total	Component Units
Primary Government								
Governmental activities								
Function 1	$xxx	$xxx	$xxx	$xxx	-$xxx	---	-$xx	$---
Function 2	xxx	xxx	xxx	xxx	-xxx	---	-xx	---
Function 3	xxx	xxx	xxx	xxx	-xxx	===	-xx	===
Total governmental activities	xxx	xxx	xxx	xxx	-xxx	===	-xx	===
Business-type activities								
Activity 1	xxx	xxx	---	xxx	---	xxx	xx	---
Activity 2	xxx	xxx	===	xxx	===	xxx	xx	===
Total business-type activities	xxx	xxx	===	xxx	===	xxx	xx	===
Total primary government	$xxx	$xxx	$xxx	$xxx	-$xxx	$xxx	$xx	$--
Component units								
Unit 1	$xxx	$xxx	$xxx	$xxx	---	---	---	xx
General revenues – detailed					xxx	xxx	xxx	xxx
Contributions to permanent funds					xxx	---	xxx	---
Special items					xxx	---	xxx	---
Transfers					xxx	-xxx	===	===
Total general revenues, contributions, special items, and transfers					xxx	xxx	xxx	xxx
Change in net position					xxx	xxx	xxx	xxx
Net position - beginning					xxx	xx	xxx	xxx
Net position - ending					xxx	xxx	xxx	xxx

A government may elect to report comparative financial statements that present the results for two or more years. When using this format, it is possible that funds designated as major in the current year were designated as non-major in a prior year. If so, the prior year designation(s) should remain in place, though it can be useful to include an explanation of the situation in the accompanying footnotes.

Reconciliation to Government-Wide Statements

A summary statement should be presented at the bottom of the fund financial statements or an accompanying schedule, reconciling them to the government-wide financial statements. The reconciliation should explain any differences between the results and balances appearing in fund financial statements and the same information in the government-wide statements. The reconciliation contains the details of assets, deferred outflows of resources, liabilities, deferred inflows of resources, revenues, and expenses that should be reported in the government-wide statements, and the financing sources and uses that should not be reported in the government-wide statements.

It may be necessary to provide additional disclosures regarding reconciling items in the accompanying notes, if the information in the reconciliation is so aggregated that it obscures the nature of individual elements.

> **Note:** If the reconciliation is included on an accompanying schedule, it is considered a continuation of the fund financial statement, and so should be on the page immediately following the fund financial statements.

If it appears necessary to include lengthy explanations of items in the reconciliation, consider doing so in the accompanying notes to the financial statements, since there is little room for this information on the face of the fund financial statements.

Sample reconciliations appear in the sample CAFR report at the end of this chapter.

Required Financial Statements – Governmental Funds

The financial reporting package for a governmental fund is comprised of a balance sheet and a statement of revenues, expenditures, and changes in fund balances. We address issues related to the specific financial statements in this reporting package in the following sub-sections.

Balance Sheet

The balance sheet states the current financial resources of each major governmental fund and in aggregate for all non-major governmental funds, along with a total column. A standard balance sheet format should be used to present assets, deferred outflows of resources, liabilities, deferred inflows of resources, and fund balances. The calculation used in the balance sheet should be:

Assets + Deferred outflows of resources = Liabilities + Deferred inflows of resources + Fund balance

For informational purposes, it can be useful to include a subtotal in the balance sheet for the following information:

- Assets + total for deferred outflows of resources
- Liabilities + total for deferred inflows of resources

A summary reconciliation should be included at the bottom of the fund financial statements or in an accompanying schedule, reconciling total government fund balances to the net position of governmental activities in the statement of net position. Reconciling items may include:

- *Capital assets.* Reporting capital assets at their historical cost and depreciating them, rather than reporting them as expenditures when incurred.
- *Long-term liabilities.* Including general long-term liabilities not due and payable in the current period.
- *Deferred inflows of resources.* Reducing deferred inflows of resources for any amounts not available to pay current-period expenditures.
- *Internal service funds.* Adding the net position balances of internal service funds.

Statement of Revenues, Expenditures, and Changes in Fund Balances

The statement of revenues, expenditures, and changes in fund balances reports information about the inflows, outflows, and balances of the current financial resources of each major governmental fund, as well as in aggregate for all non-major governmental funds. The statement should follow this general format:

Revenues (multiple line items)
Expenditures (multiple line items)
Excess (deficiency) of revenues over expenditures
Other financing sources and uses, including transfers (multiple line items)
Special and extraordinary items (possibly multiple line items)
Net change in fund balances
Fund balances – beginning of period
Fund balances – end of period

Several rules related to the classification of information in the statement of revenues, expenditures, and changes in fund balances report are as follows:

- *Revenue.* Classify revenues by major revenue source.
- *Expenditures.* Classify governmental fund expenditures by function.
- *Debt issue costs.* Classify those debt issue costs paid out of debt proceeds as expenditures. Classify those debt issue costs paid from existing resources as expenditures when the related liability is incurred.

The other financing sources and uses classification should include the following items:

- The face amount of long-term debt
- The issuance premium or discount
- Payments to escrow agents for bond refundings

- Transfers
- Sales of capital assets

A summary reconciliation should be included at the bottom of the fund financial statements or in an accompanying schedule, reconciling the total change in government fund balances to the change in net position of governmental activities in the statement of activities. Reconciling items may include:

- *Revenues.* Reporting revenues on the accrual basis.
- *Depreciation.* Reporting depreciation expense instead of expenditures for capital outlays.
- *Debt proceeds.* Reporting long-term debt proceeds as liabilities in the statement of net position rather than as other financing sources. Also, reporting debt principal payments as reductions of liabilities in the statement of net position rather than as expenditures.
- *Expenses.* Reporting other expenses using the accrual basis of accounting.
- *Internal service funds.* Adding the net revenue or expense of internal service funds.

Required Financial Statements – Proprietary Funds

The financial reporting package for a proprietary fund is comprised of a statement of net position, a statement of revenues, expenses, and changes in fund net position, and a statement of cash flows. In these statements, the financial information for each major enterprise fund should be stated in a separate column, along with a combined total column for all enterprise funds. Further, the combined totals for all internal service funds should be reported in separate columns on the financial statements, to the right of the total enterprise funds column. We address issues related to the specific financial statements in this reporting package in the following sub-sections.

Statement of Net Position

The statement of net position presents the financial position of a fund. The following rules apply to the classification and reporting of information within this statement:

- *Current and long-term differentiation.* Differentiate between the line items for current and long-term assets and liabilities.
- *Offsetting.* Do not offset assets and liabilities except when there is a right of offset.
- *Deferred outflows.* Report deferred outflows of resources in a separate section that follows assets. The total for deferred outflows can be added to the asset total to report a subtotal.
- *Deferred inflows.* Report deferred inflows of resources in a separate section that follows liabilities. The total for deferred inflows can be added to the liability total to report a subtotal.

- *Net position.* Break the net position into three parts, which are the net investment in capital assets, restricted, and unrestricted.
- *Receivable deductions.* When unearned discounts, finance charges, and interest have been added to the face amount of receivables, state these amounts in aggregate as a deduction from the receivables with which they are paired.
- *Allowances.* When there is an asset valuation allowance for expected losses, deduct it on the statement of net position from the asset(s) with which it is paired.
- *Asset restrictions.* When there are restrictions on the use of assets that alter their normal availability, report these assets separately as restricted assets.

Statement of Revenues, Expenses, and Changes in Fund Net Position

The statement of revenues, expenses, and changes in fund net position is the operating statement for proprietary funds. The following rules apply to the classification and reporting of information within this statement:

- *Revenue.* Report revenues by major source, net of discounts and allowances. Also, distinguish between operating and non-operating revenues.
- *Expenses.* Distinguish between operating and non-operating expenses.
- *Non-operating revenues and expenses.* Report non-operating revenues and expenses after operating income.
- *Subtotals.* Present a separate subtotal for operating revenues, operating expenses, and operating income.

Unless an entity's principal activity is investing, any income earned from investments should be reported as non-operating revenue. Non-operating revenue also includes revenues from appropriations between primary governments and their component units for operating purposes, or which may be used for either operating purposes or capital outlays.

Tip: Create a policy that defines operating revenues and expenses and use it consistently over time to ensure consistent classification of revenue and expense transactions.

The statement of revenues, expenses, and changes in fund net position should follow this general format:

Operating revenues (multiple line items)
Total operating revenues
Operating expenses (multiple line items)
Total operating expenses
Operating income (loss)
Non-operating revenues and expenses (multiple line items)
Income before other revenues, expenses, gains, losses, and transfers
Capital contributions, additions to permanent and term endowments, special and extraordinary items (multiple line items) and transfers
Increase (decrease) in net position
Net position – beginning of period
Net position – end of period

Statement of Cash Flows

A statement of cash flows should be included in the financial statement package for proprietary funds. Use the direct method of presenting cash flows in this statement. The statement should be presented even if the operating income of the fund is zero.

Other Topics

The amounts reported as net position and changes in net position in the proprietary fund financial statements should match the net assets and changes in net position of business-type activities in the government-wide statement of activities. If there are any differences, explain them on the face of the fund statement or in an accompanying schedule.

Required Financial Statements – Fiduciary Funds

The financial statement reporting package for a fiduciary fund is comprised of the statement of fiduciary net position and the statement of changes in fiduciary net position. These statements should encompass all fiduciary funds of the primary government, plus any component units that are fiduciary in nature.

These statements should include a separate column for each type of fund, which may include the following:

- Agency funds
- Investment trust funds
- Pension trust funds
- Private-purpose trusts

Statement of Fiduciary Net Position

The statement of fiduciary net position is used to report on assets, deferred outflows of resources, liabilities, deferred inflows of resources, and net position. Any amounts being reported as deferred outflows of resources are reported in a separate section that follows assets. In the same manner, any amounts being reported as deferred inflows of resources are reported in a separate section that follows liabilities.

It is acceptable to add together the assets total and the deferred outflows of resources total to create a subtotal in the report. It is also acceptable to add together the liabilities total and the deferred inflows of resources total to create another subtotal.

Statement of Changes in Fiduciary Net Position

The statement of changes in fiduciary net position is used to report on the additions to, deductions from and net change for the year in the net position of each type of fiduciary fund.

Agency funds should not be reported in the statement of changes in fiduciary net position.

Comparative Financial Statements

A government may elect to present the statement of net position and the flows statement for one or more preceding periods, plus the current period. When this presentation is used, include the notes to the financial statements that were presented for the preceding periods, if they continue to be significant to the reader's understanding of the financial statements. If there has been a change in the manner of presentation of financial information between the reported periods, provide an explanation for the change. For the purposes of this requirement, a "flows statement" is considered to be the government-wide statement of activities and the proprietary fund statement of revenues, expenses, and changes in fund net position.

Required Supplementary Information

Required supplementary information is that set of schedules, statistical data, and other information that the Governmental Accounting Standards Board considers to be essential to the financial reporting of a government entity. Examples of this supplementary information are:

- Budgetary comparison schedules
- Information about employee benefits
- Information concerning the modified approach for reporting infrastructure assets

This required supplementary information is presented immediately after the financial statement notes in the CAFR.

The budgetary comparison noted in the preceding list of supplementary information should be presented for the general budget, as well as for each major special revenue fund that has adopted an annual budget. If a government is unable to present this information, it must instead present budgetary comparison schedules that are based on the fund, organization, or program structure used by the government within its legally adopted budget. This comparison schedule notes the original budget, the final appropriated budget, and the actual inflows, outflows, and balances. Though not required, it is also possible to include a variance column for the difference between the final budget and actual amounts, as well as between the original and final budget amounts. The definitions of original and final budgets are as follows:

- *Original budget.* This is the first complete appropriated budget.
- *Final budget.* This is the original budget after it has been adjusted for all reserves, transfers, allocations, supplemental appropriations, and other authorized legislative and executive changes.

If there is an excess of expenditures over appropriations in the individual funds presented in a budgetary comparison and this excess represents a significant violation of finance-related legal provisions, disclose the issue in the notes accompanying the basic financial statements.

Combining Statements and Individual Fund Statements and Schedules

Combining and individual fund statements for the funds of the primary government are set forth in the financial section of the CAFR. These statements include the following:

- Non-major governmental funds
    - o Combining balance sheets
    - o Combining statements of revenues, expenditures, and changes in fund balances
- Individual fund balance sheets and statements of revenues, expenditures, and changes in fund balances, as well as the schedules needed to demonstrate compliance with finance-related legal and contractual provisions of the governmental funds
- Internal service funds and non-major enterprise funds
    - o Combining statements of net position
    - o Combining statements of revenues, expenses, and changes in fund net position
    - o Combining statements of cash flows
- Individual statements of net position; statements of revenues, expenses, and changes in fund net position and of cash flows; and the schedules needed to

demonstrate compliance with finance-related legal and contractual provisions of the proprietary funds
- Fiduciary funds
  - A combining statement of fiduciary net position
  - A combining statement of changes in fiduciary net position
  - A combining statement of changes in assets and liabilities for all agency funds

The information presented for each component unit in the combining financial statements should be the entity totals from the component units' statements of net position and activities.

The schedules supporting the financial statements should present data that is on a legally or contractually required basis that is different from GAAP, as well as other data not required by GAAP, but which management wants to include.

Narrative explanations of the financial statements should provide information not stated elsewhere in the CAFR, and which is needed to assure a reader's understanding of the information provided, as well as to demonstrate compliance with any finance-related legal and contractual provisions.

Statistical Tables

Statistical tables are used to present comparative information that spans a number of reporting periods. The tables may also contain data from sources separate from the accounting records of the reporting entity, such as economic and population data. This topic is addressed in detail in the Statistical Section chapter.

Major Component Unit Information

The financial statements of a reporting entity should allow readers to distinguish between the primary government and its component units. This can be done by presenting the component unit financial data in the statement of net position and the statement of activities, though fiduciary component units should only be included in the fund financial statements as part of the primary government's fiduciary funds. In addition, information must be provided about each major component unit in the basic financial statements of the reporting entity. This can be done in one or more of the following ways:

- By presenting each major component unit in a separate column in the statements of net position and activities.
- By including combining statements of major component units in the basic statements after the fund financial statements.
- By presenting condensed financial statements in the notes accompanying the financial statements.

If the third option is taken and condensed financial statements are presented in the accompanying notes, the following information should be included in the presentation:

- Condensed statement of net position

    o Total assets, separately noting current assets, capital assets, receivables from other funds, and other assets
    o Total deferred outflows of resources
    o Total liabilities, separately noting current liabilities, long-term liabilities, and amounts payable to other funds
    o Total deferred inflows of resources, separately noting the net investment in capital assets, restricted and unrestricted
    o Total net position

- Condensed statement of activities

    o Expenses
    o Program revenues by type
    o Net program revenue or expense
    o Tax revenues
    o Other non-tax general revenues
    o Contributions to endowments and permanent fund principal
    o Special and extraordinary items
    o Change in net position
    o Beginning net position
    o Ending net position

Account Classification Rules

The following account classification rules should be followed when preparing financial statements:

- The statement of activities should present the following information, at a minimum:

    o Activities accounted for in governmental funds by function, coinciding with the level of detail required in the governmental fund statement of revenues, expenditures, and changes in fund balance.
    o Activities accounted for in enterprise funds by different identifiable activities.

- Governmental fund revenues are to be classified by fund and source, while expenditures are classified by fund, function or program, organization unit, activity, character, and principal classes of objects.
- Proprietary fund revenues are reported by major sources, while expenses are classified in the same manner used by similar business organizations. Revenues and expenses are to be identified as operating or non-operating.

- The proceeds from general long-term debt issues are to be classified separately from revenues and expenditures in the governmental fund financial statements.
- Contributions to endowments, permanent fund principal, other capital contributions, special and extraordinary items, and transfers between governmental and business-type activities are to be reported separately from general revenues in the government-wide statement of activities. These items are to be reported separately in the proprietary fund statement of revenues, expenses, and changes in fund net position, after non-operating revenues and expenses.
- Transfers are to be classified separately from revenues and expenditures in the governmental fund statement of revenues, expenditures, and changes in fund balances.
- Special and extraordinary items should be reported after "other financing sources and uses" in the governmental fund statement of revenues, expenditures, and changes in fund balances.

Disclosures

A number of disclosures should be included in a CAFR. Some of them are noted in the following bullet points; additional disclosure commentary appears in the following chapters, in relation to the topics covered. The disclosures are:

- *Adjustments*. An estimated amount may be initially reported for an extraordinary or special item, based on the facts known at the time. When there is an adjustment in the current period to one of these items that was reported in a prior period, disclose the year of origin, nature, and amount of the adjustment.
- *Administrative overhead charges*. A government may charge funds or programs for the centralized expenses of the entity, which may result in an administrative overhead charge. The summary of significant accounting policies that accompanies the CAFR should disclose that these allocations are included in the direct expenses reported for funds or programs.
- *Fund purpose*. Disclose the purpose of each major special revenue fund, stating which revenues and other resources are reported in each of the funds.
- *Nature of transactions*. Disclose for each major component unit the nature and amount of any significant transactions with the primary government and other component units.
- *Revenue and expense policy*. Disclose the government's policy that defines operating revenues and expenses. This disclosure should appear in the summary of significant accounting policies.
- *Unusual transactions*. If there are any significant transactions or other events that are either unusual or infrequent, but not within the control of management, disclose them in the notes to the financial statements.

When a primary government is presented in more than one column of its basic financial statements, the entity should disclose in its summary of significant accounting policies the activities included in each of the following columns:

- Major funds
- Internal service funds
- Fiduciary funds

For example, the activities of an internal service fund could be described as the maintenance of government facilities to other funds on a cost-reimbursement basis.

Sample Comprehensive Annual Financial Report

This section contains a highly compressed sample version of a CAFR, not including the notes and required supplementary information, which are addressed in later chapters. The sample is based on the reporting that a city government might generate. This information is intended to expand upon the general concepts noted earlier in this chapter. The sample report is *not* intended to be a model from which a real CAFR would be constructed. The sub-headings in this section correspond to the headings that would be used in a CAFR.

Management's Discussion and Analysis

This section of Helix City's Comprehensive Annual Report (CAFR) offers readers a narrative overview and analysis of the financial activities of the City for the year ended December 31, 20X2. Readers are encouraged to consider the information presented here, in conjunction with the letter of transmittal, the basic financial statements, and the notes to the financial statements contained in this report.

Overview of the Financial Statements

Management's Discussion and Analysis is intended to provide an introduction to the City's basic financial statements. The City's basic financial statements contain three components, which are government-wide financial statements, fund financial statements, and notes to the financial statements. Following these statements, this report provides additional supplementary information. The basic financial statements include two types of statements that present unique views of the City's financial position: (1) government-wide financial statements and (2) fund financial statements.

1. Government-Wide Financial Statements

    The government-wide financial statements are intended to provide readers with a broad overview of the City's financial condition. They are presented using accounting methods very similar to those used by a privately-owned business, or the *economic resources* measurement focus, and full accrual accounting. These financial statements include the following:

- *Statement of net position.* This report presents information on all of the City's assets and liabilities, with the balance between the two reported as the net position. Over time, increases or decreases in net position can serve as an indicator of the City's financial condition.
- *Statement of activities.* This report presents information showing how the City's net position changed during the given fiscal year. All changes in net position are reported as soon as the underlying event giving rise to the change occurs, regardless of the timing of related cash flows. Capital expenditures are not included in this statement; however, capital grant revenues are reported.

2. Fund Financial Statements

The fund financial statements focus on specific elements of the City's finances and report on fund-specific operations in more detail than the government-wide financial statements. A fund is a grouping of resources that are segregated for the purpose of carrying a specific activity or attaining certain objectives in accordance with given regulations, restrictions, or limitations.

Governmental Funds

The governmental funds presentation is different from the governmental activities section of the government-wide financial statements, even though these two statements account for essentially the same activities. Governmental funds, as presented, have a budgetary or *current financial resources* measurement focus and use the modified accrual basis of accounting. That is, the governmental funds presentation focuses on the City's near-term financial position and changes thereto.

Proprietary Funds

Proprietary funds are unlike governmental funds in that they report the business-type activities of the City. Enterprise funds account for the operation of governmental programs that are intended to be supported primarily by user fees. These fees are presented as business-type activities on the government-wide financial statements but are presented in greater detail in the fund financial statements. In both cases, enterprise funds are presented using the *economic resources* measurement focus and full accrual accounting.

3. Notes to the Financial Statements

The notes to the basic financial statements provide additional information that is essential to a thorough understanding of the data provided in the government-wide and the fund financial statements.

Government-Wide Financial Statement Analysis

Assets

As of December 31, 20X2, the City had total assets of $262 million and its assets exceeded its liabilities by $232 million. The following exhibit indicates the City's net position.

Helix City's Net Position
(in millions)

	Governmental Activities		Business-Type Activities		Total	
	20X1	20X2	20X1	20X2	20X1	20X2
Current and other assets	$86.5	$105.0	$0.3	$0.3	$86.8	$105.3
Capital assets	152.5	157.1	--	--	152.5	157.1
Total assets	**239.0**	**262.1**	**0.3**	**0.3**	**239.3**	**$262.4**
Long-term liabilities	2.7	2.7	--	--	2.7	2.7
Other liabilities	9.4	12.1	0.3	0.3	9.7	12.4
Total liabilities	**12.1**	**14.8**	**0.3**	**0.3**	**12.4**	**15.1**
Deferred inflows of resources	**13.2**	**15.0**	**--**	**--**	**13.2**	**15.0**
Net position						
Net investment in capital assets	152.5	157.1	--	--	152.5	157.1
Restricted	9.5	11.7	0.1	0.1	9.6	11.8
Unrestricted	51.7	63.4	-0.1	-0.1	51.6	63.3
Total net position	**$213.7**	**$232.3**	**$0**	**$0**	**$213.7**	**$232.3**

Capital Assets

Capital assets are the largest portion of the City's total assets, representing $157 million of its total assets. Capital assets being depreciated increased during 20X2 by $1 million as a result of the completion of capital projects related to streets, traffic signals, park construction, buildings, and related activities. Capital assets not being depreciated increased during 20X2 by $7 million, due to the net increase of construction in progress for infrastructure.

Long-Term Debt

The City's long-term debt has decreased slightly. There were no additional long-term debt agreements during 20X2.

The following exhibit reflects the City's change in net position.

Changes in Helix City Net Position
(in millions)

	Governmental Activities		Business-Type Activities		Total	
	20X1	20X2	20X1	20X2	20X1	20X2
Revenues						
Program revenues						
Charges for services	$3.3	$2.9	$3.6	$4.9	$6.9	$7.8
Operating grants and contributions	6.2	6.5	--	--	6.2	6.5
Capital grants and contributions	3.5	9.1	--	--	3.5	9.1
General revenue						
Sales and use taxes	42.0	46.4	--	--	42.0	46.4
Property taxes	14.0	12.9	--	--	14.0	12.9
Other taxes	0.6	0.6	--	--	0.6	0.6
Unrestricted franchise fees	5.1	5.1	--	--	5.1	5.1
Investment income	0.2	0.2	--	--	0.2	0.2
Intergovernmental revenues not restricted to specific programs	0.6	0.5	--	--	0.6	0.5
Miscellaneous	0.4	0.9	--	--	0.4	0.9
Total revenues	**75.9**	**85.1**	**3.6**	**4.9**	**79.5**	**90.0**
Expenses						
General government	11.8	13.2	--	--	11.8	13.2
Community services	22.2	23.8	--	--	22.2	23.8
City infrastructure	24.7	24.7	--	--	24.7	24.7
Culture and recreation	2.5	1.0	--	--	2.5	1.0
Urban redevelopment	5.5	4.6	--	--	5.5	4.6
Interest on long-term debt	0.1	0.1	--	--	0.1	0.1
Land use service fees	--	--	3.1	4.0	3.1	4.0
Total expenses	**66.8**	**67.4**	**3.1**	**4.0**	**69.9**	**71.4**
Increase (decrease) before transfers	9.1	17.7	0.5	0.9	9.6	18.6
Transfers	0.5	0.9	-0.5	-.09	--	--
Increase (decrease) in net position	9.6	18.6	--	--	9.6	18.6
Net position, beginning of year	204.1	213.7	--	--	204.1	213.7
Net position, end of year	$213.7	$232.3	$--	$--	$213.7	$232.3

Governmental activities increased the City's net position by $19 million. Key elements of this net increase were as follows:

- Capital grants and contributions increased by $6 million, which included intergovernmental grants and contributions for capital road construction.
- Sales and use tax increased by $4 million, primarily as the result of higher revenues in the sales tax base, which was derived from both in-City retailers and out-of-City retailers.
- Culture and recreation expense declined by $2 million, due to a reduction in the amount of maintenance required by the City's trails, venues, and parks.

Fund Financial Statement Analysis

The City uses fund accounting to segregate resources for the purpose of carrying on a specific activity or attaining certain objectives in accordance with regulations, restrictions, or other limitations on the use of the funds.

Revenues

General Fund revenues increased $4 million in 20X2 in comparison to 20X1. Sales tax revenues increased by $3 million, due to an increase in the licensing of approximately 200 out-of-City retailers and the collection of an additional $1 million from compliance audits.

The Urban Redevelopment Authority Fund revenues declined by $1 million, as the result of lower property tax collections in the redevelopment area. Some of the properties located in this area filed a petition for the abatement of property taxes, which was approved by the County.

Capital Improvement Fund revenues increased by $6 million, as the result of funds received from intergovernmental agreements for the Westerly Road widening project during 20X2.

Expenditures

General Fund expenditures and transfers increased $15 million in comparison to 20X1. The primary change was transfers of $10 million from the General Fund to the Capital Improvement Fund, for projects associated with street construction, traffic signals, and street rehabilitation. There was also a $2 million increase in Community Services, primarily to fund contracted expenditures for public safety. There was also a $1 million increase in City Infrastructure expenditures, caused by higher contracted costs for the City's public work services.

The Urban Redevelopment Authority Fund expenditures decreased by $1 million, while the Capital Improvement Fund expenditures increased by $1 million, due to new construction for streets and intersections, as well as services for construction management.

Fund Balance

The net change in the General Fund balance was a decrease of $6 million. Economic peaks and planned savings allow the City the opportunity to increase the fund balance, while timely financial planning provides financial flexibility during economic downturns. Since its incorporation, the City has increased the balance in the General Fund in each year, with the exception of 20X0, when a significant amount was transferred to the Capital Improvement Fund for capital projects. That transfer is funding construction of the Westerly Road widening project.

The net change in the balance in the Capital Improvement Fund was an increase of $18 million, primarily due to a revised budget transfer for projects associated with street construction.

Economic Factors and Next Year's Budget

The 20X3 Budget was developed to provide desired City services at the maximum level possible while maintaining financially responsible practices. While the City has been fortunate to be relatively resilient to the impact of the downturn in overall economic conditions in prior years, the City remains cautious about the local economy over the next several years. The 20X3 and future budgets will respond to the challenge of balancing the ongoing maintenance of infrastructure with the community's standards of excellence in public works, public safety, and quality of life.

The City's budget is the long-range plan by which financial policy is implemented and controlled. The City Council's goals, City-wide objectives, ordinances and resolutions provide policy direction that respond to the needs and desires of the community. The City's budget process is a continuous cycle that begins with the Council's strategic vision and planning, continues through the planning and development stages of the budget, and finishes with the final adoption of the budget by the Council.

The total budget for 20X3 is $83 million. Department directors prepared their 20X3 budgets with a zero percent increase in expenditures over the adopted 20X2 budget, excluding increases for salaries, health care costs, and other types of expenditures beyond the control of the City, such as the costs of asphalt and concrete. Increases were also permitted for certain contractual obligations of the City, such as increases required by service providers. The 20X3 Adopted Budget includes health care cost increases of 12%, based on estimated projections.

Basic Financial Statements

Statement of Net Position

The statement of net position displays information about the financial and capital resources of the City as a whole. This report includes the primary government and its component units, but does not include fiduciary funds and component units that are fiduciary in nature.

Helix City
Statement of Net Position
December 31, 20X2
(in millions)

| | Primary Government | | |
	Governmental Activities	Business-Type Activities	Total
ASSETS			
Cash and cash equivalents	$83.4	$0.3	$83.7
Taxes receivable	20.2	--	20.2
Other receivables	0.8	--	0.8
Intergovernmental receivables	0.5	--	0.5
Prepaid expenses	--	--	--
Capital assets, not being depreciated	100.0	--	100.0
Capital assets, net of accumulated depreciation	57.2	--	57.2
Total assets	262.1	0.3	262.4
LIABILITIES			
Accounts payable	5.0	0.3	5.3
Retainage payable	0.2	--	0.2
Accrued liabilities	1.8	--	1.8
Other liabilities	0.9	--	0.9
Accrued interest payable	--	--	--
Developer contributions and deposits	4.1	--	4.1
Long-term liabilities:			
Due within one year	0.1	--	0.1
Due in more than one year	2.7	--	2.7
Total liabilities	14.8	0.3	15.1
DEFERRED INFLOWS OF RESOURCES			
Property taxes	15.0	--	15.0
NET POSITION			
Net investment in capital assets	157.1	--	157.1
Restricted for:			
Emergency reserves	2.4	0.1	2.5
Parks and open space	7.9	--	7.9
District infrastructure	1.0	--	1.0
Urban redevelopment	0.4	--	0.4
Unrestricted	63.5	-0.1	63.4
Total net position	$232.3	$--	$232.3

Statement of Activities

The statement of activities displays information about the results of the City's operations as a whole. This report includes the primary government and its component units, but does not include fiduciary funds and component units that are fiduciary in nature.

Helix City
Statement of Activities
For the Year Ended December 31, 20X2
(in millions)

| | | Program Revenues | | | Net (Expense) Revenue and Change in Net Position | | |
| | | | | | Primary Government | | |
Functions	Expenses	Charges for Services	Operating Grants and Contributions	Capital Grants and Contributions	Governmental Activities	Business-Type Activities	Total
Primary Government							
Governmental activities							
General government	$13.2	$0.2	$--	$--	-$12.9	$--	-$12.9
Community services	23.8	1.9	--	--	-21.9	--	-21.9
City infrastructure	24.7	0.8	6.5	6.2	-11.3	--	-11.3
Culture and recreation	1.0	--	--	2.9	1.9	--	1.9
Urban redevelopment	4.6	--	--	--	-4.6	--	-4.6
Interest on long-term debt	0.1	--	--	--	-0.1	--	-0.1
Total governmental activities	67.4	2.9	6.5	9.1	-48.9	--	-48.9
Business-type activities							
Land use	4.0	4.9	--	--	--	0.9	0.9
Total primary government	71.4	7.8	6.5	9.1	-48.9	0.9	-48.0
	General revenues:						
	Sales tax				38.3	--	38.3
	Use tax				3.5	--	3.5
	Property tax				12.9	--	12.9
	Auto use tax				4.6	--	4.6
	Other taxes				0.6	--	0.6
	Unrestricted franchise fees				5.1	--	5.1
	Investment income				0.2	--	0.2
	Intergovernmental revenues not restricted to specific programs				0.5	--	0.5
	Miscellaneous				0.9	--	0.9
	Transfers				0.9	-0.9	--
	Total general revenues and transfers				67.5	--	66.6
	Change in net position				18.6	--	18.6
	Net position - beginning				213.7	--	213.7
	Net position - ending				$232.3	$--	$232.3

Governmental Fund Financial Statements

The financial statements for the governmental funds are comprised of the balance sheet and a statement of revenues, expenditures and changes in fund balances. The balance sheet shows the financial position of the funds as of the balance sheet date, while the statement of revenues, expenditures and changes in fund balances reports information about the inflows, outflows, and balances of current financial resources of each major governmental fund, plus these amounts in aggregate for non-major governmental funds.

Helix City
Balance Sheet | Governmental Funds
December 31, 20X2

(in millions)	General	Urban Redevelopment Authority Fund	Capital Improvement Fund	Total Non-major Funds	Total Governmental Funds
ASSETS					
Cash and cash equivalents	$39.8	$0.4	$34.2	$9.0	$83.5
Taxes receivable	14.5	5.3	--	0.4	20.2
Other receivables	0.8	--	--	--	0.8
Intergovernmental receivables	0.5	--	--	--	0.5
Prepaid items	--	--	--	--	--
Total assets	55.6	5.7	34.2	9.4	105.0
LIABILITIES, DEFERRED INFLOWS OF RESOURCES, AND FUND BALANCES					
Liabilities:					
Accounts payable	4.0	--	0.9	0.1	5.0
Retainage payable	--	--	0.1	--	0.1
Accrued liabilities	0.6	--	1.2	--	1.8
Other liabilities	0.9	--	--	--	0.9
Developer contributions and deposits	4.1	--	--	--	4.1
Total liabilities	9.6	--	2.2	0.1	11.9
Deferred inflows of resources:					
Property taxes	9.3	5.3	--	0.4	15.0
Grants	0.1	--	--	--	0.1
Total deferred inflows of resources	9.4	5.3	--	0.4	15.1
FUND BALANCE					
Non-spendable	--	--	--	--	--
Restricted for:					
Emergency reserves	1.4	--	1.0	0.1	2.5
Parks and open space	--	--	--	7.9	7.9
District infrastructure	--	--	--	0.9	0.9
Urban redevelopment	--	0.4	--	--	0.4
Assigned to City infrastructure	--	--	31.0	--	31.0
Unassigned	35.2	--	--	--	35.2
Total fund balances	36.6	0.4	32.0	8.9	77.9
Total liabilities, deferred inflows of resources, and fund balances	$55.6	$5.7	$34.2	$9.4	$105.0

Amounts reported for governmental activities in the statement of net position are different because:

Total fund balance – governmental funds	$77.9
Capital assets used in governmental activities are not financial resources, and therefore are not reported in the funds (shown net of accumulated depreciation)	157.1
Revenues in the Statement of Activities that do not provide current financial resources are deferred in the funds	0.1
Long-term liabilities, including bonds payable, accrued interest payable, and accrued compensation absences are not due and payable in the current year, and so are not reported in governmental funds	-2.8
Total net position of governmental activities	$232.3

Helix City
Statement of Revenue, Expenditures, and Changes in Fund Balances
Governmental Funds
for the Year Ended 12/31/X2

(in millions)	General Fund	Urban Redevelopment Authority Fund	Capital Improvement Fund	Total Non-major Funds	Total Governmental Funds
REVENUE					
Taxes	$55.0	$4.6	$--	$0.4	$60.0
Intergovernmental	6.9	1.0	6.3	2.9	17.2
Charges for services	2.8	--	--	--	2.9
Franchise fees	5.1	--	--	--	5.1
Investment income	0.2	--	--	11.3	0.2
Miscellaneous	0.7	--	0.1	--	0.9
Total revenues	70.7	5.6	6.4	3.4	86.2
EXPENDITURES					
Current:					
General government	13.0	--	--	--	13.0
Community services	23.8	--	--	--	23.8
City infrastructure	13.7	--	7.3	0.1	21.1
Culture and recreation	--	--	--	1.1	1.1
Urban redevelopment	--	5.6	--	--	5.6
Capital outlay	0.8	--	7.4	0.2	8.4
Debt service					
Principal	--	--	--	0.1	0.1
Interest	--	--	--	0.1	0.1
Total expenditures	51.3	5.6	14.7	1.6	73.1
Revenue over (under) expenditures	19.5	--	-8.3	1.8	13.1
OTHER FINANCING SOURCES (USES)					
Transfers in	0.9	--	26.3	--	27.2
Transfers out	-26.3	--	--	--	-26.3
Total other financing sources and uses	-25.4	--	26.3	--	0.9
NET CHANGE IN FUND BALANCE	-5.9	--	18.0	1.8	14.0
Fund balances – beginning	42.4	0.4	13.9	7.1	63.9
Fund balances – ending	$36.5	$0.4	$31.9	$8.9	$77.9

127

Amounts reported for governmental activities in the statement of activities are different because:

Net change in fund balance – total governmental funds	$14.0
Governmental funds report capital outlays as expenditures. However, in the Statement of Activities, the costs of those assets are depreciated over their estimated useful lives (shown net of depreciation)	4.6
Repayment of long-term obligations are reported as expenditures in governmental funds, but they reduce long-term liabilities in the Statement of Net Position and do not affect the Statement of Activities	0.1
Certain revenues will not be collected for several months after the City's fiscal year-end, and so are not considered available resources	-0.1
Change in net position of governmental activities	$18.6

Proprietary Fund Financial Statements

The financial statements for the City's proprietary fund are comprised of the statement of net position, a statement of revenues, expenses and changes in net position, and a statement of cash flows. The balance sheet shows the financial position of the fund as of the balance sheet date, while the statement of revenues, expenses and changes in net position reports information about operating revenues and expenses. The statement of cash flows indicates the amounts of cash flows from operating and other sources.

Helix City
Statement of Net Position
Proprietary Fund
December 31, 20X2
(in millions)

	Business-Type Activities
	Land Use
ASSETS	
Current assets:	
Cash and cash equivalents	$0.3
Prepaid expenses	--
Total current assets	0.3
Noncurrent assets:	
Equipment, net of accumulated depreciation	0.1
Total noncurrent assets	0.1
Total assets	0.4
LIABILITIES	
Current liabilities:	
Accounts payable	0.3
Accrued liabilities	0.1
Total liabilities	0.4
NET POSITION	
Restricted for:	
Emergency reserves	0.1
Unrestricted	-0.1
Total net position	$--

Helix City
Statement of Revenue, Expenses and Changes in Net Position
Proprietary Fund
For the Year Ended December 31, 20X2
(in millions)

	Business-Type Activities
	Land Use
OPERATING REVENUE	
Building permits, licenses and fees	$4.0
Contractor's licenses and bus shelter fees	0.3
Land use permits and other income	0.6
Total operating revenue	4.9
OPERATING EXPENSES	
Personnel services	0.5
Contracted services	3.2
Services and supplies	0.3
Total operating expenses	4.0
Operating income before transfers	0.9
Transfers out	-0.9
Change in net position	--
Net position – beginning of year	--
Net position – end of year	$--

Helix City
Statement of Cash Flows
Proprietary Fund
For the Year Ended December 31, 20X2
(in millions)

	Business-Type Activities
	Land Use
Cash Flows from Operating Activities	
Cash received from customers	$4.9
Cash paid to employees	-0.4
Cash paid to vendors	-3.6
Net cash provided by operating activities	0.9
Cash Flows from Noncapital Financing Activities	
Transfers out	-0.9
Net cash used by non-capital financing activities	-0.9
Net increase in cash and cash equivalents	--
Cash and cash equivalents, beginning of year	0.3
Cash and cash equivalents, end of year	0.3
Reconciliation of operating income to net cash provided by operating activities	
Operating income	0.9
Adjustments to reconcile operating income to net cash provided by operating activities:	
Decrease in accounts payable	--
Decrease in accrued liabilities	--
Net adjustments	--
NET CASH PROVIDED BY OPERATING ACTIVITIES	$0.9

Combining Statements

In the following statements, we provide additional detail for the non-major funds that had been aggregated for reporting purposes in earlier financial statements. The reports provided are a combining balance sheet and a combining statement of revenues, expenditures and changes in fund balance.

Helix City
Combining Balance Sheet
Non-major Governmental Funds
December 31, 20X2
(in millions)

	Open Space Fund	Conservation Trust Fund	General Improvement District Fund	Total Non-major Governmental Funds
ASSETS				
Cash and investments	$5.7	$2.3	$1.0	$9.0
Taxes receivable	--	--	0.3	0.3
Total assets	5.7	2.3	1.3	9.3
LIABILITIES, DEFERRED INFLOWS OF RESOURCES, AND FUND BALANCE				
LIABILITIES				
Accounts payable	0.1	--	--	0.1
DEFERRED INFLOWS OF RESOURCES				
Property taxes	--	--	0.4	0.4
FUND BALANCE				
Restricted for:				
Emergency reserves	0.1	--	--	0.1
Parks and open space	5.6	2.3	--	7.9
District infrastructure	--	--	0.9	0.9
Total fund balance	5.7	2.3	0.9	8.9
TOTAL LIABILITIES, DEFERRED INFLOWS OF RESOURCES, AND FUND BALANCE	$5.7	$2.3	$1.3	$9.3

Helix City
Combining Statement of Revenues, Expenditures and Changes in Fund Balance
Non-major Governmental Funds
For the Year Ended December 31, 20X2
(in millions)

	Open Space Fund	Conservation Trust Fund	General Improvement District Fund	Total Non-major Governmental Funds
REVENUES				
Taxes	$--	$--	$0.4	$0.4
Intergovernmental	2.4	0.5	--	2.9
Total revenues	2.4	0.5	0.4	3.3
EXPENDITURES				
Current				
City infrastructure	--	--	0.1	0.1
Culture and recreation	0.9	0.1	--	1.0
Capital outlay	0.2	--	--	0.2
Debt service				
Principal	--	--	0.1	0.1
Interest	--	--	0.1	0.1
Total expenditures	1.1	0.1	0.3	1.5
NET CHANGE IN FUND BALANCE	1.3	0.4	0.1	1.8
Fund balance – beginning of year	4.3	1.9	0.8	7.1
Fund balance – end of year	$5.7	$2.3	$0.9	$8.9

Summary

The comprehensive annual financial report is by far the most wide-ranging and detailed financial report that a government will issue. The exact structure of this report will vary by the type and complexity of the government in question. For example, the contents of a CAFR for a school district will vary substantially from that of a city, county, or state. Consequently, the accountant who has been assigned the task of producing a CAFR might feel that a great deal of work is needed to produce the required document (which is quite true), involving sorting through the various requirements and constructing the most applicable report formats and accompanying narratives. To reduce the uncertainty associated with constructing a CAFR, the accountant would be well advised to access a sample CAFR for the most representative type of entity (which is readily available on-line), and use that as a model for the construction of the needed CAFR.

Chapter 11
Additional Financial Reporting Considerations

Introduction

A government's financial statements incorporate a number of special events or occurrences that could have a significant impact on reported results. In this chapter, we address the following financial reporting considerations:

- Related party transactions
- Subsequent events
- Going concern considerations
- Prior period adjustments
- Accounting changes and error corrections

Related Party Transactions

A government may engage in any number of transactions with related parties. For example, there could be a transaction with a joint venture in which a government is a partial owner, or with an elected official, or with a manager who works for the government, or perhaps with a pension plan that is managed by the government. There are many possible related party transactions, such as:

- The purchase or sale of property
- Accounting, engineering, and legal services
- A lending or leasing arrangement
- A guarantee of a debt or some other future payment

In short, *any* transaction can be with a related party. When there is a related party transaction, the following disclosures are required:

- The nature of the relationship
- A description of the transaction
- The dollar amount associated with the transaction
- Any amounts due from or payable to related parties, as well as the terms and manner of settlement

The preceding disclosure is not needed for compensation arrangements, expense or expenditure allowances, or other items that arise in the ordinary course of operations.

When the substance of a transaction differs significantly from its form because of the presence of a related party, record the transaction so that its substance is recognized, rather than just its legal form.

Subsequent Events

A subsequent event is one that occurs after the date of the financial statements (meaning the date of the statement of net position or similar report), but before the statements are issued. Some of these subsequent events must be recognized in the financial statements for the period that they follow. This is the case when:

- A subsequent event provides additional evidence about the conditions existing at the date of the statement of net position; and
- The event impacts the estimates used in preparing the financial statements.

In this situation, alter the estimates as appropriate, which in turn will lead to revisions in the financial statements.

Other subsequent events are not recognized in the financial statements of the period that they follow. This is the case when a subsequent event provides evidence about conditions that did not exist at the date of the statement of net position. However, depending on the event, it may be necessary to disclose the information in the notes accompanying the financial statements, because it is considered essential to a reader's understanding of the financial statements. Examples of non-recognized events include:

- Changes in the quoted prices of securities
- The issuance of bonds
- Damage to government-owned property
- The creation of a new component unit

Of the preceding list of non-recognized events, the final three would all probably be disclosed in the financial statements, since they are significant events that are essential to the financial statements.

EXAMPLE

The 20X1 financial statements for East Smithville have been prepared but not yet released. During this interval, the comptroller learns that a major company with property in the city has gone bankrupt. This will result in a loss of $120,000 in property taxes. The bankruptcy is a likely indicator of conditions that existed at the customer prior to the date of East Smithville's financial statements. This situation appears to call for recognition of a much larger allowance for doubtful accounts in East Smithville's 20X1 financial statements.

EXAMPLE

There is a major rainstorm in the East Smithville area between the date of its financial statements and their release. This causes flooding in the city's commercial district, devastating a number of major businesses. There will undoubtedly be a significant impact on sales tax receipts, since customers are now avoiding the area. This event is not indicative of conditions existing prior to the date of the financial statements, so the financials should not be adjusted.

> **Note:** It may be necessary to include information about subsequent events in the management's discussion and analysis section of the comprehensive annual financial report, especially if the events are expected to have a significant effect on the government's financial position or results of operations.

Going Concern Considerations

An underlying assumption of a government entity's financial statements is that the organization will continue to function in the future – that it is a going concern. The going concern assumption can be violated when evidence appears that a government cannot meet its obligations. Indicators of going concern issues are:

- *Negative trends.* There have been recurring periods in which:
  - Expenses have significantly exceeded revenues
  - There have been deficiencies in working capital
  - There have been recurring unsubsidized operating losses in business-type activities
  - There have been ongoing negative operating cash flows from business-type activities
  - There have been adverse financial ratios

- *Other indications of difficulties.* The entity is suffering from one or more of the following conditions:
  - It has defaulted on bond or other debt payments
  - It is approaching limits on the amount of debt it can take on
  - It is conducting a forced sale of its assets to generate cash
  - It is not in compliance with statutory reserve requirements
  - It is seeking new sources of financing
  - It is seeking to restructure its debt or has already done so
  - Suppliers are denying it normal amounts of trade credit

- *Internal matters.* The entity has experienced one or more of the following issues related to its internal operations:
  - It has experienced work stoppages
  - It is highly dependent on the success of a particular project or program
  - It is subject to long-term commitments that are not economical
  - It needs to engage in a significant revision of its operations

- *External matters.* The entity is being impacted by one or more of the following issues related to third parties:
  - Legal proceedings that may result in large payments
  - Legislation that may impact revenues and the sustainability of key programs
  - The loss by a business-unit activity of a key patent

136

- o The loss of an essential customer, taxpayer, or supplier
- o The occurrence of a catastrophe for which there is not sufficient insurance

When there is a substantial doubt about the ability of a government to continue as a going concern for 12 months beyond the financial statement date, disclose the following information (if it is appropriate to do so):

- Those conditions or events triggering doubt about the ability to continue as a going concern.
- The possible effects of those conditions or events.
- An evaluation by government officials of the significance of those conditions and events, as well as any mitigating factors.
- The possible discontinuance of government operations.
- The plans by government officials in regard to the situation.
- A discussion about the recoverability of assets, changes in the amounts of liabilities, or changes in the classification of assets or liabilities.

Note: It may be necessary to include information about going concern issues in the management's discussion and analysis section of the comprehensive annual financial report, especially if the events are expected to have a significant effect on the government's financial position or results of operations.

Prior Period Adjustments

An error may be detected in previously-issued financial statements, such as a mathematical mistake or a misuse of the facts existing when the statements were prepared. If so, the error is corrected and accounted for as a prior-period adjustment, which is an adjustment to the opening balance of net position in a single-period statement. When a government is presenting multi-period comparative statements, the proper adjustment is to alter the amounts reported in the flows statement and the statement of net position for all of the periods appearing in the financial statements. The effect of this change is not included in the net position section of the flows statement for the current period.

When there is a prior period adjustment, disclose the effects on the change in net position in the notes accompanying the financial statements. When the financial statements only cover a single period, indicate the effects of the adjustment on the beginning balance of net position, as well as on the change in net position of the preceding period. When multi-period statements are being presented, disclose the effects for each of the periods.

When there is a prior period adjustment due to an error, report the nature of the error and the effect of its correction on the government's change in net position.

Accounting Changes and Error Corrections

A government may experience several types of accounting changes and/or error corrections that impact its financial statements. An accounting change is a change in principle, estimate, or reporting entity. In the following sub-sections, we describe each one and how it should be handled in the financial statements.

Change in Accounting Principle

There is a change in accounting principle when a principle is adopted that differs from the one previously used. This situation typically arises when a government can legitimately choose between two or more options for generally accepted accounting principles, and the replacement principle is preferable to the prior principle. For example, a government could elect to start including salvage value in its depreciation calculations, or it could alter the official policy for determining which investments will be classified as cash equivalents in the statement of net position.

A change in accounting principle should be a relatively rare event, since there is a presumption that an accounting principle should not be changed, since consistently-applied principles result in more consistent financial statements over multiple reporting periods.

When there is a change in accounting principle, disclose the nature of the change and the justification for making the change (noting how it is preferable to the prior approach), as well as its effect on beginning net position. There are several issues to consider when reporting a change in accounting principle within the financial statements. These issues are:

- *Beginning net position.* Adjust the beginning net position in the period of the change for the cumulative effect of the change. It is reported as an adjustment to the amounts previously reported. The calculation is the difference between the balance of the net position at the beginning of the period and the beginning balance that would have been reported if the new principle had been applied retroactively to all prior periods.
- *Prior periods.* Present the financial statements for previous periods as they were previously reported.

It is possible that the cumulative effect of a change in accounting principle cannot be calculated. If so, disclose the effect of the change on the current-period operations and explain why there is no accounting for the cumulative effect of the change in prior periods.

Change in Accounting Estimate

The preparation of financial statements involves the use of several estimates, which are routinely altered as new information is obtained. For example, the accountant uses estimates of capital asset service lives, the uncollectability of receivables, and inventory obsolescence.

A change in accounting estimate does not trigger a retroactive adjustment in prior periods. Instead, it only impacts the current period and future periods. When there is a change in accounting estimate in the ordinary course of activities, there is no need to disclose the change in estimate. If there is a change in estimate that affects several future periods, it is acceptable to disclose the change.

EXAMPLE

The comptroller of Qanix City alters her estimate of the allowance for doubtful accounts. There is no need to disclose this change.

The comptroller also shortens the estimated useful lives of several classes of capital assets. Since this change impacts a number of future reporting periods, she discloses the change in the notes to the financial statements.

Change in Reporting Entity

There are rare situations in which the entity issuing financial statements changes to a different entity. For a government, this usually means that there is a change in the mix of organizations that comprise the reporting entity.

There are several issues to consider when reporting a change in reporting entity. First, the financial statements for all prior periods must be restated to reflect the change in entity. Second, the nature of the change should be disclosed, along with the reason(s) for it. And finally, disclose the effect of the change in entity on the beginning net position for all of the periods presented in the financial statements.

Summary

Of the special occurrences addressed in this chapter, the ones most likely to require ongoing attention are accounting changes and error corrections, specifically in regard to changes in accounting estimate and accounting errors. There may be changes in accounting estimate many times per year, while an occasional accounting error may surface. The disclosure of changes in accounting estimate is usually not necessary, since they are considered part of ongoing operations and are usually immaterial. Accounting errors may be so insignificant that they are not worthy of disclosure. Consequently, the typical government will incorporate these topics into its financial statements, but may not find it necessary to separately disclose them.

Chapter 12
Notes to Financial Statements

Introduction

The comprehensive annual financial report (CAFR) is not complete without a broad-ranging set of accompanying notes. These notes are either used to expand upon the information in the financial statements or to improve a reader's understanding of the required supplementary information section of the CAFR. In this chapter, we provide an overview of the essential notes that should always be included in a CAFR, as well as the multitude of additional disclosures that may be needed, depending on the circumstances. We also provide several sample disclosures, with particular attention to the reporting of accounting policies.

Notes Overview

The notes to the financial statements should focus on the primary government, which means that they should discuss the following:

- Governmental activities
- Business-type activities
- Major funds
- Non-major funds

Here are several additional considerations when preparing and presenting notes:

- *Location of information.* Notes are typically viewed as ancillary information that is presented after the financial statements. However, it is also possible to display some of this information on the face of the financial statements. Doing so makes it easier for readers to access information. However, an excessive amount of information on the financial statements can create too much clutter. Consequently, the amount of information presented in this manner is usually relatively limited.
- *Segregation of information.* Readers should be able to distinguish between information related to the primary government and its component units.
- *Essential vs. additional disclosures.* A large number of disclosures may be required for governmental financial statements. These disclosures can be divided into essential disclosures and additional disclosures (which are only necessary if they apply to specific circumstances).

Significant Accounting Policies

An essential disclosure is a summary of a government's significant accounting policies. These policies are the set of accounting principles (and methods used to apply them) that are considered by management to be the most appropriate for the fair presentation of the financial statements. The choice of policies used can have a significant impact on the financial statements, so users should be aware of these policies. The key disclosures are:

- *Overview.* Describe the government-wide financial statements, pointing out that fiduciary funds are not included, nor are component units that are fiduciary in nature.
- *Component units.* Describe the component units of the reporting entity, as well as their relationships to the primary government. The discussion should include the criteria used to determine which component units are included in the financial reporting entity, as well as how the component units are reported. Further, note how the reader can obtain separate financial statements for individual component units.
- *Column descriptions.* Describe the activities included within the columns in the basic financial statements for major funds, internal service funds, and fiduciary-type funds.
- *Measurement focus and basis of accounting.* Describe the measurement focus and the basis of accounting used to construct the government-wide financial statements.
- *Revenue recognition.* Note the revenue recognition policies being used in the fund financial statements.
- *Internal activities.* Describe the policy under which internal activity is eliminated in the government-wide statement of activity.
- *Inventory basis.* Describe the basis used to formulate inventory costs.
- *Asset capitalization.* Note the policy used to capitalize assets, as well as to estimate the useful lives of those assets and the methods used to compute depreciation for the major asset classes. If the modified approach is used, describe how that approach works.
- *Program transactions.* Describe the types of transactions that have been included in program revenues, as well as the policy for allocating indirect expenses to functions within the statement of activities.
- *Proprietary fund revenues.* Describe how the operating and non-operating revenues of proprietary funds are defined.
- *Cash and cash equivalents.* Define cash and cash equivalents as used in the statement of cash flows for proprietary funds.
- *Application of resources.* Describe the policy for whether to first apply restricted or unrestricted resources when an expense is incurred, in those cases where both of these resources are available.
- *Fund balance classifications.* Note the policies and procedures that apply to the government's fund balance classifications.

141

A policy should be disclosed when it involves any of the following:

- An unusual application of generally accepted accounting principles
- Principles and methods that are unique to the industry in which the government operates
- A selection from several acceptable alternatives

The summary of significant accounting policies is stated as the initial note to the financial statements.

There are a number of other essential disclosures related to specific parts of the financial statements. Those disclosures are addressed in the chapters pertaining to those parts of the statements.

Additional Disclosures

There are a number of additional disclosures that may be required, depending on the circumstances. The following list indicates the extent of these additional notes. The list is not all-inclusive. The accountant will need to use judgment in determining the level of disclosure needed to provide a reasonable amount of detail. There may be a temptation to be excessively exuberant in adding information to the notes – try not to do so, since unnecessary and immaterial information can overwhelm the reader. Conversely, enough material should be included in the notes to ensure that readers are aware of all material items. A good rule for deciding whether to include information is to do so if its omission would cause the financial statements to be misleading.

Summary of Additional Disclosures

Accountability for related organizations	Lending and mortgage banking activities
Accounting changes and error corrections	Long-term construction-type contracts
Asset valuation allowances	Major special revenue funds
Bankruptcy disclosures	Minimum fund balance policies
Change in manner of corresponding item presentation	Nature of reconciling items
Condensed statements for major component units	Net position restricted by enabling legislation
Conduit debt obligations	Non-exchange financial guarantees
Debt extinguishments	Non-exchange transactions
Deferred resource inflows and outflows	Non-monetary transactions
Demand bonds	On-behalf payments for compensation
Derivative instruments	Pension plans
Disaggregation of receivable and payable balances	Pollution remediation obligations
Discounts that reduce gross revenues	Post-employment benefit plans
Disposals of government operations	Property taxes
Effects of prior-period adjustments	Regulated business-type activities
External investment pools	Related-party transactions
Fair value measurements	Research and development arrangements
Foreign currency transactions	Retail land sales operations
Fund balance classification details	Revenue anticipation notes
Future revenues that are pledged or sold	Reverse repurchase agreements
Going concern issues	Risk management activities
Government combinations	Securities lending transactions
Idle impaired capital assets	Segment information for enterprise funds
Impairment losses	Service concession arrangements
Inconsistencies caused by different fiscal year-ends	Short-term debt instruments
Insurance enterprises	Short-term obligations
Insurance recoveries	Significant transactions not within management control
Interest expense included in direct expenses	Special assessment debt
Interfund eliminations	Stabilization arrangements
Investments in common stock	Tax abatements
Joint ventures and jointly-governed entities	Termination benefits
Landfill closure and post-closure care	Troubled debt restructurings

A selection of disclosures is summarized in the following bullet points.

- *Classes of capital assets.* Present the beginning and end-of-year balances, as well as accumulated depreciation, capital acquisitions, and sales or other dispositions. Also note the current-period depreciation expense, separating out the amounts charged to each of the functions listed in the statement of activities.
- *Collections.* If collections have not been capitalized, describe the collections and the reason(s) for not capitalizing them.
- *Long-term liabilities.* Present the beginning and end-of-year balances, as well as increases and decreases in liability levels and the portion of each liability that is due within one year.
- *Funds used for liquidations.* Note which government funds have been used to liquidate other long-term liabilities in prior years.
- *Donor-restricted endowments.* Disclose the following information regarding endowments that have been restricted by donors:
  - The amount of net appreciation available for authorization for expenditure
  - How the amount of net appreciation is reported in the net position of the entity
  - The relevant state law pertaining to the ability to spend net appreciation
  - The entity's policy for authorizing and spending investment income
- *Short-term debt.* Describe short-term debt activity during the year, including a schedule of changes from the beginning to ending balances. Also state the reason why the debt was issued.
- *Disaggregations.* Break out the different types of receivables and payables stated on the statements of net position and the balance sheet when aggregation has obscured significant items.
- *Interfund balances.* Disclose the following information about interfund balances that have been reported in the fund financial statements:
  - The amounts due from other funds, breaking out individual major funds, and the following funds in aggregate: non-major governmental funds, non-major enterprise funds, internal service funds, and fiduciary funds
  - The reason for the interfund balances
  - Any interfund balances that are not expected to be repaid within one year
- *Interfund activity.* Disclose the following information about interfund transfers that have been reported in the fund financial statements:
  - The amounts transferred from other funds, breaking out individual major funds, and the following funds in aggregate: non-major governmental funds, non-major enterprise funds, internal service funds, and fiduciary funds

- The purpose of the transfers
- The purpose and amount of significant transfers that do not occur on a routine basis, or which are inconsistent with the activities of the fund making the transfer

- *Future revenues pledged.* When future revenues have been pledged to secure debt, disclose the following information about the revenues being pledged:

  - The revenue that has been pledged and the amount of the pledge
  - The debt associated with the pledged revenue and its purpose
  - The duration of the pledge period
  - The proportion of the revenue stream that has been pledged
  - A comparison of the pledged revenues to the associated debt

- *Future revenues sold.* When future revenues have been sold, disclose the following information:

  - The revenue that has been sold and the assumptions used in determining the approximate amount sold
  - The period to which the sale applies
  - The proportion of the revenue stream that has been sold
  - A comparison of the sale proceeds to the present value of the future revenues sold and the assumptions used in determining the present value figure

- *Deferred inflows and outflows.* Provide details regarding the different types of deferred inflows and outflows of resources that have been reported at an aggregate level in the statement of net position or balance sheet. This is necessary when significant amounts have been obscured due to the aggregation.

Disclosure Sequence

The preceding list of disclosures was in alphabetical order, which is not necessarily the best order in which to present these items in the notes. The order of presentation is more informative when it is presented in a logical sequence. There is no ideal sequence for the notes, since the order of presentation depends on the unique characteristics of each set of financial statements. Nonetheless, the following sequence could be used as a general guideline for the order in which to present information within the notes:

I. Summary of significant accounting policies

   a. Description of the government-wide financial statements
   b. Description of the component units of the financial reporting entity
   c. Basis of presentation of the government-wide financial statements
   d. Basis of presentation of the fund financial statements
   e. Basis of accounting

     f.   Assets, liabilities, and net position and fund balances, in their order of appearance

     g.   Revenues, expenditures/expense

II.   Stewardship, compliance and accountability

     a.   Violations of legal and contractual provisions and remedies taken

     b.   Deficit fund balances of individual funds

III.   Detail notes on all activities and funds

     a.   Assets

     b.   Liabilities

     c.   Interfund receivables and payables

     d.   Revenues and expenditures/expenses

     e.   Donor-restricted endowment disclosures

     f.   Interfund transfers

     g.   Encumbrances outstanding

IV.   Segment information – enterprise funds

V.   Individual major component unit disclosures

VI.   The nature of the primary government's accountability for related organizations

VII.   Joint ventures and jointly governed organizations

VIII.   Related party transactions

IX.   Summary disclosure of significant contingencies

     a.   Litigation

     b.   Compliance audits for federally assisted programs

X.   Significant effects of subsequent events

Notes Minimization

The information contained within the notes should not be repetitive. Rather than duplicating text presented elsewhere in the financial statements, provide references to the information presented elsewhere in the statements.

A number of other statements and schedules may accompany the basic set of financial statements. If so, only provide information for these items that is not included in the basic financial statement package. The following guidelines can be of assistance in deciding whether to include additional information:

- The information is needed to assure an understanding of the combining and individual statements and schedules.
- The information is needed to demonstrate compliance with legal and contractual requirements.

Sample Disclosure of Accounting Policies

This section contains a sample set of abbreviated accounting policies for a city government. The general format and text of these policies could be used as the starting point for constructing similar disclosures for another entity.

NOTE – SUMMARY OF SIGNIFICANT ACCOUNTING POLICIES

The accounting and reporting policies of the City conform to accounting principles generally accepted in the United States of America (U.S. GAAP) as applicable to governmental units. The Governmental Accounting Standards Board (GASB) is the accepted standard-setting body for establishing governmental accounting and financial reporting principles.

The City's basic financial statements consist of government-wide statements including a Statement of Net Position and a Statement of Activities, and fund financial statements that provide a more detailed level of financial information. The following summary of significant accounting policies is presented to assist the reader in evaluating the City's financial statements.

Measurement Focus, Basis of Accounting, and Financial Statement Presentation

Government-Wide and Proprietary Fund Financial Statements

The government-wide financial statements are reported using the *economic resources measurement focus* and the *accrual basis of accounting*, as is the proprietary fund. Revenues are recorded when earned and expenses are recorded when a liability is incurred, regardless of the timing of related cash flows. For example, revenues from property taxes are recognized in the fiscal year for which the taxes are levied. Depreciation is computed and recorded as an operating expense. Expenditures for property and equipment are shown as increases in assets and redemption of bonds and notes are recorded as a reduction in liabilities. Contributed infrastructure assets are recorded as capital contributions when received.

Governmental Fund Financial Statements

Governmental funds are reported using the *current financial resources measurement focus* and the *modified accrual basis of accounting*. Revenues are recognized as soon as they are both measurable and available. Revenues are considered to be available if they are collectible within the current period or soon enough thereafter to pay liabilities of the current period. For this purpose, the City considers revenues to be available if they are collected within 60 days of the end of the current fiscal period. The major sources of revenue susceptible to accrual are taxes, intergovernmental revenues, franchise fees, and investment income. All other revenue items are considered to be measurable and available only when cash is received by the City.

Expenditures, other than interest on long-term obligations, are recorded when the fund liability is incurred or the long-term obligation is paid. Principal and interest on long-term debt are recognized when due. General capital asset acquisitions are reported as expenditures in governmental funds. Compensated absences are recorded only when payment is due.

Proprietary Fund Financial Statements

Proprietary funds distinguish operating revenues and expenses from non-operating items. Operating revenues and expenses generally result from providing services and producing and delivering goods in connection with a proprietary fund's principal ongoing operations. Operating revenues consist of charges to customers for service provided. Operating expenses for enterprise funds include the cost of sales and services, administrative expenses, and depreciation of assets. All revenues and expenses not meeting this definition are reported as non-operating revenues and expenses or capital contributions.

When both restricted and unrestricted resources are available for a specific use, it is the City's policy to use restricted resources first, then unrestricted resources as they are needed.

Assets, Liabilities, and Net Position/Fund Balance

Cash and Investments

The City's cash and cash equivalents include amounts that are readily convertible to cash and are not subject to significant risk from changes in interest rates. Cash and cash equivalents include cash on hand, demand deposits, and short-term investments with original maturities of three months or less from the date of acquisition.

Investments are reported at their fair value.

The City follows the practice of pooling cash of most funds to maximize daily investment earnings. Except when required by trust or other agreements, all cash is deposited to, and disbursed from, applicable fund operating accounts. Cash in excess of immediate operating requirements is swept from operating accounts to investment accounts.

Receivables

Receivables are reported net of an allowance for uncollectible accounts, where applicable.

Property Taxes Receivable

Property taxes attach as an enforceable lien on property on January 1 and are levied by the City Council based on assessed valuations determined by the County Assessor each year. The levy is set annually by December 15, by certification to the County Commissioners. The County Treasurer collects the determined taxes during the ensuing calendar year. The taxes are payable by April, or if in equal installments at the taxpayer's election, in February and June. Delinquent taxpayers are notified in August and generally sales of the tax liens on delinquent properties are held in November. The County Treasurer remits the taxes collected monthly to the City.

Property taxes are levied for the previous year, but collected in the subsequent year, are recorded in the governmental funds as taxes receivable and deferred inflows of resources in the year there is an enforceable lien and the amount is measurable. Amounts deferred are subsequently recorded as revenue in the year they are available or collected.

Prepaid Expenses

Certain payments to vendors reflect costs applicable to future years and are recorded as prepaid expenses/items in both government-wide and fund financial statements using the consumption method.

Capital Assets

Capital assets are reported in the applicable governmental or business-type activities column in the government-wide financial statements and in the proprietary fund in the fund financial statements. Purchases or construction of capital assets are recorded as expenditures in the governmental funds.

Capital assets are defined by the City as machinery and equipment with an individual cost of $5,000 or greater, land, easements and buildings, and infrastructure with the same individual cost threshold, and an estimated useful life in excess of one year. Such assets are recorded at historical cost or estimated historical cost if the actual historical cost is not available. Donated capital assets are recorded at estimated fair value at the date of donation. Contributed infrastructure by developers or other governmental entities is recorded as capital contributions and additions to the systems at fair value at the date of contribution. Interest accrued during construction is not capitalized.

Intangible assets included in capital assets not being depreciated consist of easements and rights of way and are capitalized at historical cost.

The costs of normal maintenance and repairs that do not add to the value of the asset or materially extend the life of the asset are not capitalized. Improvements are capitalized and depreciated over the remaining useful lives of the related capital assets, as applicable.

Capital assets are depreciated using the straight-line method of depreciation over the estimated economic useful lives as follows:

Buildings	50 years
Machinery and equipment	5 years
Infrastructure:	
Bridges	50 years
Storm drainage system	75 years
Streets and walkways	20 years
Signals	10 years
Signs	20 years

Notes to Financial Statements

Deferred Inflows of Resources

Deferred inflows include property taxes earned, but levied for a subsequent year. In addition, grants not available as current financial resources are reported as deferred inflows in the governmental fund financial statements.

Compensated Absences

The City's compensated absences policy allows employees to accumulate earned but unused paid time off (PTO) benefits of at least 3.0 hours per pay period, depending on length of service and employment status. Employees may carry over PTO hours equivalent to the annual accrual for the employee during the immediately preceding year. Such carry-over leave must be used within the year into which it is carried over. PTO hours accrued above the carry-over amount during the preceding calendar year and not used by December 31 will be forfeited. In the event of separation from the City, an employee is paid 100% of accumulated PTO benefits.

In the governmental fund financial statements, compensated absences are recognized as current salary costs when paid. In the government-wide and proprietary fund financial statements, compensated absences are reported when earned. The City's General Fund is used to liquidate compensated absences of the governmental activities.

Long-Term Obligations

In the government-wide financial statements, long-term debt and other long-term obligations are reported as liabilities in the Statement of Net Position. Bonds payable are reported net of the applicable bond premium or discount.

In the fund financial statements, governmental funds recognize bond premiums and bond discounts in the year of issue. The face amount of the debt issued is reported as other financing sources.

Issuance costs, whether or not withheld from the debt proceeds received, are reported as current expenses or expenditures.

Net Position

Net position represents the difference between assets and liabilities. Net investment in capital assets consists of capital assets, net of accumulated depreciation, reduced by the outstanding balance of any borrowing used for the acquisition, construction or improvements of those assets. Net position is reported as restricted when there are limitations imposed on their use through external restrictions imposed by creditors, grantors, laws, or regulations of other governments.

Fund Balance

In the fund financial statements, governmental funds report fund balances based on financial reporting standards that establish criteria for classifying fund balances into specifically defined classifications to make the nature and extent of constraints more useful and understandable. The classifications comprise a hierarchy based primarily on the extent to which the City is bound to honor constraints on the specific purposes for which amounts in those funds can be spent. Fund balances may be classified as non-spendable, restricted, committed, assigned, or unassigned. Definitions of these classifications are as follows:

- *Non-spendable fund balance.* Non-spendable amounts are those that cannot be spent because they are either not in spendable form, or legally or contractually to be maintained intact. Examples are items that are not expected to be converted to cash, including inventories and prepaids.
- *Restricted fund balance.* Restricted amounts are those that are restricted for a specific purpose. The spending constraints placed on the use of fund balance amounts are externally imposed by creditors, grantors, contributors, laws or regulations of other governments, or imposed by law through constitutional provisions or enabling legislation that are legally enforceable.
- *Committed fund balance.* Committed amounts are those that can only be used for specific purposes pursuant to constraints imposed by the City Council by ordinance. The committed amounts cannot be used for any other purpose unless the City Council removes or changes the specified use by taking the same type of formal action it employed to previously commit those amounts. This classification also incorporates contractual obligations to the extent that existing resources in the fund have been specifically committed for use in satisfying those contractual requirements.
- *Assigned fund balance.* Assigned amounts are those that are constrained by the City's intent to be used for specific purposes, but are neither restricted nor committed.
- *Unassigned fund balance.* The unassigned fund balance is applicable only to the General Fund and represents the remaining fund balance after amounts are set aside for other classifications.

As of December 31, 20X2, the City had in place a minimum fund policy which states that the overall fund balance of the General Fund shall equal no less than 25% of annual expenditures, including transfers. Additionally, the City had in place a 10% operating reserve in the General Fund, which is to be used for emergency purposes as designated by the City Council.

Estimates

The preparation of financial statements in conformity with accounting principles generally accepted in the United States requires management to make estimates and assumptions that affect the amounts reported in the financial statements and accompanying notes. Actual results may differ from those estimates.

Sample Disclosure of Assets and Liabilities

This section contains a sample set of abbreviated disclosures related to the asset and liability line items found on the statement of net position.

Cash and Cash Equivalents

A summary of cash and investments as of December 31, 20X2 is as follows:

(in millions)	
Cash deposits	$13.9
Investments	69.9
Total	$83.8

Investments

The City is required to comply with State statutes and the City's Investment Policy, which specify instruments meeting defined rating, maturity, and concentration risk criteria in which local governments may invest, which include the following:

- Obligations of the United States and certain U.S. government agency securities
- Certain corporate or bank securities
- General obligation and revenue bonds of U.S. local government entities
- Bankers' acceptances of certain banks
- Commercial paper
- Written repurchase agreements collateralized by certain authorized securities
- Certain money market funds
- Guaranteed investment contracts
- Local government investment pools

The City's policy is to invest funds to attain a market rate of return throughout budgetary and economic cycles while preserving and protecting capital in the overall portfolio; the primary investment goals are safety, liquidity, and maximizing yield while avoiding speculation.

At December 31, 20X2, the City's investment balances were as follows:

(in millions) Investment	S&P Rating	% of Total	Fair Value	Maturities Less than 1 Year	1-2 Years	3-5 Years
U.S. Agency Securities	AA+	14.2%	$9.9	$--	$5.5	$4.4
U.S. Treasury Securities	N/A	4.6%	3.2	0.8	2.5	--
Corporate Notes	AA+	0.7%	0.5	--	0.5	--
Corporate Notes	AA	2.1%	1.5	1.0	--	0.5
Wells Fargo Money Market	AAAm	1.4%	1.0	1.0	--	--
Local Government Investment Pools	AAAm	77.0%	53.8	53.7	--	--
Totals		100.0%	$69.9	$56.5	$8.5	$4.9

Notes to Financial Statements

Investment Risks

Interest Rate Risk. The City's investment policy limits the final maturity of investments in U.S Treasury and Agency securities to a maximum of five years, or as dictated by state statutes governing said investments. Likewise, investments in corporate notes cannot have a final maturity exceeding three years from the date of purchase.

Credit Risk. The City's investment policy limits investments in U.S. Agency securities to a five year maturity. Securities rated in the highest rating category by each of the nationally recognized statistical rating organizations (NRSROs) may be purchased, subject to maturity limits. In the event that an agency security carries a rating lower than the highest category set by any NRSRO, the security is eligible for purchase, subject to any statutory limits regarding final maturity and rating as permitted by State law. Corporate notes must be rated at least AA- or the equivalent by two or more NRSROs. Commercial paper must be rated at least A-1 or the equivalent at the time of purchase by at least two NRSROs and rated not less by all NRSROs that rate the commercial paper. State statutes limit investments in money market funds to those that maintain a constant share price, with a maximum remaining maturity in accordance with the Securities and Exchange Commission's Rule 2a-7, and either assets of one billion dollars or the highest rating issued by an NRSRO.

Concentration of credit risk. The City's investment policy requires that at no time shall the aggregate investment in corporate notes, commercial paper, and banker's acceptances exceed 40% of the City's total investment portfolio. Furthermore, investments in corporate notes and commercial paper shall not individually exceed 20% of the City's investment portfolio, and no more than 10% of the portfolio may be invested in the obligations of any one issuer of corporate debt or commercial paper. Investments in U.S. agency securities shall not exceed 85% of the total portfolio, and no more than 30% of the portfolio can be invested in any one issuer of agency securities.

Interfund Transfers

The following schedule summarizes the City's interfund transfer activity for the year ended December 31, 20X2.

(in million)	Transfers In		
Transfers Out	Capital Improvement Fund	General Fund	Total
General Fund	$26.3	$--	$26.3
Land Use Fund	--	0.9	0.9
Totals	$26.3	$0.9	$27.2

The $26.3 million transfer from the General Fund to the Capital Improvement Fund was made to provide needed funding for 20X2 budgeted capital projects. The $0.9 million transfer from the Land Use Fund to the General Fund was to reimburse the General Fund for past contributions.

Capital Assets

An analysis of the changes in capital assets for the year ended December 31, 20X2 is as follows:

(in millions)	Balance at 12/31/X1	Increases	Decreases	Balance at 12/31/X2
Governmental Activities:				
Capital assets not being depreciated	$92.7	$7.6	$0.3	$100.0
Capital assets being depreciated	128.9	1.0	--	129.9
Less accumulated depreciation	69.1	3.6	--	72.7
Total capital assets being depreciated, net	59.8	-2.6	--	57.2
Governmental activities capital assets, net	$152.5	$5.0	$0.3	$157.2
Business-Type Activities:				
Total capital assets being depreciated	$0.2	--	--	$0.2
Total accumulated depreciation	0.1	--	--	0.1
Total capital assets being depreciated, net	0.1	--	--	0.1
Business-type activities capital assets, net	$0.1	$--	$--	$0.1

Depreciation expense of the governmental activities was charged to the city infrastructure and general government programs in the amounts of $3.5 million and $0.1 million, respectively.

Long-Term Obligations

Long-term obligation transactions as of December 31, 20X2 are summarized below.

(in millions)	Balance at 12/31/X1	Additions	Reductions	Balance at 12/31/X2	Due within 1 Year
Governmental Activities:					
Bonds payable					
Buffalo GID bonds	$2.6	$--	$0.1	$2.5	$0.1
Total bonds payable	2.6	--	0.1	2.5	0.1
Compensated absences	0.2	0.3	0.3	0.2	--
Total long-term obligations	$2.8	$0.3	$0.4	$2.7	$0.1

General Obligation Bonds

In 20X1, Buffalo General Improvement District issued $3.0 million of general obligation bonds with interest rates varying from 3.3% to 5.1%, payable semi-annually on June 1 and December 1 commencing on June 1, 20X1 through December 20X7. The bonds were issued for the purposes of (i) financing or reimbursing all or any part of the costs of acquiring, construction, and installing a

Notes to Financial Statements

system of water pipelines to furnish municipal water service within the District; (ii) providing capitalized interest to pay a portion of debt service on the bonds; and (iii) paying the costs of issuance of the bonds.

Bonds outstanding and related interest requirements as of December 31, 20X2 are as follows:

(in millions) Year	Principal	Interest	Total
20X3	$0.1	$0.1	$0.2
20X4	0.1	0.1	0.2
20X5	0.1	0.1	0.2
20X6	0.1	0.1	0.2
20X7	2.1	0.1	2.2
Totals	$2.5	$0.5	$3.0

Sample Disclosure of Contingencies

This section contains a sample abbreviated disclosure for the contingencies to which a City might be subjected.

The City entered into construction contracts for various capital projects which are not complete as of December 31, 20X2. The total unexpended commitments at December 31, 20X2 are stated in the following table.

(in millions) Project	Total Contract Amount	Remaining Contract Amount
Baseline Road improvements	$4.7	$2.9
Fiber installation	0.5	0.2
Baseline interchange upgrade	3.2	2.1
Charleston & Evans intersection	0.8	0.2
	$9.2	$5.4

Sample Disclosure of Risk Management

This section contains a sample disclosure of the risk management practices of a city government.

The City is exposed to various risks of loss related to torts; thefts, damage to, or destruction of, assets; errors or omissions; injuries to employees; or acts of God. The City is a member of the State Intergovernmental Risk Sharing Agency (SIRSA). SIRSA is a joint self-insurance pool created by intergovernmental agreement of 150 municipalities to provide property, workers' compensation, general and automobile liability and public officials' coverage to its members.

Coverage is provided through the pooling of self-insured losses and the purchase of excess insurance coverage. SIRSA has a legal obligation for claims against its members to the extent that funds are available in its annually established loss fund and that amounts are available from insurance providers under excess specific and aggregate insurance contracts. Losses incurred in excess of loss funds and amounts recoverable from excess insurance are direct liabilities of the participating members. It is the intent of the members of SIRSA to create an entity in perpetuity which will administer and use funds contributed by the members to defend and indemnify, in accordance with the bylaws, any member of SIRSA against stated liability of loss, to the limit of the financial resources of SIRSA.

It is also the intent of the members to have SIRSA provide continuing stability and availability of needed coverages at reasonable costs. All income and assets of SIRSA shall be at all times dedicated to the exclusive benefit of its members.

Sample Disclosure of Subsequent Events

This section contains a sample disclosure of a subsequent event that might happen to a city government.

> On February 1, 20X3 the Buffalo General Improvement District ("Buffalo") issued general obligation refunding bonds in the amount of $2.5 million. Proceeds from this issuance were used to refund $2.5 million of general obligation bonds that were originally issued for acquiring, construction, and installation of a system of water pipelines to furnish municipal water service within the District. Principal is due on the bonds each December 1st. Interest accrues at rates varying from 2.3% to 4.8%, and is payable semi-annually on June 1st and December 1st.

Summary

A great many disclosures are included in the notes to the financial statements – so many that the accountant might feel oppressed by the prospect of spending an inordinate amount of time writing them each year. The situation is not that bad, since the circumstances of the typical government do not change that much from year to year. It is quite likely that the same disclosures can be used for multiple years, with adjustments for any numeric values included in the text. However, there is a danger that an accountant relying too much on prior year disclosures will not add new disclosures or will not delete less relevant text. Consequently, part of the report preparation process is to critically review the financial circumstances of a government to see if there are any new occurrences requiring disclosure, or if previously-reported items are no longer relevant. This task is made easier when the team in charge of preparing the financial statements has been doing so for several years, and so can bring a historical perspective to the task.

Chapter 13
Budgetary Reporting

Introduction

A complete set of financial statements should include in the reporting package a set of budgetary comparison schedules, which are intended to show how well the reporting entity has been able to match its actual performance to its original and final appropriated budgets. In this chapter, we cover the requirements for when these comparison schedules should be used and provide several examples.

Overview of Budgetary Reporting

A government should present budgetary comparisons for the general fund, as well as for each major special revenue fund that has a legally adopted annual budget associated with it. When presenting a comprehensive annual financial report (CAFR), similar schedules should also be included for individual non-major special revenue funds and other governmental funds of the primary government. Each of these comparisons should present both the original and final appropriated budgets for the reporting period, as well as the actual inflows, outflows, and balances reported by the government. Also, governments are encouraged to include a separate column to report the variance between the final budget and actual amounts, though doing so is not required.

> **Note:** The budget submitted by the executive branch to the legislature is called the *executive budget*. After discussion between the executive and the legislature, an original budget is created. The *original budget* is the first complete appropriated budget that covers the entire fiscal period, while the *final budget* is the original budget adjusted by all subsequent reserves, transfers, allocations, supplemental appropriations, and other legally authorized changes.

Budget information can be included in a budgetary comparison statement that is part of the basic financial statements. If so, they are reported with the fund financial statements after the statement of revenues, expenditures, and changes in fund balances. Alternatively, the information can be provided later in the document, with the other required supplementary information.

A budgetary comparison schedule may be presented using the same format, terminology, and classifications used in the budgeting document, or as used in the financial statements. No matter which approach is used, the comparison must be accompanied by information that reconciles the budgetary information to GAAP. This reconciliation may need to adjust for differences in the following:

- *Accounting basis.* The basis of accounting used to develop the budget may differ from the basis used to report on the applicable fund. For example, a government would normally use the modified accrual basis of accounting for its general fund, but could prepare its general fund budget on the cash basis.
- *Timing.* There can be a number of differences in the timing applied to budget transactions versus financial statements, which may be caused by continuing appropriations, project appropriations, automatic re-appropriations, and biennial budgeting. For example, a capital project may be budgeted for several years, while the fund accounting for construction activities uses an annual budget.
- *Perspective.* The structure of a budget may differ from the structure used to assemble financial statements, such as differences in fund structures that establish which assets, liabilities, equities, and revenue and expenditure/expense flows are included in a fund. For example, there may be several funds paying for a project, but the related budget is associated with a single project.
- *Entity.* An appropriated budget could include organizations, programs, activities, and functions that are not reported in the same manner in the financial statements.

The accompanying notes should also disclose the budgetary basis of accounting and any excesses of expenditures over appropriations in the individual funds presented in the budgetary comparison.

The preparation of a reconciliation between the budget and the financial statements can be fairly difficult, especially when there are multiple causes for differences, as just stated (accounting basis, timing, perspective, and entity). One way to reduce the amount of reconciliation required is to work with the budget preparers to develop a budget that conforms in as many respects as possible to the actual financial statements with which they will be compared.

Additional Reporting

It is acceptable if the accountant wants to include additional budgetary comparisons in the financial reporting package, which usually involves non-major funds. If so, the additional reports cannot be included in the required supplementary information section of the reporting package, since (as the name of this section implies) the additional reports are not *required*. The only required budgetary comparisons are for the general fund and each major special revenue fund that has a legally adopted annual budget associated with it. Instead, these additional reports should be presented as supplementary information.

Sample Budgetary Comparison Reports

This section contains three sample budgetary compliance schedules, as well as a disclosure note that provides a financial statement reader with information about a city's budgeting process. The schedules present several variations on the types of revenue and expenditure line items that may be encountered in a budgetary comparison report. The sample disclosures are as follows:

- Note regarding budgetary information
- Comparison schedule for general fund
- Comparison schedule for redevelopment authority fund
- Comparison schedule for capital improvement fund

Budgetary Information

The City adopts an annual budget for all governmental funds on a basis consistent with generally accepted accounting principles. Budgetary comparisons for the Enterprise Fund are presented on a non-GAAP budgetary basis. Capital outlay is budgeted as an expenditure, and depreciation is not budgeted.

The following procedures are followed in establishing the budgetary data reflected in the financial statements:

- Prior to September 30th, the City Manager submits to the City Council a proposed operating budget by fund, department and object for the fiscal year commencing the following January 1. The operating budget includes proposed expenditures and the means of financing them.
- Upon receipt of the proposed budget, the City Council publishes a notice indicating that such proposed budget is available for inspection and open for public hearing.
- Prior to December 10th, the budget is legally adopted through a City Council resolution. All operating budget appropriations lapse at year-end, although unexpended appropriations may be re-appropriated for the next year.
- The legal level of budgetary control is exercised at the fund level. The City Manager is authorized to transfer budgeted amounts between departments within the same fund, with subsequent notification to the City Council. The Council must approve any revisions that alter the total expenditures of any fund.

Helix City
Budgetary Comparison Schedule
General Fund
For the Year Ended December 31, 20X2

(in millions)	Budget Amounts		Actual Amounts	Variance with Final Budget Positive (Negative)
	Original	Final		
REVENUES				
Sales tax	$33.7	$36.6	$38.3	$1.7
Use tax	1.6	2.3	3.5	1.2
Property tax	8.1	7.9	7.9	--
Auto use tax	3.7	4.3	4.6	0.3
Other taxes	0.6	0.6	0.6	--
Franchise fees	5.1	5.1	5.1	--
Court fines	2.0	1.8	1.8	--
Charges for services	0.6	0.6	1.1	0.5
Investment income	0.2	0.2	0.2	--
Intergovernmental	6.5	6.6	6.9	0.3
Miscellaneous	0.6	1.1	0.7	-0.4
Total revenues	62.7	67.1	70.7	3.6
EXPENDITURES				
Current				
General government	9.6	10.9	9.0	1.9
Finance & administration	4.4	4.8	4.0	0.8
Community services	24.1	23.9	23.8	0.1
City infrastructure	14.1	14.9	13.2	1.7
Planning & development	0.5	0.6	0.5	0.1
Capital outlay	--	--	0.8	-0.8
Total expenditures	52.7	55.1	51.3	3.8
REVENUE OVER (UNDER) EXPENDITURES	10.0	12.0	19.4	7.4
OTHER FINANCING SOURCES (USES)				
Transfers in	0.3	0.4	0.9	0.5
Transfers out	-19.0	-26.3	-26.3	--
Total other financing sources (uses)	-18.7	-25.9	-25.4	0.5
NET CHANGE IN FUND BALANCE	-8.7	-13.9	-6.0	7.9
FUND BALANCE – BEGINNING OF YEAR	33.8	42.5	42.5	--
FUND BALANCE – END OF YEAR	$25.1	$28.6	$36.5	$7.9

Helix City
Budgetary Comparison Schedule
Urban Redevelopment Authority Fund
For the Year Ended December 31, 20X2

(in millions)	Budget Amounts		Actual Amounts	Variance with Final Budget Positive (Negative)
	Original	Final		
REVENUE				
Property tax	$5.4	$4.8	$4.6	-$0.2
Intergovernmental	1.1	1.0	1.0	--
Miscellaneous	0.1	0.1	--	-0.1
Total revenue	6.6	5.9	5.6	-0.3
EXPENDITURES				
Sales tax sharing pass-through	1.1	1.0	1.0	--
Property tax sharing pass-through	5.4	4.8	4.5	0.3
Professional services	0.1	0.1	0.1	--
Contingencies	--	0.4	--	0.4
Total expenditures	6.6	6.3	5.6	0.7
NET CHANGE IN FUND BALANCE	--	-0.4	--	0.4
FUND BALANCE – BEGINNING OF YEAR	--	0.4	0.4	--
FUND BALANCE – END OF YEAR	$--	$--	$0.4	$0.4

Helix City
Budgetary Comparison Schedule
Capital Improvement Fund
For the Year Ended December 31, 20X2

(in millions)	Budget Amounts		Actual Amounts	Variance with Final Budget Positive (Negative)
	Original	Final		
REVENUE				
Intergovernmental revenue	$0.2	$6.4	$6.3	-$0.1
Developer contributions	0.2	1.9	0.1	-1.8
Total revenue	0.4	8.3	6.4	-1.9
EXPENDITURES				
Rehabilitation				
Street rehabilitation program	6.6	7.0	6.9	0.1
Major/minor structures	0.2	0.2	--	0.2
Professional services	0.3	0.4	0.3	0.1
Capital outlay				
Streets	3.4	21.8	6.9	14.9
Sidewalks	0.1	1.6	0.1	1.5
Traffic control and signals	0.7	2.3	0.1	2.2
Major capital project reserve	7.9	11.9	0.3	11.6
Buildings	0.2	3.3	--	3.3
Total expenditures	19.4	48.5	14.6	33.9
REVENUE OVER (UNDER) EXPENDITURES	-19.0	-40.2	-8.2	32.0
OTHER FINANCING SOURCES				
Transfers in	19.0	26.3	26.3	--
NET CHANGE IN FUND BALANCE	--	-13.9	18.1	32.0
FUND BALANCE – BEGINNING OF YEAR	0.3	13.9	13.9	--
FUND BALANCE – END OF YEAR	$0.3	$--	$32.0	$32.0

Budgetary Control

Budgets are not just used for reporting purposes; they are also used to provide some measure of control over a government's revenues and expenditures. This is best achieved by loading the final budget into the accounting system and entering budget information at the legal level of control. The *legal level of control* is the lowest budgetary level at which management is not allowed to reassign resources without first gaining legislative approval. Once this information is loaded, the budget is compared to actual expenditures, as well as any encumbrances (which show commitments associated with unfilled purchase orders or contracts). Ideally, the comparison to the loaded budget would include the following elements:

+	Liquidated expenditures (those obligations that have been settled)
+	Unliquidated expenditures (those obligations for which a bill has been received but not yet paid)
+	Encumbrances (those purchases not yet made, but for which there is a commitment to do so)

For example, a government has an annual supplies budget of $80,000. The government has so far incurred liquidated expenditures of $42,000 and unliquidated expenditures of $16,000. An encumbrance for future purchases of $10,000 has also been recorded. Netting these items together reveals that the government has $12,000 of budgeted funds remaining that can be used to purchase additional supplies.

A set of journal entries that could be used to record encumbrances is stated in the Common Accounting Transactions chapter.

Summary

The budgetary comparison is unique to governmental accounting. Many for-profit organizations structure their financial statements so that a budgetary comparison is included, but it is not required. Also, a for-profit organization usually only releases a budgetary comparison report as part of its internal financial statement reporting package; it is rarely released to outsiders, which is not the case with budgetary comparisons reported by a government entity.

Chapter 14
Cash Flows Statements

Introduction

Certain types of government entities are required to include a statement of cash flows in their financial reporting packages. A statement of cash flows is intended to provide information about the cash receipts and cash disbursements of the reporting entity over the course of a reporting period. This statement is used by readers to assess an entity's ability to generate future net cash flows and meet its obligations as they come due for settlement, as well as its need for external financing. In this chapter, we cover the contents of the statement of cash flows and the manner in which it is presented.

Reporting Requirements

Proprietary funds and governmental entities engaged in business-type activities are required to present a statement of cash flows for each period for which they are reporting the results of operations. Examples of these entities are governmental utilities and hospitals, as well as public colleges and universities. Trust funds are exempt from this requirement.

Note: A proprietary fund that has no operating income or loss must still present a statement of cash flows.

Report Contents

A statement of cash flows is intended to report on the net cash provided to or used by a government's ongoing operations, its capital and non-capital financing transactions, and its investing transactions. The report also contains a reconciliation of the entity's operating income to its net cash flow from operating activities; this is done by adjusting operating income to remove the effects of depreciation, amortization, and other deferred inflows and outflows. Changes during the period in receivables, inventory, and payables should be separately reported. The reconciliation should separately report all major classes of reconciling items. A sample reconciliation appears in the final section of this chapter.

Cash and Cash Equivalents

The central focus of a statement of cash flows is changes in the amount of cash and cash equivalents over a reporting period. The report shows the beginning and ending cash balances, which should be traceable to similar line items in the statements of financial position as of the same dates.

> **Note:** A *cash equivalent* is a short-term, highly liquid investment that is readily convertible into known amounts of cash, and which is so near its maturity that it presents an insignificant risk of changes in value due to changes in interest rates. Examples of cash equivalents are Treasury bills, commercial paper, and money market funds.

Gross and Net Cash Flows

Most cash flows should be reported at a gross level, where cash inflows are not netted against related cash outflows. By doing so, the reader has more information with which to assess the cash flows of the organization.

It is allowable to report some cash flows at their net amounts, where cash inflows *are* offset against related cash outflows. This reporting is allowed when a transaction has rapid turnover, occurs in large amounts, and involves short maturities. Examples of items that may be reported net are investments, loans receivable, and debt, as long as the original maturity is three months or less.

It is also allowable for governmental enterprises to report the purchases and sales of their highly liquid investments at net, rather than at gross. This reporting approach is allowed when substantially all of the enterprise's assets were highly liquid investments during the reporting period, and the enterprise has a minimal amount of debt in relation to average total assets.

Negative Cash Balances

A government may have a cash balance on its books that is a negative number. When reporting the cash balance in the statement of cash flows, this negative balance is assumed to be zero. To increase the negative balance to zero, report an *inflow* in the noncapital financing activities classification of the statement. By doing so, it appears as if a cash management pool or bank financed the negative cash situation. In the following period, the "loan" is assumed to have been repaid, so that a noncapital financing *outflow* in the same amount is reported. A sample line item dealing with this situation appears in the final section of this chapter.

When Cash Flow Occurs

When reporting information in the statement of cash flows, it can be confusing to decide whether a cash transaction has occurred. As a general guideline, cash flows only if it has changed hands, so that legal ownership of the cash has been transferred to a new entity. For example, a government qualifies for a loan with a local lender, and the lender grants the loan. There is no cash flow until the bank shifts the funds into the government's bank account.

Cash Flows from Operating Activities

One of the main classifications in a statement of cash flows is cash flows from operating activities. The results listed within this classification typically result from providing services and producing and delivering goods. It can also be a catchall classification that includes results that do not readily fall into any of the other classifications (which are covered in the following sections). As a general rule, results included in cash flows from operating activities are those involving transactions and other events that are included in the determination of operating income. The cash inflows and outflows usually broken out within this classification are as follows:

Cash inflows from operating activities

- Cash received from the sale of goods or services, including the collection of receivables
- Cash received from the provision of interfund services
- Cash received from grants for specific activities that the granting entity considers to be operating activities
- Cash received from interfund reimbursements
- All other cash receipts not relating to the other reporting classifications

Cash outflows from operating activities

- Cash paid to buy materials for the provision of goods and services, including the payment of supplier invoices for such materials
- Cash paid to suppliers for other types of goods and services
- Cash paid to employees in exchange for their services
- Cash paid as grants to other entities for activities that the grantor considers to be operating activities
- Cash paid for taxes, fines, and other fees or penalties
- Cash paid for interfund services used
- All other cash payments not relating to the other reporting classifications

Additional line items can be added if the resulting detail is considered useful.

Cash Flows from Noncapital Financing Activities

The second classification used in the statement of cash flows is cash flows from noncapital financing activities. The line items within this classification include the borrowing of money for any activity that does not include the acquisition, construction, or improvement of capital assets, as well as the repayment of these borrowings. Also, any proceeds from borrowings that are not clearly associated with capital assets are stated here. The cash inflows and outflows usually broken out within this classification are as follows:

Cash inflows from noncapital financing activities

- Cash received from the issuance of bonds, notes, and other borrowings not clearly associated with capital asset activities

- Cash received from grants or subsidies, not including any cash specifically restricted for capital uses and those designated for activities that are classified as operating activities by the granting entity
- Cash received from other funds, not including any cash specifically attributable to capital asset activities, interfund services provided, or interfund reimbursements
- Cash received from tax collections for the enterprise and which are not restricted for capital asset activities

Cash outflows from noncapital financing activities

- Cash paid to reduce borrowings that were not intended for capital asset activities
- Cash paid to reduce the interest obligation to lenders on borrowings not associated with capital asset activities
- Cash paid as grants or subsidies to other entities, except in relation to activities considered to be operating activities by the grantor
- Cash paid to other funds, except in relation to the usage of interfund services

Cash Flows from Capital and Related Financing Activities

The third classification used in the statement of cash flows is cash flows from capital and related financing activities. The line items within this classification primarily address the acquisition and disposition of capital assets. The cash inflows and outflows usually broken out within this classification are as follows:

Cash inflows from capital and related financing activities

- Cash received from the issuance of bonds, mortgages, notes and other borrowings clearly associated with the acquisition, construction, or improvement of capital assets
- Cash received from capital grants
- Cash received from contributions made by other funds or other entities in order to defray the cost of acquiring, constructing, or improving capital assets
- Cash received from the sale of capital assets
- Cash received from insurance on capital assets that have been destroyed or stolen
- Cash received from taxes or special assessments levied specifically to finance capital asset activities

Cash outflows from capital and related financing activities

- Cash paid to acquire, construct, or improve capital assets
- Repayments of amounts borrowed to acquire, construct, or improve capital assets

- Other trade credit payments to suppliers related to capital asset activities
- Cash paid for the interest associated with capital asset activities

There can be some confusion in deciding whether to classify a cash flow as capital financing or non-capital financing in nature. The following rules can be used to make the determination:

- *Relationship to capital assets.* Debt that is not clearly attributable to the construction, acquisition, or improvement of capital assets should be classified as noncapital debt. Also, the debt proceeds and all subsequent principal and interest payments are considered noncapital financing.
- *Subsequent sale of assets.* When principal and interest payments are being made on debt that was originally used to acquire, construct or improve a capital asset, and that asset has since been disposed of in some way, continue to classify the payments as capital and related financing.
- *Debt refunding.* When debt is being recalled and then reissued, the proceeds of a debt issuance that is intended to refund capital debt is classified as a cash inflow within the capital and related financing category. Also, payments made to recall the original capital debt is classified as a cash outflow in the same category. Further, all subsequent principal and interest payments made against the refunding debt are classified as cash outflows in the capital and related financing category.

Cash Flows from Investing Activities

The fourth classification used in the statement of cash flows is cash flows from investing activities. The line items within this classification primarily address the issuance and collection of loans, as well as the acquisition and disposal of debt or equity securities. The cash inflows and outflows usually broken out within this classification are as follows:

Cash inflows from investing activities

- Cash received from collecting payments on loans made by the governmental enterprise, as well as from the sale of the debt instruments of other entities that had been purchased by the enterprise
- Cash received from the sale of equity securities
- Cash received from interest and dividends
- Cash received from the withdrawal of funds from investment pools

Cash outflows from investing activities

- Cash paid to acquire the debt instruments of other entities
- Cash paid to acquire equity securities
- Cash paid as deposits into investment pools

Specific Cash Flow Classifications

In this section, we address the proper cash flow treatment of a number of highly specific transactions in which a government may engage. This information is useful for slotting cash flows into the correct classifications within the statement of cash flows. The transactions are as follows:

- *Bond issuance costs, deducted.* If a government issues bonds and the related issuance costs and underwriting fees are deducted from the proceeds, then present the net amount of the bond proceeds in either the capital or noncapital financing classifications, depending on the nature of the borrowing.
- *Bond issuance costs, paid later.* If a government issues bonds and pays the related issuance costs and underwriting fees separately, then present the cash inflow from the bond proceeds in either the capital or noncapital financing classifications, depending on the nature of the borrowing. The related issuance costs and fees are then classified as cash outflows within the same classification.
- *Rent income.* A government may earn rental income from its properties. There is no specific directive for how the related cash inflow is to be classified. If the nature of the transaction does not align with the criteria for one of the more specific classifications, rent income is classified as a cash inflow from operating activities, since that is the default cash flow classification.
- *Royalty income.* A government may earn royalty income, usually from its intangible assets. There is no clear definitive classification for royalty income. One should evaluate the asset underlying the royalties to determine whether the income is a cash inflow from investing activities. If not, it is classified as a cash inflow from operating activities, since that is the default cash flow classification.
- *Contributions, capital assets.* When a government receives capital assets from developers or others, they are disclosed in an accompanying schedule (see the next section, concerning information about noncash activities).
- *Contributions, noncapital.* When an enterprise fund receives a noncapital contribution, it is treated the same as a grant or subsidy, and so is classified as a noncapital financing cash inflow.
- *Grants received.* When a grantor issues a grant to a government and the amount is not related to capital asset activities, it is probably a subsidy of the entity's ongoing operations or a purchase of services, and so should be reported within the operating activities classification.
- *Insurance proceeds.* If there are insurance proceeds related to the loss or theft of capital assets, present them in the capital and related financing activities classification. Report all other insurance proceeds within the operating activities classification, since that is the residual classification to be used when a cash flow cannot be classified anywhere else.
- *Interest earnings.* All interest earnings are reported as a cash inflow within the investing activities classification. This is the case even with the interest

earnings on cash and cash equivalents, as well as when there are interest earnings on customer deposits.

- *Interfund loans.* If interfund cash flows are not related to capital asset activities, then they are reported as noncapital financing activities. If the cash flows *are* related to capital asset activities, then they are reported within the capital and related financing activities classification.

- *Investment gains and losses.* Gains and losses associated with investments are not reported in the statement of cash flows. Only proceeds from the sale of investments (which incorporate any gains and losses) are reported; these amounts appear as cash inflows in the investing activities classification.

- *Miscellaneous items.* When there are cash flows associated with miscellaneous income and expenses, classify them as cash inflows or outflows within the operating activities classification. This is the case even when the items are non-operating in nature.

- *Property taxes for capital debt service.* When a government imposes a property tax to assist with the financing of the debt associated with its capital assets, the payment is reported as a cash inflow within the capital and related financing activities classification. This treatment is used because the property taxes are indirectly financing the capital assets.

- *Refundable customer deposits.* Customers may pay a government entity a deposit, which will be refunded to them at a later date. These cash inflows and outflows are classified as operating activities, because they do not fit the requirements for classification in the financing or investing classifications. The deposits are not treated as loans from customers, and so are not considered financing activities.

- *Subsidies for capital debt service.* When a government receives a subsidy to assist with the financing of the debt associated with its capital assets, the payment is reported as a cash inflow within the capital and related financing activities classification. This treatment is used because the subsidy is indirectly financing the capital assets.

- *Tap fees.* A customer may pay a tap fee to defray the costs associated with connecting the customer to a utility system. The cash inflow associated with this fee is included in the operating activities classification. However, if part of the fee is associated with the acquisition, construction, or improvement of capital assets, then that portion is presented within the cash flows from capital and related financing activities classification.

Information about Noncash Activities

A government may occasionally engage in activities that do not involve cash. Examples of these noncash transactions are:

- The acquisition of an asset by assuming a related liability
- The acquisition of a structure by incurring a mortgage
- The acquisition of equipment by entering into a lease

- The exchange of one asset for another
- The receipt of a donated capital asset
- Transfers of capital assets between funds

These transactions should be reported in a separate schedule if the transactions affect recognized assets or liabilities *and* they can be classified as investing, capital, or financing activities. Noncash operating transactions are not reported in the schedule.

The schedule of noncash transactions can be in either a tabular or a narrative format. If sufficient space is available, this schedule can appear on the same page as the statement of cash flows.

Some of these transactions involve cash and noncash elements. For example, a government could swap one copier for another, plus a payment of $5,000. Only the cash portion of these transactions should appear in the statement of cash flows.

Sample Statement of Cash Flows

The following presentation of a sample statement of cash flows is designed for a utility fund. It includes all four of the cash flow classifications, as well as a narrative discussion of noncash activities.

Cash Flows Statements

Sample Utility Fund
Statement of Cash Flows
For the Year Ended December 31, 20X2

Cash flows from operating activities:		
Cash received from customers	$570,000	
Cash payment to employees for services	-132,400	
Cash payments to suppliers for goods and services	-195,600	
Cash payment to general fund for lease	-21,000	
Net cash provided by operating activities		$221,000
Cash flows from noncapital financing activities:		
Cash payment (subsidy) to (from) city	-161,000	
Transfer from the Electrical Utility Fund	2,000	
Negative cash balance implicitly financed	1,000	
Net cash used for noncapital financing activities		-158,000
Cash flows from capital and related financing activities:		
Construction and improvement of plant	-600,000	
Debt principal payments	-108,000	
Debt interest payments	-12,000	
Contributions in aid of construction from developers	80,000	
Net cash used for capital and related financing activities		-640,000
Cash flows from investing activities:		
Interest and dividends on investments	117,000	
Proceeds from sales and maturities of investments	1,450,000	
Purchases of investments	-1,000,000	
Net cash provided by investing activities		567,000
Net decrease in cash and cash equivalents		-10,000
Cash and cash equivalents at beginning of year		10,000
Cash and cash equivalents at end of year		$--

172

Reconciliation of operating income to net cash provided by operating activities:

Operating income		$32,600
Adjustments to reconcile operating income to net cash provided by operating activities:		
Depreciation	$190,000	
Change in assets and liabilities:		
Increase in accounts receivable	-2,400	
Decrease in inventory	1,600	
Increase in accounts payable	4,000	
Decrease in accrued wages	-4,800	
Total reconciling adjustments		188,400
Net cash provided by operating activities		$221,000

In addition to the $2,000 cash transfer, the Electrical Utility Fund also received certain assets of the Sample Utility Fund. The net book value of the assets at the time of the transfer was $26,000. In addition, there was a net increase in the fair value of the Sample Utility Fund's investments of $3,920.

Summary

The statement of cash flows can be the most difficult of the financial statements to prepare, since its contents are not necessarily generated automatically by a government's accounting system. Instead, the accounting system may produce a rough, high-level statement of cash flows that requires considerable fine-tuning to ensure that it provides a detailed view of all material cash flows. It may also be necessary to shift certain transactions among different reporting classifications, depending on one's judgment regarding the reasons for the transactions. Consequently, this report requires a considerable amount of manual intervention to ensure that it fairly represents a government's actual cash flows.

Chapter 15
Segment Information

Introduction

When a government separately reports enterprise funds or uses enterprise fund accounting, it must include segment information for those activities in the notes that accompany the financial statements. In this chapter, we cover the requirements for segment reporting.

Segment Reporting

A segment is an identifiable activity that is reported within an enterprise fund or similar entity that has one or more bonds or similar debt instruments outstanding, where some portion of its revenue stream is pledged to support repayment of the debt. Further, the activity's revenues, expenses, gains, losses, assets, and liabilities are required to be accounted for separately by an external party. For example, there may be a provision in a bond indenture agreement that requires a government to provide this information.

A condensed set of financial information must be presented for each segment in the notes to the financial statements. The following information must be presented for each segment:

Condensed statement of net position

- *Total assets.* Distinguish between the segment's current assets, capital assets, and other assets. Separately note any amounts receivable from other funds or component units.
- *Outflows.* State the total deferred outflows of resources.
- *Total liabilities.* Distinguish between current and long-term liabilities. Separately note any amounts payable to other funds or component units.
- *Inflows.* State the total deferred inflows of resources.
- *Total net position.* Distinguish between the net investment in capital assets, restricted net position, and unrestricted net position.

Condensed statement of revenues, expenses, and changes in net position

- *Operating revenues.* State operating revenues by major source.
- *Operating expenses.* State operating expenses, with depreciation and amortization identified separately.
- *Results.* State the operating income or loss.
- *Non-operating revenues/expenses.* State the non-operating revenue and expense, with separate reporting of major revenues and expenses.

- *Contributions*. State the amount of capital contributions, as well as additions to the permanent and term endowments.
- Special and extraordinary items
- Transfers
- Change in net position
- Beginning net position
- Ending net position

Condensed statement of cash flows

- *Cash flows*. Distinguish between the net cash provided by or used by operating activities, noncapital financing activities, capital and related financing activities, and investing activities.
- *Cash balances*. State the beginning and ending cash and cash equivalent balances.

Segment reporting is not required when an individual fund is classified as a segment and is also being reported as a major fund.

Sample Segment Reporting

The following sample of a segment report provides the condensed financial information for a utility fund, along with an explanatory footnote.

Segment Information

The City issues two revenue bonds to finance its water and wastewater departments. The City accounts for the two departments as a single public utility fund, but investors rely entirely on the revenue generated by each individual department for repayment. Summary financial information for each of these departments is presented in the following table. The water department operates the City's reservoir system, while the wastewater department operates the City's sewage collection, pumping, and treatment facilities.

(000s)	20X2	
	Water Department	Wastewater Department
CONDENSED STATEMENT OF NET POSITION		
Assets:		
Current assets	$10,459	$13,840
Capital assets, net	77,906	184,383
Total assets	88,365	198,223
Deferred outflows of resources	255	--
Liabilities:		
Interfund payables	--	350
Other current liabilities	3,041	5,968
Noncurrent liabilities	10,952	98,854
Total liabilities	13,993	105,172
Net position:		
Net investment in capital assets	65,545	79,952
Unrestricted	9,082	13,099
Total net position	$74,627	$93,051
CONDENSED STATEMENTS OF REVENUES, EXPENSES, AND CHANGES IN NET POSITION		
Operating revenues	$8,319	$14,341
Depreciation expense	-1,100	-1,226
Other operating expenses	-5,286	-6,204
Operating income	1,933	6,911
Non-operating revenues (expenses):		
Investment income	435	475
Interest expense	-806	-2,396
Capital contributions	2,320	972
Transfers out	--	-580
Change in net position	3,882	5,382
Beginning net position	70,745	87,628
Ending net position	74,627	93,010
CONDENSED STATEMENT OF CASH FLOWS		
Net cash provided (used) by:		
Operating activities	4,004	1,701
Noncapital financing activities	--	-580
Capital and related financing activities	-3,368	-3,282
Investing activities	435	475
Net increase (decrease)	1,071	-1,686
Beginning cash and cash equivalents	6,179	11,270
Ending cash and cash equivalents	$7,250	$9,584

Summary

Segment reporting falls outside of the normal set of financial statements and disclosures, and so can be easy to forget. To ensure that this is not the case, carry forward the segment reporting for the prior year's financial statements, and also see if there are any contractual obligations that have occurred since that date, requiring the government to issue segment reports to any third parties. This investigation should be included in the mandated action steps that the accounting staff completes as part of its procedure for closing the books and producing financial statements.

Chapter 16
Reporting Entity and Component Unit Presentation and Disclosure

Introduction

A government may create a number of separate legal entities to perform a selection of the functions that it would otherwise take on itself. For example, a separate water utility may be created in order to pledge its highly predictable revenue stream to the debt service on bonds issued to pay for water systems. Or, a nonprofit entity is given the power to engage in activities that the founding government is not permitted to do, such as buying or selling land.

When a government issues its comprehensive annual financial report (CAFR), the report should present information about the reporting entity, while also providing an overview of its discretely presented component units. When assembling a CAFR, questions may arise about exactly which of these entities to include in the financial statements. In this chapter, we define the financial reporting entity, the component unit, and several reporting issues pertaining to component units, including equity investments, intra-entity transactions, and reporting periods.

The Financial Reporting Entity Defined

The financial reporting entity is the primary government and any other organizations for which the primary government is financially accountable. Included in this definition are the primary government's blended component units (described later in this chapter) and discretely presented component units. The managers of the primary government may also decide that the government's financial reporting include entities that fall outside of the financial accountability criterion, because not doing so would be misleading for the readers of the financial statements; if so, these entities are treated as component units.

> **Note:** *Discrete presentation* means that separate columns and rows are used in the government-wide statements to provide an overview of component unit financial data. Discrete columns are placed to the right of the financial data for the primary government.

The Component Unit Defined

A component unit is a legally separate organization for which the elected officials of a primary government are financially accountable. This entity may be a governmental organization, a nonprofit corporation, or a for-profit corporation.

When a primary government issues financial statements, it should include an overview of the entity, while still allowing readers to distinguish between the primary government entity and its component units. This usually means that financial information should be discretely presented in the government-wide statements. This is not the case for component units that are fiduciary by nature; these units should only be included in the fund financial statements with the primary government's fiduciary funds. These statements are the statements of fiduciary net position and changes in fiduciary net position.

A component unit of a primary government may have its own component units. When the primary government reports a component unit within its own financial statements, it should include the data from these "second tier" component units. When doing so, the proper accounting is to complete the financial reporting at the lowest tier, which is then included in the reporting for the next highest tier, and so forth.

EXAMPLE

A power generation district is a component unit of Minnetonka City, because the city appoints the governing board of the district and the district imposes a financial burden on the city. The power generation district is financially accountable for a building authority that manages the power grid for the city. The building authority is a component unit of the power generation district, while the power generation district is a component unit of Minnetonka City. The building authority is not a formal component unit of the city, but its financial data should be included in the city's financial reporting entity as part of the power generation district.

Component units are discretely presented in the financial statements of the financial reporting entity. Discrete presentation is made when the financial data of a component unit is made in columns and rows that are separate from the primary government's financial data. This data should only be reported in the government-wide financial statements. The combined data of the component units should be stated within one or more columns in the government-wide statement of net position and statement of activities. These columns should be positioned to the right of the total column for the primary government, thereby distinguishing between the financial data of the primary government and its discretely presented component units.

Major Component Unit Information

Certain additional information should be presented when a component unit is considered to be a major unit. In general, the designation as a major unit depends on the nature and significance of a unit's relationship with the primary government. The following factors are considered when determining whether a component unit is to be classified as major:

- The services provided by it to citizens are considered so significant that separate reporting of the unit is essential to the readers of the financial statements;
- There are significant transactions between the unit and the primary government; or
- The unit has a significant financial burden or benefit relationship with the primary government.

When a component unit is classified as major, the following reporting should be applied to them:

- Present each major component unit in a separate column in the statements of net position and activities;
- Include combining statements for the major component units in the primary government's basic financial statements, following the fund financial statements; or
- Include the unit's condensed financial statements in the notes accompanying the parent government's financial statements.

When reporting units are not classified as major, they are aggregated into a single column in the primary government's applicable financial statements. It is possible, but not required, to present a combining statement for the non-major component units as supplementary information to the financial statements.

If the decision is made to include component unit information in the notes, one should include the following information:

Condensed statement of net position

- *Total assets.* State the total asset figure, differentiating between current assets, capital assets and other assets. Also, separately note any amounts receivable from the primary government or other component units.
- *Deferred inflows.* State the total amount of all deferred inflows to the component unit.
- *Total liabilities.* State the total liabilities figure, differentiating between current liabilities and long-term liabilities. Also, separately note any amounts payable to the primary government or other component units.
- *Total net position.* State the total net position, differentiating between the net investment in capital assets, restricted net position, and unrestricted net position. When reporting the restricted net position, separately report its expendable and non-expendable components.

Condensed statement of activities

- *Expenses.* State expenses by major functions, separately reporting depreciation.
- *Revenues.* Separately state program revenues.

- *Net result*. State the net program revenue or expense.
- Tax revenues
- Other non-tax general revenues
- *Contributions*. Separately state any contributions made to endowments and permanent fund principal.
- Special and extraordinary items
- Change in net position
- Beginning net position
- Ending net position

The preceding information should be presented in the form of aggregated totals, matching the entity totals stated in the component units' statements of net position and activities.

Also disclose in the accompanying notes the nature and amount of any significant transactions between the primary government and its component units.

Blending Component Units

The operations of some component units may be so intertwined with those of the primary government that they are essentially part of the primary government. These units are reported as part of the primary government in the government-wide financial statements and fund financial statements (known as *blending*). Blending should be used under any of the following circumstances:

- *Governance*. The governing body of the component unit is essentially the same as that of the primary government, and there is a financial burden or benefit relationship between the entities, or the primary government has operational responsibility for the component unit.
- *Service relationship*. The component unit provides services or benefits almost entirely to the primary government. The unit is essentially an internal service fund, where services are not provided directly to citizens.
- *Repayment*. The resources of the primary government are to be used to entirely or almost entirely repay the component unit's total debt outstanding.
- *Nonprofit member*. The primary government is the sole corporate member of the component unit, which is organized as a nonprofit corporation.

The funds of a blended component unit are included for presentation purposes with the primary government's other funds. However, the general fund of a blended component unit is presented as a special revenue fund, since report users prefer to see the general fund of the reporting entity on a standalone basis.

EXAMPLE

A state government creates a financing authority that is tasked with issuing debt for the state's public safety and transportation functions. The financing authority can also issue debt to fund a small number of school districts in the poorest neighborhoods of the state; this amount comprises roughly 20% of the total debt issued. The state government appoints every member of the financing authority's board and has also pledged a significant portion of the state's gasoline taxes to repay all of the authority's outstanding debt.

The financing authority should be classified as a *blended* component unit, since the authority's debt is to be repaid with resources provided by the state. The use of debt to fund school districts is irrelevant to the classification decision. However, if the debt related to the school districts had instead been paid with local property taxes, then the state is no longer paying for *all* of the debt. In this case, the state would instead classify the financing authority as a component unit.

In those cases where a government is only engaged in business-type activities that only involve the presentation of information in a single column in the financial statements, it is allowable to blend the data for a component unit into the single column presentation for the primary government. This also involves the presentation of combining information in the accompanying notes. At a minimum, such a condensed combining presentation should include the following information:

Condensed statement of net position

- *Total assets.* State the total asset figure, differentiating between current assets, capital assets and other assets. Also, separately note any amounts receivable from the primary government or other component units.
- *Deferred outflows.* State the total amount of all deferred outflows.
- *Total liabilities.* State the total liabilities figure, differentiating between current liabilities and long-term liabilities. Also, separately note any amounts payable to the primary government or other component units.
- *Deferred inflows.* State the total amount of all deferred inflows of resources.
- *Total net position.* State the total net position, differentiating between the net investment in capital assets, restricted net position, and unrestricted net position. When reporting the restricted net position, separately report its expendable and non-expendable components.

Condensed statement of revenues, expenses, and changes in net position

- *Revenues.* State the amounts of operating revenues by major source.
- *Expenses.* State the amounts of operating expenses, separately noting the amount of depreciation and amortization.
- *Income.* State the amount of operating income.
- *Non-operating activity.* Separately state the amounts of non-operating major revenues and expenses.
- *Contributions.* Separately state any contributions made to permanent and term endowments.
- Special and extraordinary items
- Transfers

- Change in net position
- Beginning net position
- Ending net position

<u>Condensed statement of cash flows</u>

- *Net cash.* State the amounts of net cash provided (used by) each of the following: operating activities, noncapital financing activities, capital and related financing activities, and investing activities
- Beginning cash and cash equivalent balances
- Ending cash and cash equivalent balances

Equity Interests in Component Units

There may be instances in which a government owns a majority of the equity interest in a separate organization. In this situation, the presentation of that equity interest depends on the government's intent in owning the equity interest. The alternatives are:

- *To provide services.* When the government's intent is to enhance its ability to provide services, then report the entity as a component unit. If the government discretely presents this component unit, report the equity interest as an asset of the fund that has the equity interest.
- *To provide an investment.* When the government's intent is to earn a return on its investment, it reports the equity interest as an investment, even if its ownership of the entity is not total.

EXAMPLE

Qanix City has been having difficulty obtaining sand for its road sanding operations, and so decides to buy all of the outstanding shares of a local quarry corporation to ensure its supply of sand. Qanix should report the quarry as a component unit.

Qanix City buys an interest in the local producer of a ride-sharing app, with the intent of earning a return on its investment. Qanix should report the producer as an investment.

Intra-Entity Transactions

It is possible that resources will flow back and forth between a primary government and component units that are being reported on a blended basis in its financial statements. These resource flows are classified as internal activities from the perspective of the blended financial statements.

The treatment of intra-entity transactions between a primary government and any discretely presented component units is somewhat different, as noted in the following bullet points:

- *Payables and receivables.* Any amounts payable or receivable between a primary government and any discretely presented component units (or between those units) are reported on a separate line.
- *Resource flows.* Any resource flows between a primary government and any discretely presented component units, other than those affecting just the statement of financial position, are reported as revenues and expenses.

Reporting Periods

It is possible that a primary government and its component units will have different fiscal year-ends. To avoid this situation, governments are encouraged to mandate identical fiscal year-ends for the primary government and its component units. If it is not practical to have a common fiscal year-end, the financial reporting entity should use those financial statements of a reporting entity that end during the fiscal year of the reporting entity. If the unit's fiscal year ends during the first quarter of the reporting entity's fiscal year, it is possible to use the financial results of the unit's next fiscal year, though only if doing so does not interfere with the timely release of the reporting entity's financial statements.

Note Disclosures

The following disclosures related to the reporting entity and its component units may be added to the notes accompanying the financial statements:

- *Overview.* Describe the component units in the notes, as well as their relationship to the primary government. State why each component unit is being included in the financial reporting entity, also noting whether it is being discretely presented, included in the fiduciary fund financial statements, or blended.
- *Additional information.* State how to obtain the separate financial statements for individual component units.
- *Inconsistencies.* When component units have different fiscal years, there may be inconsistencies in the transactions recorded between them. If so, describe these inconsistencies in the notes.
- *Fiscal year changes.* When there is a change in the fiscal year of the component units included in the reporting entity, disclose the change.

A sample overview disclosure that incorporates several of these requirements is as follows:

> The Lincoln Trade School Foundation is a legally separate, tax-exempt component unit of Lincoln Trade School. The foundation is a fund raising organization that is intended to supplement the resources available to the school to fulfill its program goals. The five-member board of the foundation is self-perpetuating and is comprised of graduates and associates of the school. Although the school has no control over the timing or amount of funds received from the foundation, the majority of resources that the foundation holds and invests are restricted to the activities of the school by donors. Since these restricted resources can only be used by or for the benefit of the school, the foundation is considered a component unit of the school and so is discretely presented in the school's financial statements.

> During the year ended 20X2, the foundation distributed $303,200 to the school for both restricted and unrestricted purposes. The foundation's complete financial statements can be obtained from its administrative office, which is located at 123 Main Street, Anywhere CO 80123 or from the foundation's website.

In general, disclosures should distinguish between information pertaining to a primary government and its discretely presented component units.

Presentation Issues

There may be circumstances under which a primary government will issue financial statements that do not include the financial data for its component units. If so, disclose that the financial statements do not include the financial data for its component units that would normally be included. Similarly, there may be cases in which a component unit will separately issue its own financial statements. If so, state that the unit is a component of another government. For example, the following text could appear in the header block of a financial statement:

> Helix City School District, a component unit of Helix City

In addition to this change to the header block, the separate financial statements of a component unit should also disclose the name of the primary government of which it is a part, and describe the relationship between the entities.

A primary government may appoint some or all of the governing board members of other entities that are not treated as component units. These entities may be related organizations, joint ventures, jointly governed organizations, or component units of another government. A *related organization* is an entity for which a primary government is accountable due to the primary government's ability to appoint a majority of its board, but for which it is not financially accountable. When a primary government has a relationship with a related organization, it should disclose the nature of its accountability for the other organization.

EXAMPLE

Qanix City establishes an airport authority for the purpose of stimulating commerce and increasing the number of visitors to the city. The mayor of Qanix appoints four members of the seven-member governing council of the airport authority, but the city does not appoint the airport authority's management team. The board members can only be removed for cause. The authority develops its own budget, issues bonds, and sets rates without any input from the city. The city does not provide any financial support to the airport authority, nor does it receive any benefit. Given the structure of this relationship, where there is no financial burden or benefit and the city does not control the airport authority, the entity is not classified as a component unit of the city. However, since the mayor appoints a voting majority of its board, the airport authority should be disclosed in the city's financial statements as a related organization.

Summary

To be clear, there are three options for how a primary government can report a component unit. When the relationship between a primary government and a component unit is very close, their financial data are *blended*, as though the unit is part of the primary government. Or, a component unit operates sufficiently separate from a primary government that it is *discretely presented* in the financial statements; this is the most common approach. The third option is available when a component unit is fiduciary in nature; in this case, the component unit is only included in the fund financial statements with the *fiduciary funds* of the primary government.

Chapter 17
Statistical Section

Introduction

Statistical information may be presented within the supplementary information section of a government's comprehensive annual financial report (CAFR). The information required for the statistical section is extensive, covering a number of financial and operational issues that the readers of a government's financial statements may need in order to properly assess its condition. In this chapter, we cover the contents of the statistical section.

Overview of the Statistical Section

The information presented in the statistical section is intended to provide the readers of financial statements with additional context, detail, and historical perspective, so that they can better understand and assess a government's economic condition.

General Content

The statistical section of a government's financial statements presents comparative information for multiple time periods, sometimes covering a decade or more. This section may also contain non-accounting information of various kinds, such as the following:

- Assessed valuations
- Economic data
- Population data
- Tax rates
- The legal debt margin

This information is grouped into five categories, which are as follows:

- *Financial trends information.* Used to understand and assess how a government's financial information has changed over time.
- *Revenue capacity information.* Used to understand and assess those factors impacting a government's ability to generate its own-source revenues.
- *Debt capacity information.* Used to understand and assess a government's debt obligations and the extent to which it can issue additional debt.

- *Demographic and economic information.* Used to explain the socio-economic environment within which a government operates, as well as providing a comparison of financial statement information over a period of time.
- *Operating information.* Presents operational and resource information to be used in the assessment of a government's economic condition.

> **Note:** The term *own-source revenues* refers to those revenues generated by a government itself, such as by levying taxes or charging fees. This revenue is still considered own-source revenue, even if the revenue is collected on behalf of the government by another entity (such as local sales taxes collected by a state government).

In order to give readers a proper perspective on a government's operating results, the default presentation is to present information for the last 10 years, in a tabular format.

Additional disclosure information pertaining to each of these categories is covered in the following sections.

Focus of the Data

The focus of the information presented in the statistical section should be on the primary government (which includes any blended component units). However, it may be useful to include information about a component unit if doing so would be beneficial to readers in their assessment of the economic condition of the primary government.

Limitations

A government only needs to include a statistical section if it is preparing a comprehensive annual financial report. This information is not required for any other financial statement reporting package that a government might prepare. However, if a government chooses to include a statistical section in any other financial statement reporting package, it should follow the guidelines laid out in this chapter.

If a government does not fully implement the stated requirements for a statistical section, then it should not refer to that portion of its financial statements as a statistical section.

Financial Trends Information

The general classifications of information to be presented within the financial trends section are net position and changes in net position. These topics are addressed further in the following sub-sections.

Net Position

Net position information should be broken down into the net investment in capital assets, restricted net position and unrestricted net position, and presented separately for governmental activities, business-type activities, and the total primary government. A sample net position disclosure appears next.

Acorn City
Net Position by Component
Last 10 Fiscal Years

	Fiscal Year		
(000s)	20X1	20X2	20X3
Governmental activities			
Net investment in capital assets	$130,732	$127,796	$134,744
Restricted	10,434	11,039	11,127
Unrestricted	14,505	17,799	17,883
Total governmental activities net position	155,671	156,634	163,754
Business-type activities			
Net investment in capital assets	--	--	--
Restricted	--	--	--
Unrestricted	--	--	--
Total business-type activities net position	--	--	--
Primary government			
Net investment in capital assets	130,732	127,796	134,744
Restricted	10,434	11,039	11,127
Unrestricted	14,505	17,799	17,883
Total primary government net position	$155,671	$156,634	$163,754

Note: Only the last three years are shown in this sample statement.

Changes in Net Position

The accountant should separately present the following information for governmental and business-type activities:

- Expenses by program, function, or identifiable activity
- Program revenues by category, which may include charges for services, operating grants, operating contributions, and capital grants and contributions
- Total net expense or revenue
- General revenues and other changes in net position by type
- Total change in net position

- The most significant charges for services revenue, categorized by program, function, or identifiable activity

If a government is only engaged in business-type activities, it should report revenues by major source, as well as distinguish between operating and non-operating revenues and expenses. This information should appear in their separately-issued financial reports.

If a government is only engaged in fiduciary activities, it should report the following information in its separately-issued financial reports:

- Additions by source
- Deductions by type
- Total change in net position

In addition, the following information should be presented for each individual pension or other post-employment benefit plan that is reported as a pension trust fund:

- Benefit and refund deductions by type of benefit, such as age and service benefits
- Benefit and refund deductions by refund, such as death or separation payments

When a government reports about government funds, it should also present information about fund balances and changes in fund balances. This reporting should include:

- The required classifications of fund balances for the general fund
- The required classifications of fund balances for all other governmental funds in aggregate
- The following information for total governmental funds:
  o Revenues by source
  o Expenditures by function[2]
  o Other financing sources and uses
  o Other changes in fund balances by type
  o Total change in fund balances
  o The ratio of total debt service expenditures to non-capital expenditures[3]

It is acceptable to provide a greater level of detail on the face of the schedule or in a separate, accompanying schedule.

---

[2] The interest and principal components of debt service expenditures are presented separately.
[3] Non-capital expenditures are calculated as total expenditures minus capital outlay and expenditures for capitalized assets stated within the functional expenditure categories.

A sample changes in net position disclosure appears next, along with a statement of fund balances and a statement of changes in fund balances.

Acorn City
Change in Net Position | Last 10 Fiscal Years

(000s)	Fiscal Year		
	20X1	20X2	20X3
Governmental activities			
Expenses			
General government	$4,727	$5,534	$6,748
Community services	19,258	20,839	21,354
City infrastructure	20,549	20,657	17,721
Culture and recreation	--	91	85
Urban redevelopment	--	607	952
Interest on long-term debt	156	165	146
Total governmental activities expenses	44,690	47,893	47,006
Program revenues			
Charges for services			
General government	47	47	75
Community services	1,612	2,060	2,301
City infrastructure	176	203	354
Urban redevelopment	--	684	1,980
Operating grants and contributions	4,389	4,318	4,070
Capital grants and contributions	3,286	4,039	5,258
Total governmental activities program revenues	9,510	11,351	14,038
Total governmental activities net program expense	35,180	36,542	32,968
General revenues and other changes in net position			
Taxes			
Sales tax	17,570	18,736	18,621
Use tax	1,127	1,237	3,265
Property tax	7,440	7,526	7,989
Auto use tax	3,514	3,994	3,522
Other taxes	958	964	891
Unrestricted franchise fees	4,209	4,253	4,829
Investment income	1,265	1,658	832
Issuance of debt	66	265	534
Insurance proceeds	45	--	--
Contributions	150	--	--
Transfers	-961	-1,129	-394
	35,383	37,504	40,089
	$203	$962	$7,121

Note: Only the last three years are shown in this sample statement.

Statistical Section

Acorn City
Change in Net Position | Last 10 Fiscal Years

	Fiscal Year		
(000s)	20X1	20X2	20X3
Business-type activities			
Expenses			
Land use fund	$3,274	$4,029	$3,549
Total expenses	3,274	4,029	3,549
Revenues			
Land use service fees	2,313	2,900	3,155
Total revenues	2,313	2,900	3,155
Operating income (loss) before transfers	-961	-1,129	-394
Transfers	961	1,129	394
Total business-type activities change in net position	--	--	--
Total primary government change in net position	$203	$962	$7,121

Note: Only the last three years are shown in this sample statement.

Acorn City
Fund Balances, Governmental Funds | Last 10 Fiscal Years

	Fiscal Year		
(000s)	20X1	20X2	20X3
General fund			
Reserved	$1,350	$1,491	$1,298
Unreserved	13,017	13,200	13,508
Non-spendable	--	--	--
Restricted	--	--	--
Assigned	--	--	--
Unassigned	--	--	--
Total general fund	14,367	14,691	14,806
All other governmental funds			
Reserved	7,184	9,684	9,917
Unreserved	6,453	7,293	6,875
Non-spendable	--	--	--
Restricted	--	--	--
Assigned	--	--	--
Total all other governmental funds	$13,637	$16,977	$16,792
Total all governmental funds	$28,004	$31,668	$31,598

Note: Only the last three years are shown in this sample statement.

Acorn City
Fund Balances, Governmental Funds
Last 10 Fiscal Years

(000s)	Fiscal Year		
	20X1	20X2	20X3
Revenues			
Taxes	$30,610	$32,458	$34,288
Intergovernmental	7,674	8,154	9,121
Charges for services	1,836	2,994	4,709
Franchise fees	4,209	4,253	4,828
Investment income	1,265	1,657	833
Miscellaneous	67	265	534
Total revenues	45,661	49,781	54,313
Expenditures			
Current			
General government	4,414	5,535	6,708
Community services	19,456	20,878	21,354
City infrastructure	15,252	13,730	13,843
Culture & recreation	--	91	85
Urban redevelopment	--	607	952
Capital outlay			
General government	--	21	7,839
Capital improvement	1,116	3,949	3,006
Debt service			
Principal	1,306	15	56
Interest and fiscal charges	203	161	147
Total expenditures	41,747	44,987	53,990
Revenue over expenditures	3,914	4,794	323
Other Financing Sources (Uses)			
Transfers in	5,059	3,880	900
Transfers out	-6,020	-5,009	-1,294
Contributions	150	--	--
Issuance of debt	45	--	--
Total other financing sources (uses)	-766	-1,129	-394
Net change in fund balances	$3,148	$3,665	-$71
Debt service as a percent of noncapital expenditures	3.9%	0.4%	0.5%

Note: Only the last three years are shown in this sample statement.

193

Revenue Capacity Information

The general classifications of information to be presented within the revenue capacity section are revenue base, revenue rates, and principal revenue payers. These topics are addressed in the following sub-sections.

Revenue Base Information

The accountant should report revenue base information by major component, such as by different classes of real and personal property, or by type of rate payer. Further, state the total direct rate applied to this revenue base. The *total direct rate* is the weighted average of every individual direct rate applied by a government. A *direct rate* is the amount applied to a unit of a revenue base, such as a sales tax of 4% of a retail sale, or a $0.25 charge for every 100 gallons of water used.

    If a government reports revenue base information for a property tax, it must present the following information:

- *Assessed value.* Report the assessed value of taxable property by major component. Examples of these components are residential property and commercial property.
- *Estimated actual value.* Report the estimated actual value of the taxable property. This is the fair value of taxable real or personal property (or some similar measure of fair value), which is commonly considered its market value.

If the government uses an assessment method that does not generate a reasonable basis for estimating actual property value, disclose the situation on the face of the schedule and state why the information has not been presented.

    A sample report of revenue base information appears next.

Walnut City
Assessed Value and Actual Value of Taxable Property
Last 10 Fiscal Years

(000s)	Taxable Real and Personal Property			
Fiscal Year	Residential Property	Commercial Property	Industrial Property	Vacant Land
20X0	$796,434	$539,134	$4,763	$30,745
20X1	853,955	574,216	4,300	32,639
20X2	858,295	575,249	4,074	30,690
20X3	825,768	669,232	5,189	39,676
20X4	836,720	692,471	4,343	41,196
20X5	805,653	628,640	3,950	33,667
20X6	806,330	639,120	3,750	31,862
20X7	828,687	674,005	3,854	28,528
20X8	829,760	638,792	3,204	27,077
20X9	1,015,628	762,947	4,519	32,702

Walnut City
Assessed Value and Actual Value of Taxable Property
Last 10 Fiscal Years
(continued)

(000s)		Taxable Real and Personal Property			
Fiscal Year	Other Property	Total Taxable Assessed Value	Mill Levy	Actual Value	Assessed Value as % of Actual Value
20X0	$76,889	$1,447,965	5.031	$12,251,482	11.82%
20X1	86,587	1,551,697	4.958	13,133,259	11.82%
20X2	95,876	1,564,184	5.054	13,215,858	11.84%
20X3	91,294	1,631,159	5.047	13,150,665	12.40%
20X4	89,318	1,664,048	5.077	13,363,879	12.45%
20X5	105,985	1,577,895	5.077	12,783,755	12.34%
20X6	112,373	1,593,435	5.129	12,843,507	12.41%
20X7	117,278	1,652,352	5.073	13,250,415	12.47%
20X8	114,500	1,613,333	5.015	12,681,268	12.72%
20X9	106,859	1,922,655	5.015	15,296,547	12.57%

Revenue Rates Information

The accountant should separately state each individual direct rate applied by the government to the revenue base, as well as the total direct rate. In addition, disclose any legal restrictions on the ability of the government to raise its direct rates. This may happen when (for example) a municipality must obtain the approval of a majority of its voters in order to raise a rate.

The revenue rates presentation may involve *overlapping rates*, where there are rates applied by governments that overlap, in part or in full, with the entity preparing the statistical section information. When this is the case, some overlapping taxing entities may levy their taxes for different fiscal periods, which can cause inconsistencies in the reporting of rates. Consequently, when preparing this schedule, the rates stated should be based on the taxes payable by taxpayers in the same year. Two sample revenue rate schedules are presented next.

Walnut City
Direct Sales Tax Rates
Last 10 Fiscal Years

Fiscal Year	Walnut City	State of Arizona	Maricopa County	Cultural District	Football District	Total
20X0	1.50%	5.60%	0.70%	0.10%	0.10%	8.00%
20X1	1.50%	5.60%	0.70%	0.10%	0.10%	8.00%
20X2	1.50%	5.60%	0.70%	0.10%	0.10%	8.00%
20X3	1.50%	5.60%	0.70%	0.10%	0.10%	8.00%
20X4	1.50%	5.60%	0.70%	0.10%	0.10%	8.00%
20X5	1.50%	5.60%	0.70%	0.10%	0.10%	8.00%
20X6	1.50%	5.60%	0.70%	0.10%	0.10%	8.00%
20X7	1.50%	5.60%	0.70%	0.10%	0.00%	7.90%
20X8	1.50%	5.60%	0.70%	0.10%	0.00%	7.90%
20X9	1.50%	5.60%	0.70%	0.10%	0.00%	7.90%

Almond City
Direct and Overlapping Sales Tax Rates
Last 10 Fiscal Years

Fiscal Year	City Direct Rates			Overlapping Rates		
	Basic Rate	Debt Service	Total Direct Rate	School District	Mayfield County	Fire Control District
20X0	$1.72	$0.25	$1.97	$2.15	$0.92	$0.08
20X1	1.72	0.25	1.97	2.15	0.92	0.08
20X2	1.70	0.25	1.95	2.18	0.95	0.08
20X3	1.70	0.25	1.95	2.18	0.95	0.08
20X4	1.70	0.25	1.95	2.18	0.95	0.08
20X5	1.68	0.25	1.93	2.20	0.95	0.08
20X6	1.68	0.25	1.93	2.20	0.95	0.08
20X7	1.68	0.25	1.93	2.21	0.96	0.08
20X8	1.75	0.25	2.00	2.21	0.96	0.08
20X9	1.75	0.25	2.00	2.21	0.96	0.08

There are a few restrictions on the requirement to report revenue rates, which are as follows:

- *State governments.* State governments do not have to present information about the revenue rates of the overlapping governments situated within their borders.
- *Non-state governments.* A non-state government is not required to present information about any overlapping state government revenue rates.
- *Regional governments.* Regional governments are encouraged to report about the revenue rates of their overlapping governments, but this is not required.

The total direct rate may be difficult to calculate when a government has a complex rate structure. If so, an effective tax rate can be used instead. If an effective rate is used, it should be clearly labeled in the revenue base and revenue rate schedules, along with a note stating why an effective tax rate is being used instead of the total direct rate.

> **Note:** An *effective tax rate* is the average rate that is calculated by dividing either total revenue or total collections by the total revenue base for a reporting period.

Principal Revenue Payers Information

The accountant should identify the payers of a government's most significant own-source revenue, the amount of revenue base attributable to each, and the percentage of each amount in relation to the total revenue base. The 10 largest payers should be presented (either by revenue base or taxes levied), unless a smaller number can be used to attain 50% of the total revenue base or total taxes levied. This information should be presented for the current year and the preceding nine years.

When a government is legally prohibited from reporting individual revenue payers, it should instead provide other information that helps users to understand the degree of concentration of its own-source revenue.

The preceding disclosures related to principal revenue assume that a government has a single, most-significant revenue source that does not change over time. This may not be the case; for example, one revenue source may start small and grow so much that it becomes the dominant revenue source. In this case, it could make sense to present information for both the prior largest revenue source and the new largest revenue source.

A sample schedule that contains principal revenue payer information appears next. The schedule is designed to show the changes in principal revenue payers over a 10-year period, using the current period and the period from nine years ago.

Cacao City
Principal Property Taxpayers
For 20X0 and 20X9

For the Year 20_0			
(000s)		Taxable Assessed Value	Percent of Total City Assessed Value
Ranking	Taxpayer		
1	Pensive Corporation	$7,250	0.50%
2	Newton Enterprises	7,079	0.49%
3	Red Herring Fish Company	6,235	0.43%
4	Arizona Teachers Pension Fund	5,945	0.41%
5	Milagro Corporation	5,897	0.41%
6	Spade Designs, Inc.	5,220	0.36%
7	Snuggable Pillows, Inc.	5,122	0.36%
8	Mulligan Imports	4,582	0.32%
9	Nascent Corporation	4,495	0.31%
10	Pianoforte International	3,770	0.26%
	Total	$55,595	3.85%

For the Year 20_9			
		Taxable Assessed Value	Percent of Total City Assessed Value
Ranking	Taxpayer		
1	Milagro Corporation	$13,392	0.83%
2	Nascent Corporation	12,843	0.80%
3	Red Herring Fish Company	11,980	0.74%
4	Pensive Corporation	11,644	0.72%
5	Electronic Inference Corporation	8,541	0.53%
6	Snuggable Pillows, Inc.	7,850	0.49%
7	Grizzly Golf Carts	7,320	0.45%
8	Hodgson Industrial Design	6,708	0.42%
9	Radiosonde Communications	6,140	0.38%
10	New Centurion Corporation	6,003	0.37%
	Total	$92,421	5.73%

Property Tax Levies and Collections

When a government levies a property tax, the accountant should present the following information for the last 10 years about property tax levies and collections:

- The amount levied for the period
- The amount collected before the end of the period, as well as the percentage of the levy that the collection figure represents
- The amount of the levy collected in later years, the total amount collected to date, and the percentage of the levy that the to-date collection figure represents

A sample schedule that contains this information appears next.

Walnut City
Property Tax Levies and Collections
Last 10 Fiscal Years

(000s)		Collected in Fiscal Year of the Levy	
Fiscal Year	Taxes Levied for Collection in the Fiscal Year	Amount	Percentage of Levy
20X0	$7,484	$7,440	99.4%
20X1	7,629	7,526	98.7%
20X2	8,088	7,989	98.8%
20X3	8,173	8,133	99.5%
20X4	8,451	8,323	98.5%
20X5	8,340	8,286	99.4%
20X6	8,173	7,984	97.7%
20X7	8,105	8,243	101.7%
20X8	8,538	8,463	99.1%
20X9	8,308	8,294	99.8%

Debt Capacity Information

Governments should present information about their debt capacity. To do so, they should present information about ratios of outstanding debt, direct and overlapping debt, debt limitations, and pledged revenue coverage. These topics are covered in the following sub-sections.

Ratios of Outstanding Debt

An outstanding debt ratio should be presented. This ratio is calculated by dividing total debt outstanding by total personal income. The total amount of personal income should be presented alongside this ratio, or with the demographic and economic information (as discussed in a later section of this chapter). If the total amount of personal income is not available, it is allowable to replace it with the estimated actual value of taxable property or some other relevant economic base.

A per capita ratio of total outstanding debt should also be presented. Depending on the circumstances, there may be a more relevant alternative to the population figure used in this ratio. For example, a government-run cable television utility might prefer to divide outstanding debt by the number of its customers, rather than the entire population of the area that the utility serves.

A government may issue general bonded debt. If so, it should provide additional information about ratios of general bonded debt. Each type of this debt should be shown individually and totaled. If the government has accumulated resources that are restricted for use in repaying the principal on this debt, then the debt should be shown net of these resources and presented as net general bonded debt.

If general bonded debt is present, a government should present a general bonded debt ratio. The ratio is calculated by dividing total general bonded debt by the total estimated actual value of taxable property. The numerator may instead be net general bonded debt, if applicable. If these bonds are not to be repaid with property taxes, it is allowable to use an alternative revenue base.

A per capita ratio of total general bonded debt should also be presented. Depending on the circumstances, there may be a more relevant alternative to the population figure used in this ratio, as was the case for the per capita ratio of total outstanding debt.

These ratios require the use of current information about personal income and population. If this information is not yet available by the time the financial statements are published, here are several alternative ways to deal with the situation:

- Access tentative personal income data published by the U.S. Bureau of Economic Analysis, and recalculate the related ratios in later years, after the tentative data has been finalized.
- Use the personal income or population data from the most recent year available and recalculate the related ratios in later years, when more definitive data is made available.
- Use an alternative source for the needed information.
- Internally produce personal income and population data.

Whenever these alternative methods are used, be sure to disclose the source of the data.

A sample schedule that addresses the preceding requirements appears next.

Cashew City
Ratios of:
Outstanding Debt by Type,
Outstanding General Bonded Debt
and Legal Debt Margin
Last 10 Fiscal Years

(000s)	Fiscal Year		
Outstanding Debt by Type	20X1	20X2	20X3
Governmental activities			
General obligation bonds	$3,050	$3,035	$2,980
Total primary government outstanding debt	$3,050	$3,035	$2,980
Percentage of personal income	0.1%	0.1%	0.1%
Per capita	$30	$31	$29
Outstanding general bonded debt			
General obligation bonds	$3,050	$3,035	$2,980
Percentage of personal income	0.1%	0.1%	0.1%
Per capita	$30	$31	$29
Legal debt margin			
Debt limit	$367,544	$393,998	$401,642
Total net debt applicable to limit	3,050	3,035	2,980
Legal debt margin	$364,494	$390,963	$404,622
Legal debt margin as percent of the debt limit	99.2%	99.2%	99.2%

Note: Only the last three years are shown in this sample statement.

Direct and Overlapping Debt

Information should be presented for a government's direct and overlapping debt. When there is debt attributable to the governmental activities of an overlapping governmental entity, the statistical section should include the following information for the current year:

- The total amount outstanding
- The percentage of overlap between the reporting and overlapping governments
- The product of the debt outstanding, multiplied by the percentage of overlap

If a government only engages in business-type activities, there is no need to present information about direct and overlapping debt.

The total amount of debt outstanding should agree with the amount stated in the entity's basic financial statements. This means that the disclosure of the total amount outstanding should incorporate all debt premiums and/or discounts, and other accounting adjustments.

The products for the overlapping debt are then totaled and presented, along with total direct debt and total direct and overlapping debt.

> **Note:** *Direct debt* is a government's outstanding long-term debt instruments, such as bonds, loans, and notes. *Overlapping debt* is the outstanding long-term debt instruments of governments that overlap geographically with the territory of the government preparing statistical section information.

There is no requirement for state governments to present direct and overlapping debt information in the statistical section. Further, non-state entities are not required to present the debt of overlapping state governments. County and regional governments are not required to present direct and overlapping debt information, but are encouraged to do so.

The overlap percentage between the reporting entity and the overlapping entity is calculated by dividing the amount of the revenue base from which the debt is repaid that is located within the overlapping area by the total revenue base of the overlapping entity.

EXAMPLE

An overlapping government's debt is repaid with property taxes. To calculate the overlap percentage, divide the value of the property in the overlap area by the total value of the property of the overlapping government.

If there is not adequate information available for the relevant revenue base associated with the calculation of an overlap percentage, an alternative base can be used, such as personal income. Whatever the method used, the statistical section should include an explanation of the methodology and denominator used to calculate the percentage of overlap for each type of debt.

A sample schedule that addresses the preceding requirements appears next.

Hickory City
Direct and Overlapping Governmental Activities Debt
as of December 31, 20X2

(000s) Governmental Unit	General Obligation Debt Outstanding	Estimated Percentage Applicable	Estimated Share of Overlapping Debt
Chestnut Water District	$200	100.0%	$200
Cottonwood Metropolitan District	8,510	35.9%	3,055
Hawthorn School District	129,060	45.0%	58,077
Hemlock Wastewater Authority	325	100.0%	325
Hickory Public Schools	458,270	17.8%	81,572
Larch Metropolitan District	48,515	42.1%	20,425
Locust Recreation District	3,680	26.7%	983
Maple Metropolitan District	394	100.0%	394
Oak Metropolitan District	4,110	100.0%	4,110
Spruce Metropolitan District	3,430	8.5%	292
Sycamore School District	141,696	36.2%	51,294
Subtotal overlapping debt	798,190		220,727
Ocelot Water System District	15,700	100.0%	15,700
Subtotal direct debt	15,700		15,700
Total direct and overlapping debt	$813,890		$236,427

Debt Limitations

When a government has a legal debt limitation, it should report the information used as the basis for its legal debt margin for the current year. A typical presentation would be as follows:

- The relevant revenue base
- The debt limit amount
- The debt applicable to the limit, any reserves to be deducted, and the total net debt applicable to the limit
- The legal debt margin amount

In addition, the accountant should include an explanation of the nature of the debt limitation. Further, the following information should be presented for the last 10 years:

- The debt limit amount
- The total net debt applicable to the limit
- The legal debt margin amount
- The ratio of the legal debt margin amount or the total net debt applicable to the debt limit, divided by the debt limit

Pledged-Revenue Coverage

If a government has pledged any of its revenue to pay for debt, it should present information about the level of pledged-revenue coverage. For each type of debt that has been backed by pledged revenues, present the gross revenues, principal and interest requirements and a coverage ratio. Discuss the nature of the revenues being pledged for each type of debt.

> **Note:** A *coverage ratio* measures the magnitude of the resources available to pay the interest and principal associated with debt that is backed by pledged revenues. It is calculated by dividing pledged revenues (or pledged revenues net of certain operating expenses) by the total amount of interest expenses and principal repayments.

A sample presentation of pledged-revenue coverage appears next.

Orange City
Pledged Revenue Coverage
Special Assessment Bonds
Last 10 Years

Fiscal Year	Special Assessment Collections	Debt Service - Principal	Debt Service - Interest	Coverage
20X0	$9,200	$1,200	$8,000	1.1
20X1	9,085	1,300	7,785	1.1
20X2	9,070	1,400	7,670	1.0
20X3	9,055	1,500	7,555	1.0
20X4	9,040	1,600	7,440	0.9
20X5	9,025	1,700	7,325	0.9
20X6	9,010	1,800	7,210	0.9
20X7	8,995	1,900	7,095	0.9
20X8	8,980	2,000	6,980	0.8
20X9	8,965	2,100	6,865	0.8

Additional Debt Reporting Topics

A government should separately present each type of outstanding debt, of which there may be many types, such as:

- Certificates of participation
- General obligation bonds
- Loans
- Revenue-backed bonds

When reporting each type of outstanding debt, distinguish between debt that is related to governmental activities and debt related to business-type activities. The presentation should include a total for all debt.

Demographic and Economic Information

Governments should present relevant demographic and economic indicators, as well as information about the principal employers within their boundaries. These topics are discussed in the following sub-sections.

Demographic and Economic Indicators

The following demographic and economic indicators should be presented:

- Population
- Total personal income
- Per capita personal income
- Unemployment rate

If any of this information is not available for some or all of the 10 years required for presentation, either indicate that it is unavailable, use information from an alternative source, use information from a nearby jurisdiction, or provide estimates.
    A sample schedule that addresses these requirements appears next.

Acorn City
Demographic and Economic Statistics
Last 10 Fiscal Years

Fiscal Year	Population	(000s) Personal Income	Per Capita Personal Income	Median Age	High School Graduation Rate	Unemployment Rate
20X0	100,300	$3,294,100	$32,842	35.5	94.6%	5.1%
20X1	98,800	3,440,300	34,821	36.0	94.8%	5.3%
20X2	99,200	3,586,500	36,154	37.5	95.0%	5.5%
20X3	99,700	3,732,700	37,439	39.5	95.2%	5.9%
20X4	100,400	3,878,900	38,634	40.0	95.6%	6.0%
20X5	101,900	4,025,100	39,500	40.0	95.8%	5.6%
20X6	102,600	4,171,200	40,655	40.5	95.7%	5.3%
20X7	103,700	4,227,700	40,769	40.5	95.3%	4.8%
20X8	106,100	4,384,900	41,328	41.0	95.0%	4.0%
20X9	107,200	4,433,400	41,356	41.0	94.9%	4.2%

Principal Employers

The following information about employers should be presented for the current year and the previous nine years:

- The principal employers within the government's jurisdiction
- The number of persons employed by each principal employer
- The percentage of total employment represented by each principal employer

The 10 largest employers should be presented, based on the number of individuals employed. A smaller number can be reported if fewer are needed to reach 50% of the total employment within the government's jurisdiction. The information presented should be for *all* employers, including for-profit, nonprofit, and governmental employers.

A sample schedule that addresses these requirements appears next.

Hitchcock City
Principal Employers
Ten Year Comparison

Top Ten Employers	Current Year Rank	Top Ten Employers	10 Years Ago Rank
Active Exercise Machines	1	Blitz Communications	1
Gatekeeper Corporation	2	Gulf Coast Insurance	2
Blitz Communications	3	International Automation	3
Gulf Coast Insurance	4	Viking Fitness	4
Medusa Medical	5	Rubens Trailers	5
Aphelion Corporation	6	Nefarious Industries	6
Rapunzel Hair Products	7	Tsunami Products	7
International Automation	8	Active Exercise Machines	8
Nefarious Industries	9	Treadway Corporation	9
Coronary Associates	10	Subterranean Access	10
Employees by NAICS Industries		Employees by NAICS Industries	
Finance, insurance, and real estate	6,300	Finance, insurance, and real estate	9,200
Professional, scientific and management	8,700	Professional, scientific and management	9,900
Construction	2,500	Construction	5,100
Retail trade	6,000	Retail trade	3,900
Education services and health care	10,900	Education services and health care	6,300
Arts and entertainment	3,900	Arts and entertainment	6,700
Wholesale trade	2,000	Wholesale trade	3,500
Information	2,400	Information	2,800
Other services	2,600	Other services	1,300
Public administration	1,600	Public administration	1,200
Manufacturing	3,400	Manufacturing	500
Transportation and warehousing	2,200	Transportation and warehousing	700
Agriculture and mining	600	Agriculture and mining	200
Total	53,100	Total	51,300

Operating Information

Governments should present operating information that encompasses the number of government employees, operating indicators, and capital assets. These topics are discussed in the following sub-sections.

Government Employees

A government should present the number of people that it employs, reporting this information by function, program, or identifiable activity. Some other basis of presentation is acceptable, if the resulting information would be more meaningful to readers.

> **Note:** There is no specification for how to measure the number of workers, such as by headcount or full-time equivalents. The method used should be applied to all reporting periods, in order to provide consistent information.

The measurement of government employees can be derived in any manner, such as by counting employees as of a specific date or by using a headcount average for the entire reporting period. Whichever method is used should be consistently applied.

A sample schedule that addresses these requirements appears next.

Acorn City
Full-Time Equivalent Employees as of December 31
Last Ten Years

	20X0	20X1	20X2	20X3	20X4	20X5	20X6	20X7	20X8	20X9
General government	5.0	8.0	12.0	13.5	12.5	10.0	13.5	17.3	25.3	24.5
Community services	11.0	11.0	5.0	5.0	6.0	5.0	5.5	4.5	3.0	9.5
Finance & administration	12.0	13.0	13.0	13.0	16.0	17.0	13.5	15.0	17.5	19.5
Planning & development	1.0	9.0	15.5	14.0	14.0	13.0	9.0	8.5	5.0	3.5
City infrastructure	--	--	1.0	1.5	1.5	5.0	5.0	3.0	3.5	6.0
Totals	29.0	41.0	46.5	47.0	50.0	50.0	46.5	48.3	54.3	63.0

Operating Indicators

A government should present indicators of demand or level of service. There is no requirement for the number of indicators to be provided. Examples of these indicators are:

- Number of applications processed
- Number of arrests made
- Number of inspections performed
- Number of permits issued
- Number of properties assessed

A sample schedule that addresses these requirements appears next.

Birchwood City
Operating Indicators by Function | Program
Last Ten Fiscal Years

| | Fiscal Year | | |
	20X1	20X2	20X3
General Government			
Administrative Services			
Citations processed	14,500	17,800	20,700
Employment applications processed	700	770	760
New hires processed	10	25	20
Computer service requests	180	260	530
Finance			
Accounts payable checks issued	1,600	1,800	2,000
Purchasing card transactions	300	400	700
Sales/use tax accounts	4,300	3,600	2,800
City Management			
Ordinances and resolutions approved by City Council	140	160	150
Citizen surveys received	1	2	1
Community Development			
Building permits issued	3,900	4,300	4,000
Building inspections performed	11,600	13,000	13,200
Code enforcement cases	800	1,500	2,100
Public Safety			
Calls for services	48,900	48,700	46,700
Average response time to high priority calls (minutes)	6.5	6.6	10.0
Hours spent on proactive patrol, per day per deputy	4.4	4.2	3.7
Total arrests	4,900	4,800	3,700
Public Works			
Vehicles in fleet	2	6	6
Lane miles receiving snow & ice control	89,100	62,500	41,800
Lane miles swept	7,300	5,600	8,500

Note: Only the last three years are shown in this sample statement.

Capital Assets

A government should present indicators of the volume, usage, or nature of its capital assets. Examples of this information are:

- Average daily water consumption
- Estimated vehicle-miles traveled on its highways
- Lane-miles of streets and highways
- Miles of sewers
- Miles of water mains
- Number of cars in the central pool
- Square feet of administrative office space

A sample schedule that addresses these requirements appears next.

Marmot City
Capital Asset Statistics by Function | Program
Last Ten Fiscal Years

	20X0	20X1	20X2	20X3	20X4	20X5	20X6	20X7	20X8	20X9
Recreation										
Acres of developed parks	9.7	9.7	9.7	9.7	9.7	9.7	17.1	17.1	17.1	17.1
Acres of open space parks	42.3	42.3	49.8	49.8	49.8	49.8	54.6	54.6	54.6	54.6
Public Works										
Maintenance facility	--	--	--	1	1	1	1	1	1	1
Miles of streets	392	392	393	397	397	408	408	411	411	417
Number of street lights	3,642	3,711	3,979	3,987	3,992	4,057	4,042	4,043	4,222	4,222
Number of fleet vehicles	2	2	4	4	4	6	6	6	6	7

Sources, Assumptions, and Methodologies

Some additional discussion is needed regarding background information that pertains to the financial statement reporting package. The following information should be included:

- Identify the sources of all information in the statistical section that do not appear in the basic financial statements, the notes to the basic financial statements, or the required supplementary information.

- Explain the methodologies used to produce the information in the statistical section.
- Explain any significant assumptions made.

Summary

The information presented in the statistical section can match or exceed the information presented in the rest of a financial statement reporting package. This can result in a considerable overload of data for a reader, so it is useful to add narrative explanations to enhance the understandability of the information provided. The inclusion of a brief narrative can be useful in the following circumstances:

- When it makes it easier for someone to locate information
- When it improves a reader's understanding of significant changes in the information
- When it explains occurrences that impact the presented information
- When it provides context between information in the basic financial statements and the statistical section
- When it helps readers understand a government's economic condition

A narrative explanation should be largely analytical in nature, encompassing the following types of discussions:

- Explain the objectives of this section, the main categories of statistical information, and the individual schedules being presented.
- Explain any basic concepts that may be unfamiliar to readers.
- Identify relationships among the information presented in the various schedules, as well as between the statistical section and information in other parts of the reporting package.
- Explain unusual trends and anomalous data that readers might not otherwise understand.

A sample statement of the objectives of the statistical section appears next.

Statistical tables are used to provide a historical financial review. The various tables provide information which is useful in analyzing the existing financial position of the City and identifying potential trends.

Financial Trends

These schedules contain trend information to help the reader understand how the City's financial performance and well-being have changed over time.

Revenue Capacity

These schedules contain information to help the reader assess the City's significant local revenue sources, which are sales and use tax and property tax.

Debt Capacity

These schedules present information to help the reader assess the affordability of the City's current levels of outstanding debt and the City's ability to issue additional debt in the future.

Demographic and Economic Information

These schedules offer demographic and economic indicators to help the reader understand the environment within which the City's financial activities take place.

Operating Information

These schedules contain service and infrastructure data to help the reader understand how the information in the City's financial report relates to the services the City provides and the activities it performs.

Chapter 18
Fair Value Measurement

Introduction

A government is required to incorporate fair value into its recordation of certain assets and liabilities. In this chapter, we cover fair value principles, applicable valuation techniques, required disclosures, and several related topics, with particular attention to the fair value hierarchy.

Fair Value Definition

Fair value is defined as the price that a government would receive if it were to sell an asset, or the amount it would pay to settle an obligation in an orderly transaction between market participants at the measurement date. Given the length of that definition, it may be worthwhile to examine its components. Key features of the definition are:

- *Orderly transaction.* This is a transaction that has had a sufficient amount of time for normal marketing activities to be completed. Thus, the transaction is not being forced, where (for example) the seller of an asset has the time to search for buyers and evaluate their bids.
- *Market participants.* The parties engaged in a transaction, who are located in the most advantageous market for the asset or liability being sold or settled (respectively), and where the parties are independent of each other, are knowledgeable, and are willing and able to enter into a transaction without being forced to do so.
- *Measurement date.* This is the date on which the fair value of the asset or liability in question is determined.

From the perspective of the entity that is holding an asset or is obligated under a liability, fair value is the *exit price* – that is, the price the seller of an asset would receive or the price the holder of a liability would pay in order to settle an obligation.

Fair Value Principles

The determination of fair value is based on several underlying principles, which are noted in the following sub-sections.

Characteristics of the Asset or Liability

The fair value of an asset or liability depends in part on the characteristics of the individual item. For example, the fair value of an asset is directly influenced by the amount of wear it has incurred, any liens associated with it, and its location. The impact that these characteristics have on fair value will depend on how they are perceived by market participants.

Markets

When making a fair value measurement, the assumption is that a presumed transaction to sell an asset or settle a liability will be made in either a government's principal market or its most advantageous market (if there is no principal market). A *principal market* is that market having the greatest transaction volume for an asset or liability. The *most advantageous market* is that market in which a government would maximize the amount to be received from the sale of an asset, or which would minimize the amount paid to settle a liability, after factoring in transaction and transportation costs. The market in which a government usually enters into transactions is usually considered its principal market or most advantageous market.

If there is a principal market for a government's asset or liability, the related fair value measurement should be based on the price in that market, even if the price could potentially be better in a different market.

Transaction Costs

When determining the fair value of an asset or liability based on its principal market, the price is not adjusted for transaction costs. *Transaction costs* are directly attributable to the sale of an asset or settlement of a liability, result directly from the transaction, and would not have been incurred in the absence of the transaction. However, transaction costs do not include transportation costs. Thus, the fair value calculation is adjusted for the cost that would be incurred to transport an asset from its current location to the market in which it would be sold.

Bid-Ask Spread

When measuring fair value, the accountant may find that an asset or liability has a bid price and an ask price associated with it. The bid price is the price at which a seller is willing to sell, while the ask price is the price at which a buyer is willing to buy. The price within this bid-ask spread that is most representative of fair value should be used. If there is no price within the bid-ask spread that is most representative of fair value, then either the bid price or the ask price can be used.

Valuation Techniques

Valuation techniques are employed to determine the fair value of an asset or liability. Three techniques are available, and are outlined in the following sub-sections. The technique used to derive fair value should maximize the use of observable inputs, while minimizing the use of unobservable inputs. An *observable input* is developed using market data, such as publicly available market information about actual transactions. An *unobservable input* is based on the best information available in the absence of market data.

A single valuation technique may be sufficient in those cases where there is a close match in the principal market, such as when there are quoted prices available in an active market for an identical asset. When this is not the case, several valuation techniques can be used, which may result in a range of values. If so, the fair value is considered to be that point within the range that is most representative of fair value under the circumstances.

The valuation techniques used should be consistently applied from period to period. However, a different technique can be used when the result is more representative of fair value. This situation may arise, for example, when new information becomes available, market conditions change, or when information that had previously been used is no longer available.

Market Approach

The first valuation technique is the market approach, which uses prices and other information from market transactions that involve identical or similar assets or liabilities. For example, an asset could be assigned a fair value based on quoted market prices for similar assets. Two variations on the concept are:

- *Market multiples technique*. This approach uses multiples, such as the price-earnings ratio for similar assets or liabilities, to develop a fair value. For example, an investment in a company can be valued based on the price-earnings ratios of a selection of similar businesses.
- *Matrix pricing technique*. This approach uses the relationship of a security to a benchmark quoted price to develop a fair value.

Cost Approach

The second valuation technique is the cost approach, where fair value is assumed to be the amount that would be required in the current period to replace an asset's present service capacity. This means that fair value is based on the cost to acquire or construct a substitute asset that has a comparable utility to that of the asset being valued, adjusted for obsolescence.

Income Approach

The final valuation technique is the income approach, where fair value is based on the present value of the future cash flows associated with an asset or liability. This calculation is based on the most recent estimate of what those future cash flows may be.

Fair Value Hierarchy

There are three levels of information that can be used as inputs to the preceding valuation techniques. These levels are known as the fair value hierarchy. The three levels are defined as follows:

- *Level 1*. These are quoted prices for identical assets or liabilities in active markets.
- *Level 2*. These are inputs that are directly or indirectly observable for an asset or liability.
- *Level 3*. These are unobservable inputs for an asset or liability.

The following rules apply when using the fair value hierarchy:

- When developing a fair value, Level 1 inputs are given the highest priority, while Level 3 inputs are given the lowest priority.
- If fair value is measured using inputs from multiple levels of the hierarchy, the measurement is considered to have been based on the input from the lowest priority level that is significant to the entire measurement.
- If an observable input is adjusted with an unobservable input, where the unobservable input results in a significant adjustment in fair value, the resulting measurement is classified as being within Level 3 of the fair value hierarchy.

We provide additional information about the levels of the fair value hierarchy in the following sub-sections.

Level 1 Inputs

Level 1 inputs provide the most reliable evidence for the determination of fair value, and so should be used without adjustment whenever possible. These inputs can be found in exchange markets, such as the New York Stock Exchange, or in brokered markets, where brokers try to match buyers with sellers. These types of inputs are commonly available for many financial assets and financial liabilities, such as common stock and options.

A Level 1 input should not be adjusted, except in one of the following situations:

- A government holds a large number of similar assets or liabilities, and a quoted price is available, but not readily accessible for each individual item.
- The quoted price in an active market is not representative of fair value as of the measurement date. This could happen, for example, when the accountant knows of significant events occurring after the close of a market on the measurement date that would have impacted the quoted price.
- A liability is being measured based on the price being quoted for an identical asset, and that price must be adjusted due to factors applicable only to the asset, not the liability.

> **Tip:** Create a policy that clearly states the circumstances under which a Level 1 input should be adjusted. For example, specifically state those events that might impact a quoted closing price. By doing so, a government only alters its Level 1 inputs on a consistent basis.

A government may be holding a large number of identical assets or liabilities, which are measured using Level 1 inputs. The quoted market price for these items should be applied to all of the assets or liabilities, even when the market's normal trading volume could not absorb the quantity held by the government, where an order to clear out the government's position would affect the market price.

Level 2 Inputs

Level 2 inputs in the fair value hierarchy include the following:

- Quoted prices in active markets for similar assets or liabilities
- Quoted prices in less active markets for identical or similar assets or liabilities
- Observable inputs other than quoted prices, such as credit spreads, implied volatilities, and interest rate yield curves

It may be necessary to adjust a Level 2 input depending on issues specific to the asset or liability, such as its condition or location, and the activity level in the markets from which information has been obtained.

Level 3 Inputs

Level 3 inputs should be derived using the best information available, which may include data generated by the government itself. When deriving this information, a government does not need to go to great lengths to obtain information about market participant assumptions, but should take into account all information that is readily available. It may be necessary to include a risk adjustment if there is significant measurement uncertainty; this is the case in either of the following two situations:

- There has been a significant decline in the trading volume for the asset or liability, such as when there are few recent transactions, there is a wide bid-ask spread, or price quotations vary substantially among market makers. In this situation, it may be necessary to use multiple valuation techniques to derive a fair value. When a wide range of valuations result from these techniques, it may be necessary to conduct further analysis.
- The accountant believes that a transaction price or quoted price does not reflect actual fair value. For example, if a transaction does not appear to have been conducted in an orderly manner (such as on a rush basis), one should place little reliance on the use of that transaction price. A quoted price may be inaccurate when it is based on a reduced volume of transactions. The accountant can place more reliance on quoted prices that represent binding offers.

Measurement Principles

There may be cases in which an accounting standard requires that a non-financial asset be measured at its fair value. If so, the determination of fair value takes into account the ability of the asset holder to generate resources by utilizing the asset according to its highest and best use. The *highest and best use* is that use of a nonfinancial asset that would maximize the value of the asset. The employment of an asset is only considered to be its highest and best use when the employment is physically possible, financially feasible, and legally permissible.

EXAMPLE

Acorn City's accountant is trying to determine the fair value of a parcel of land. One consideration is to use it as the basis for a commercial operation. However, the current zoning laws do not allow commercial use of the land. Since commercial application is not legally permissible, this is not the highest and best use of the land parcel.

The highest and best use is employed when deriving the fair value of an asset, even when the asset is not currently used in that manner. However, the current use of an asset is presumed to *be* its highest and best use, unless other factors suggest that a different use would maximize its value.

The highest and best use of an asset may be obtained by selling the asset, in which case its valuation is based on its prospective sale price.

As was the case with assets, there may be instances in which an accounting standard requires that a liability be measured at its fair value. If so, an underlying assumption of the measurement is that the liability will be transferred to a third party at the measurement date. Since the liability is being transferred, the assumption is that it remains outstanding, and that the transferee will now fulfill the obligation.

There may not be an observable market for the transfer of liabilities. However, there may be an observable market for the *reverse*, where these items are being held by other parties as assets. If so, a government could use the perspective of the asset holder to derive a valuation that is based on the quoted price for an item held as an asset. It may be necessary to adjust this quoted price if there are factors specific to the asset that do not apply to the fair value measurement for the liability.

When measuring the fair value of a liability, take into account the effect of the government's credit standing and other concerns that might influence the probability that the obligation will not be fulfilled.

Disclosures

The following information should be disclosed for each type of asset or liability that is measured at fair value in the statement of net position after its initial recognition:

- The fair value measurement as of the end of the reporting period.

- The level of the fair value hierarchy from which information was derived to determine fair value.
- A description of the valuation techniques used.
- The description of any changes in the fair value techniques used, when the changes have had a significant impact on the result. Also note the reason for the change.

There may be cases in which fair value measurements are nonrecurring, where they are only required in specific situations. When there are nonrecurring fair value measurements, note the reasons for the measurements.

SAMPLE DISCLOSURE

The City classifies its fair value measurements within the fair value hierarchy, as established by generally accepted accounting principles. The hierarchy is based on the valuation inputs used to measure the fair value of an asset or liability. Level 1 inputs are quoted prices in active markets for identical assets. Level 2 inputs are significant other observable inputs, and Level 3 inputs are significant unobservable inputs.

The following fair value measurements were included in the City's statement of net position as of December 31, 20X2:

- U.S. Treasury securities of $37 million are valued using quoted market prices (which are Level 1 inputs).
- Corporate bonds of $6 million are valued using a matrix pricing model (which is a Level 2 input).

The City also has a nonrecurring fair value measurement as of the same date for a closed elementary school; there is no intent to use the school again, so it is considered to be impaired. Based on an appraisal of the property (which is a Level 3 input), the school has been written down from $4.2 million to $2.6 million.

Summary

The reporting of fair value inputs within the fair value hierarchy might seem like an excessively detailed amount of information for the readers of a government's financial statements. However, there is a point to the presentation – Level 1 inputs are considered much more reliable than Level 3 inputs, so a government reporting the bulk of its inputs as being Level 1 is much more likely to be fairly representing the value of its assets and liabilities. Conversely, a large proportion of Level 3 inputs may result in fair values that are considerably more suspect.

Chapter 19
Claims Accounting

Introduction

A government may engage in risk management activities in order to minimize its risk of loss in certain areas. These activities can include any actions taken in advance to minimize the risk of losses ever occurring, as well as the use of risk transfers to an insurer, which will compensate the government after-the-fact for any losses incurred. It is also possible that a government may choose to retain risk, so that it incurs monetary losses when adverse events occur. Another option is to participate in a public entity risk pool, where payments are made by multiple governments into a central pool, from which claims are reimbursed. In this chapter, we cover the accounting for claim recognition, risk financing activities, public entity risk pools, contingencies, and several related topics.

Risk Transfers

When accounting for claims made for loss reimbursement, a key point is whether risk has actually been transferred to the party that is receiving the claim. Risk is typically transferred when the insuring party is entitled to a payment from the applicable government that is independent of the amount of claims subsequently made. Thus, if a premium is paid and a lesser amount of claims is later sent to the insurer, the insurer is not obligated to repay any of the premium to the government. Or, in the reverse situation, if the claims amount turns out to be higher than the premium, the government is not obligated to send any additional payments to the insurer.

When the situation indicates that a risk transfer has not taken place, it is more likely that the "insurer" is really a claims processor that handles the administration of claims.

Claim Recognition

When a government has not transferred risk to a third party and a loss occurs, it should report an estimated loss from the claim as a liability and an expenditure or expense, but only if the following two conditions apply:

- It is probable that an asset has been impaired or a liability incurred; and
- It is reasonably possible to estimate the amount of the loss.

When the prospective loss falls within a range of possible amounts, accrue a loss for the best estimate within the range. If there is no best estimate, accrue a loss for the minimum amount in the range.

It is possible that an incident will occur prior to the balance sheet date, but a claim is not reported to the insurer by the balance sheet date. This situation can arise not only for a known incident for which a claim will later be presented, but also for unknown incidents that will trigger claims, as well as expected future changes to claims already made. When this type of claim can be reasonably estimated and it is probable that a claim will be made, recognize an associated liability and expenditure or expense.

The amount to be recorded for a claim should be derived from the estimated ultimate cost of settling the claim. To derive the estimated ultimate cost, it may be necessary to apply past experience, adjusted for any other factors that would modify past experience. Any incremental costs associated with a claim, such as outside legal advice, should be included in the determination of the cost of a claim.

Discounting

A government may have entered into a structured settlement, where a claim liability is settled by contracting with a third party to pay out a stream of future payments. If so, the government should record the liability at its discounted present value, rather than at the total amount of the payment. When calculating a present value for these payments, apply a discount rate that has been derived based on the government's investment yield rate, as well as the discount rate at which such a liability can be sold.

Annuity Contracts

A government may buy an annuity contract in the name of a claimant, so that payments are made to the claimant at periodic intervals for a period of time. If the need to make additional payments beyond the cost of this contract is remote, then the government can consider itself to have settled the liability. In this case, there is no need to report the annuity contract and the related liability in the entity's government-wide and proprietary fund financial statements.

If the determination is made at a later date that the primary liability will revert back to the government, the liability must be added back to the government's financial statements.

Risk Financing Activities in an Internal Service Fund

A government may shift its risk financing activities to an internal service fund. If so, the internal service fund recognizes claims expenses and liabilities in the normal manner. These amounts may be reduced by any amounts expected to be recovered via excess insurance (where the insurer provides insurance in excess of a certain loss amount).

EXAMPLE

Acorn City is part of a regional risk pool, where 100+ municipalities contribute funds to the pool and will be paid back a maximum of $3 million per claim if they incur certain types of losses. In addition, Acorn purchases excess insurance to compensate it if a claim exceeds $3 million. Acorn experiences a $3.2 million claim, so it receives $3 million from the pool and $200,000 from the insurer. The $200,000 receipt is considered excess insurance.

The designated internal service fund can charge its costs to other funds within the government using any allocation basis. The charges made are recorded by the internal service fund as revenue, and as expenditures or expenses by the receiving funds. A deficit in the internal service fund can be charged back to the other funds over a reasonable period of time. If this deficit is not charged back within a reasonable time period, it should be charged back to the other funds and reported by them as an expenditure or expense.

If the internal service fund charges an excess amount to the other funds, report the excess as an internal transfer.

Participation in Public Entity Risk Pools

A government may participate in a risk-sharing pool, where risks are shared among the group. If so, contributions made to the pool should be classified as an insurance expenditure or expense in its government-wide and fund financial statements. If the pool agreement can require participants to pay additional amounts, the government should periodically assess whether such additional payments are probable and can be reasonably estimated; if so, report an additional expenditure/expense and associated liability for the expected additional payment.

A pool agreement may not allow for additional member assessments. If so, monitor the pool to see if it reports an operational deficit. If so, and it appears that the pool will not be able to meet its obligations, consider the probability that the government will need to pay its own obligations following the failure of the pool. This may require the accountant to report an additional expenditure/expense and associated liability for the expected additional payment.

When governments join together to form a public entity risk pool, they may be required to make capitalization contributions to the pool in order to meet statutory capitalization minimums. This capitalization contribution should be classified as a deposit, but only if it is probable that the contribution will be returned when the pool is dissolved or the government withdraws from the pool. This deposit is classified as a non-spendable fund balance. If it is not probable that the deposit will be returned, then it is initially reported as prepaid insurance and recognized as expense over the periods for which the pool is expected to provide coverage. If the duration is not readily determinable, then charge the deposit to expense over a period of not more than 10 years. If the contribution is being reported in a governmental fund, an option is to recognize the entire amount as an expenditure in the period of the contribution.

Insurance Transactions

In this section, we address the accounting for claims-made policies, retrospectively-rated policies, and policyholder dividends.

Claims-Made Policies

A government may enter into a claims-made policy, which covers losses from claims filed against the policy holder during the policy period, no matter when the triggering event actually occurred. This type of policy does not transfer any risk associated with claims not filed during the policy period, so the government must account for any of these other claims as noted previously in the Claim Recognition section.

Retrospectively-Rated Policies

A government may enter into a retrospectively-rated policy, where the total premium paid is based largely on the entity's loss experience. The minimum amount of these premiums should be accounted for through the coverage period as an expenditure or expense. In addition, accrue estimated losses from reported and unreported claims that exceed the amount of the minimum premium. This accrual is capped at the maximum premium that can be paid.

Policyholder Dividends

If a government receives a dividend as an insurance policy holder or as a participant in an insurance pool, recognize the dividend as a reduction of expenditure or expense. This recognition should occur as soon as the dividend is declared.

Contractual Actions

A government may be subject to a variety of claims arising from contractual arrangements, ranging from claims for contract delays to nonpayment of contractually committed amounts. For these types of claims, a government should recognize a loss liability when it is probable that an asset has been impaired or a liability incurred, and the amount of the loss can be reasonably estimated.

Contingencies

A contingency is an existing condition or situation that involves some degree of uncertainty in regard to a possible gain or loss, with resolution based on a future event. The accounting treatment discussed in this section relates to specific types of loss contingencies, which are as follows:

- The collectability of receivables
- Guarantees of the indebtedness of other parties in an exchange transaction
- Receivable repurchase agreements

- Claims related to contractual delays or inadequate specifications

When there is a risk of loss, it should be classified along a continuum that ranges from probable to remote. These classifications are:

- *Probable*. The event is likely to occur.
- *Reasonably possible*. The event is more than remote but less than likely.
- *Remote*. There is no more than a slight chance that the event will occur.

A loss contingency should be accrued if both of the following are true:

- The amount of the loss can be reasonably estimated.
- It is probable that an asset has been impaired or a liability incurred as of the financial statements date. At this point, it should be probable that a future event will occur that confirms the fact of the loss.

When the prospective loss falls within a range of possible amounts, accrue a loss for the best estimate within the range. If there is no best estimate, accrue a loss for the minimum amount in the range.

EXAMPLE

Qanix City invests $500,000 of excess funds in the common stock of a major consumer electronics company, which later unexpectedly declares bankruptcy. There is no longer a quoted price for the common stock, though a reasonable estimate of loss is in the range of $320,000 to $480,000. There is no amount within that range that appears to be a better estimate of loss than the other stated amounts. Consequently, Qanix records a loss contingency of $320,000, matching the minimum amount in the range of possible losses.

Presentation Issues

Claims expenses are treated as direct expenses, in that they are directly associated with a service, program, or department. If a claim is instead classified as an extraordinary item (quite a rare event), report it separately at the bottom of the statement of activities.

Disclosures

If applicable, a government should disclose the following information in the notes to its financial statements:

- *Risk exposure*. Describe the government's exposure to risks of loss and how these risks are handled.
- *Insurance reductions*. Note any significant reductions in insurance coverage from the prior year by major risk categories. Also point out whether the

settlements amount was greater than the insurance coverage in each of the last three years.

- *Risk pools.* If the government participates in a risk pool, describe the nature of its participation, including the rights and responsibilities of both sides.
- *Risk retention.* If a government retains the risk of loss, provide the following information:
  - o The basis for estimating its unpaid claims liability.
  - o The carrying amount of liabilities for unpaid claims that are stated at their present value, as well as the range of discount rates used.
  - o The total amount of claims liabilities for which annuities have been purchased on behalf of the claimants, and for which the related liabilities are no longer reported.
  - o A reconciliation of the changes in claims liabilities for the current and prior fiscal years, using a tabular format. The table should include the amount of beginning claims liability, claims incurred during the year, claims payments, other transactions, and the amount of ending claims liability.

The following disclosures may be required, based on the occurrence of risk-related events:

- *Unrecorded claims.* It is possible that a government will not record a liability for a claim, perhaps because it is not probable that a liability has been incurred or because it is not possible to estimate the amount of the claim. If it is at least reasonably possible that a loss has been incurred, disclose the nature of the contingency in the accompanying footnotes, along with an estimate of the possible loss or the range within which the loss is situated. Alternatively, state that an estimate cannot be made. It is not necessary to make a disclosure regarding an unreported claim if:
  - o There has been no indication of a potential claimant; unless
  - o It is probable that a claim will be asserted; and
  - o There is a reasonable possibility of an unfavorable outcome.

- *Annuity contracts.* A government may have settled a claim by acquiring an annuity contract in the name of the claimant. If so, and the annuity and associated liability are no longer stated on the entity's financial statements, the aggregate outstanding amount should still be disclosed until such time as the liability is settled.
- *Deficit fund balance.* If an internal service fund accounts for the risk financing activities of a government and the fund has a deficit balance, disclose this balance.
- *Contingencies – probable.* If a loss contingency has been recorded, note the nature of the contingency and the amount accrued.
- *Contingencies – reasonably possible.* If there is at least a reasonable possibility of loss in excess of the amount accrued, note the additional

exposure to loss. If no accrual was made for a loss contingency, disclose the existence of the contingency as long as there is at least a reasonable possibility of loss, indicating the nature of the contingency and showing the range of the potential loss (or state that such an estimate cannot be made).

- *Contingencies – remote*. It may still be necessary to disclose a contingency even when the possibility of loss is remote. This situation usually arises when there is a guarantee in an exchange transaction, such as a guarantee of the indebtedness of another party or a guarantee to repurchase receivables that have been sold. The disclosure should describe the nature and amount of the guarantee.

SAMPLE DISCLOSURE

The City has exposure to a number of risks of loss related to torts, damage to its assets, errors and omissions, natural disasters, and injuries to its employees. During the fiscal year 20X1, the City established a risk management fund (the Fund) to account for and finance those of its risks that are uninsured. Under the terms of this program, the Fund provides coverage for up to $200,000 for each workers' compensation claim, $100,000 for each general liability claim, and $25,000 for each property damage claim. The City purchases commercial insurance for claims exceeding the coverage provided by the Fund, as well as for all other types of risk. Settled claims have not exceeded this commercial coverage in any of the past three years.

All of the City's funds participate in the risk management program and make payments to the Fund based on actuarial estimates of the amounts needed to pay prior and current year claims, as well as to build a reserve for catastrophic losses. The amount of this reserve was $215,000 as of year-end.

The City purchases annuity contracts from commercial insurers in order to satisfy certain liabilities; accordingly, no liability is reported for those claims. As of year-end, $92,000 of those covered claims were still outstanding.

Changes in the claims liability amount in 20X1 and 20X2 are noted in the following table.

Fiscal Year	Beginning Liability	Current Year Claims and Changes in Estimates	Claim Payments	Balance at Year-End
20X1	$772,000	$141,000	$109,000	$804,000
20X2	804,000	98,000	113,000	789,000

Summary

Governments routinely deal with claims of various kinds, especially larger entities that have many employees and engage in a broad range of activities. Given the relatively high volume and significant amount of these claims, the accountant should routinely update his or her knowledge of the probability and amount of claims – otherwise, there is a risk that the financial statements will be incorrect to a material extent. It is also necessary to periodically update the disclosures related to contingencies that are classified as reasonably possible or remote, so that financial statement readers are made aware of possible losses that may later appear in the basic financial statements if they are reclassified as probable.

Chapter 20
Landfill Closure and Postclosure Costs

Introduction

Many government entities must deal with the costs of landfills that are being closed or which have already been closed. In the accounting standards, these landfills are classified as municipal solid waste landfill (MSWLF). An MSWLF is considered to be an area of land that receives household waste. In this chapter, we cover the accounting requirements related to MSWLF operations.

Operating Methods

When a landfill is in operation, usually only a portion of the landfill, known as a "cell," is used at one time. Waste containment and monitoring systems are installed before a cell is ready for use. Final cover is applied to a cell once it has been filled. If a landfill operates as a single large cell, then final cover may not be applied until the entire landfill stops accepting additional waste.

Note: *Final cover* is a multi-layered system of materials that is used to reduce the amount of storm water that will enter a landfill after closing.

Estimated Total Current Cost of MSWLF Closure and Postclosure Care

The owner of a MSWLF must incur several types of costs to protect the environment from the landfill, both during its operation and the postclosure period. These costs include:

- Cost of equipment and facilities, such as the leachate collection systems and final cover
- Cost of services, such as postclosure maintenance and monitoring costs

Note: *Leachate* is the liquid that drains from a landfill.

A government that is planning to close a landfill will need to separately classify some of these costs as the estimated total current cost of MSWLF closure and postclosure care. These costs result in disbursement close to or after the date when a MSWLF stops accepting solid waste. In general, this classification includes costs irrespective of whether they are capital or operating in nature. In more detail, the costs to be classified in this manner are as follows:

- *Equipment and facilities.* Includes the cost of all equipment and facilities that will be installed or constructed near or following the date when the MSWLF stops accepting solid waste, as well as during the postclosure period. These items should be limited to just those that will be used exclusively by the MSWLF. Examples of these items are:
  - Gas monitoring and collection systems
  - Ground water monitoring wells
  - Leachate treatment facilities
  - Storm water management systems
- *Final cover.* Includes the cost of final cover expected to be applied to the MSWLF once it stops accepting solid waste.
- *Monitoring and maintenance.* Includes the cost required to monitor and maintain the expected usable landfill area through the postclosure period. Examples of these costs are:
  - Environmental hazard containment
  - Equipment repair and replacement
  - Final cover maintenance
  - Groundwater monitoring
  - Leachate collection and treatment
  - Methane monitoring and collection

> **Note:** The *expected usable landfill area* is the area within a landfill that is expected to receive solid waste during the operating life of the landfill. This area is estimated based on environmental factors that may call for the early closure of the landfill, permit periods, and the probability of permit renewals.

When equipment or facilities are shared by several MSWLFs, their costs are assigned to each one based on the percentage of usage.

When deriving the estimated total current cost of MSWLF closure and postclosure care, do so based on those applicable laws that have been approved as of the balance sheet date, even if their effective date is at some point later in the future.

EXAMPLE

Acorn City plans to construct a small power generation facility adjacent to one of its landfill operations, with the intent of generating electricity from the methane gas naturally occurring in the landfill. This facility is not a required part of landfill closure and postclosure care, and so should not be included in the landfill liability. Instead, it should be accounted for separately as a capital asset.

Reevaluations

The estimated current cost of MSWLF closure and postclosure care should be reevaluated each year, with adjustments for inflationary effects. Also adjust the current cost under the following circumstances:

- There are changes in the closure or postclosure care plan.
- Landfill operating conditions alter estimated costs. Here are several circumstances that can impact estimated costs:
  - Changes in legal or regulatory requirements
  - Changes in technology
  - Changes in the expected usable landfill area
  - Price changes that vary from the general inflation rate
  - The types of equipment and facilities expected to be used

Proprietary Fund Reporting

A MSWLF may be reported in the financial statements of a proprietary fund. If so, a portion of its estimated total current cost closure and postclosure care should be recognized in each period. This recognition takes the form of an expense and a liability within each period for which the MSWLF is accepting solid waste. This recognition should begin as soon as the MSWLF begins accepting solid waste, and should continue through all subsequent operating periods, to be completed when it no longer accepts solid waste. This cost should be apportioned to each period based on usage, such as in cubic yards. Apportionment based on the passage of time is not acceptable. Thus, the following formula should be used to calculate the apportionment of costs:

$$\frac{\text{Estimated total current cost} \times \text{Cumulative capacity used}}{\text{Total estimated capacity}} - \text{Amount previously recognized}$$

EXAMPLE

Sunflower City operates a municipal landfill. Thus far, 1.2 million cubic yards of the landfill have been used out of the 4 million total cubic yards within the landfill area. The following total current cost of closure and postclosure care is estimated for the facility:

Maintenance of leachate treatment facility	$400,000
Expected renewal of storm water control facilities	920,000
Monitoring well replacements	25,000
Maintenance of final cover	680,000
Groundwater and gas monitoring	480,000
Off-site leachate treatment	1,100,000
Total	$3,605,000

Sunflower's to-date expense for closure and postclosure care is calculated as follows:

$$\frac{\$3,605,000 \text{ Estimated total current cost} \times 1,200,000 \text{ Cumulative capacity used}}{4,000,000 \text{ Total estimated capacity}}$$

$$= \$1,081,500 \text{ to-date closure and postclosure care expense}$$

When equipment and facilities are included in the estimated total current cost of closure and postclosure care, they should not also be reported as capital assets. All equipment, facilities, services, and final cover that have been included in the estimated total current cost should, when they are acquired, be reported as a subtraction from the accrued liability for MSWLF closure and postclosure care.

Capital assets should be fully depreciated by the time a MSWLF stops accepting solid waste, under the following conditions:

- The assets are used exclusively for the MSWLF; and
- The assets are excluded from the calculation of the estimated total current cost of closure and postclosure care.

When a capital asset is associated with a single cell, its depreciation period should be the same as the estimated useful life of the associated cell. When a capital asset is used by several MSWLFs, the cost assigned to each MSWLF should be depreciated through the date when each one no longer accepts solid waste.

Governmental Fund Reporting

A MSWLF may be reported in the financial statements of a governmental fund. If so, the measurement of the liability is the same as was just described for a proprietary fund. The basis of accounting used in this case is the modified accrual basis, so the following additional accounting and presentation actions apply:

- A governmental fund liability and expenditure should be recognized as payments come due in each period as goods are used and services are received.
- The long-term liability for landfill closure and postclosure care costs does not trigger an outflow of current financial resources, and so does not result in the recognition of any additional fund liability or expenditure, though the liability is reported in the governmental activities column in the government-wide statement of net position.
- Report equipment and facilities acquisitions that have been included in the estimated total current cost as closure and postclosure care expenditures in the statement of revenues, expenditures, and changes in fund balances.

Government-Wide Financial Statement Reporting

The same reporting previously noted for proprietary funds also applies to government-wide financial statements. This reporting applies to assets, deferred outflows of resources, liabilities, deferred inflows of resources, revenues, and expenses.

Changes in Estimates

When there is a change in the estimated total current cost of closure and postclosure care, the change is reported at once, in the period of change. An exception to this rule is when the change in estimate applies to the horizontal expansion of the waste boundaries of an existing MSWLF; in this case, the change is only to the capacity of the landfill, so the change is recognized as the new capacity is used.

A change in the estimated total current cost may arise after the date on which a landfill no longer accepts solid waste. These changes should be reported as soon as the change is probable and can be reasonably estimated.

Assets Placed in Trust

The owners or operators of a MSWLF may be called upon to place assets with a trustee, in order to provide financial assurance about their ability to operate the landfill. Any amounts held in trust should be reported in the fund where the landfill operations are reported, as "amounts held by trustee." If there are any investment earnings on these amounts held in trust, report them as revenue and not as reductions in the estimated total current cost and associated accrued liability.

Responsibility Assumed by a Different Entity

The operator or owner of a MSWLF may transfer some portion (or all) of its closure and postclosure care responsibility to a third party. If it appears that the assuming entity will not be able to meet its obligations and it is probable that the original operator or owner will be forced to pay closure and postclosure care costs, then this obligation should still be reported, as specified earlier in this chapter.

Disclosures

If a government is subject to landfill closure and postclosure care requirements, it should disclose the following information in the notes to its financial statements:

- *Requirements*. State the nature and source of the requirements, referring to specific laws or regulations.
- *Basis of recognition*. Note that the liability for closure and postclosure care costs is based on the amount of landfill capacity used to date.

- *Liability and remaining cost recognition.* Report the liability associated with the closure and postclosure care costs, as well as the estimated total current cost of closure and postclosure care that has not yet been recognized.
- *Capacity usage.* Note the percentage of landfill capacity that has been used to date, as well as the estimated landfill life that remains (in years).
- *Financial assurance.* State how any financial assurance requirements associated with the closure and postclosure care costs are being met. Further, describe any assets that have been restricted for the payment of closure and postclosure care costs, if this information is not readily apparent in the financial statements.
- *Change issues.* Describe the nature of the estimates made and the possibility for further changes due to inflation or deflation, laws and regulations, or technology.

SAMPLE DISCLOSURE

State laws and regulations require the City to place a final cover on its Stony Lane landfill site when it stops accepting waste, as well as to perform certain maintenance and monitoring functions at the site for 25 years following its closure. Even though closure and postclosure care costs will be paid near or after the landfill closure date, the City reports a portion of these costs as an operating expense in each period, based on the proportion of landfill capacity used in each successive period. The $1.1 million reported as landfill closure and postclosure care liability at December 31, 20X2 represents the cumulative amount reported to date based on the use of 30% of the estimated capacity of the landfill. The City will recognize the remainder of the estimated cost of $2.5 million as the remaining estimated capacity is filled. The City expects to close the landfill in the year 20X9. The actual cost incurred may be higher due to inflation, changes in regulations, or changes in technology.

The City is required by state laws and regulations to make annual contributions to a trust, to be used to finance landfill closure and postclosure care. The city is in compliance with these requirements, and has so far shifted $3.0 million into the trust. These funds are reported as restricted on the statement of net position. The City expects that the additional cost of inflation will be paid from the interest earned on these funds. If interest earnings prove to be inadequate or additional postclosure care is required, these costs may need to be paid through charges to future landfill users or from additional tax revenue.

Summary

The costs of landfill closure and postclosure care can be quite significant – to the point where an error in the accounting for them can represent a material error in a government's financial statements. Consequently, it is worthwhile to create a detailed timetable and procedure for the ongoing examination and updating of these costs, preferably before the financial statement closing process begins. By updating landfill cost information in a slower part of the accounting work schedule, the accountant will have more time available for a thorough examination of the calculation, underlying assumptions, and changes in costs.

Chapter 21
Nonexchange Transactions

Introduction

A large part of the revenue generated by a government is likely to come from nonexchange transactions. In this chapter, we describe the different types of these transactions and note the proper accounting for each one, along with several related topics.

Overview of Nonexchange Transactions

In a nonexchange transaction, a government either gives value without receiving an equal value in exchange, or the reverse occurs – the government receives value without giving an equal amount of value in exchange. Nonexchange transactions fall into four categories, which are as follows:

- *Derived tax revenues.* These are assessments imposed by a government on an exchange transaction. For example, a government can impose taxes on retail sales, corporate income, and personal income. In all cases, the government is imposing on the entity that acquires income, goods, or services, and does so when there is an exchange transaction.
- *Imposed nonexchange revenues.* These are assessments imposed by a government on nonexchange transactions. For example, a government can impose taxes on property, levy fines, and seize assets. In these cases, the government is acting based on an action committed (such as property ownership) or omitted (such as breaking the speed limit) by the payer.
- *Government-mandated nonexchange transactions.* These are situations in which a government at one level provides resources to a government at another level, stipulating that the resources be used for a specific purpose. For example, a state government could provide funds to municipal governments as long as the funds are used for road repairs.
- *Voluntary nonexchange transactions.* These are legislative or contractual agreements between parties, such as grants and donations. Both parties may be governments, or one may be some other entity. There may be restrictions on the use of the resources provided. These transactions are not imposed on the recipient, and eligibility requirements must be fulfilled.

Note: An *exchange transaction* occurs when there is a reciprocal transfer between two parties that results in one of them acquiring assets or services or settling obligations by surrendering other assets or services or incurring other obligations.

EXAMPLE

A state government imposes a 4% tax on the sale of goods by retailers. The tax is based on the net sale amount and is collected by retailers from their customers at the point of sale. Most retailers are required to submit their sales tax receipts to the state government on a monthly basis, though low-volume retailers can do so on a quarterly or annual basis. This situation is an example of derived tax revenues.

EXAMPLE

Qanix City adopts a property tax levy ordinance that links the taxes to the City's appropriation ordinances for its 20X2 fiscal year. The City has an enforceable claim on the taxes as of the assessment date, which is defined by statute as the first day of the fiscal year to which the appropriation ordinance applies. This situation is an example of imposed nonexchange revenues.

EXAMPLE

A developer has completed an industrial park. As required by city law, the developer contributes the park's infrastructure to the city. The amount of this contribution is based on the assessed value of the developed property, which the city recognizes as revenue when the infrastructure is substantially complete. This situation is an example of imposed nonexchange revenues.

EXAMPLE

A state government's department of education reimburses school districts for certain costs related to the safety features of school buildings, which is capped at a certain amount per school and school district per year. To obtain reimbursement from the department of education, each school district submits an annual expenditure report to the government. This situation is an example of a government-mandated nonexchange transaction.

EXAMPLE

A wealthy benefactor offers money to a local trade school that must be used for scholarships to needy applicants. Any residual (unused) amount left at the end of the year is to be returned to the benefactor. This situation is an example of a voluntary nonexchange transaction.

The accounting for nonexchange transactions depends upon the category within which they are classified, based on their characteristics. It can be misleading to place a transaction within one of these categories just based on its title, when its detailed characteristics indicate that a different treatment might be more accurate.

EXAMPLE

Mole Industries pays $500,000 to the mechanical engineering department of a public university, labeling the payment as a grant to be directed at tunneling devices. However, the details of the transaction indicate that Mole will receive a 50% split of all royalties generated by the resulting research. Despite the misleading title of the payment, this transaction is actually an exchange transaction, since there is a reciprocal transfer of benefits between the parties.

Accounting for Nonexchange Transactions

Governments must recognize nonexchange transactions in their financial statements, unless the related amounts cannot be reasonably estimated or collection is not probable. The accounting for these transactions varies by the type of nonexchange transaction, as noted in the following sub-sections.

Requirements and Restrictions

A provider of resources or enabling legislation may mandate that resources provided in a nonexchange transaction be used within a certain date range and/or used for a specific purpose. For example:

- Granted funds must be used within the current fiscal year
- Granted funds cannot be used until after the current fiscal year
- Granted funds must be used within the next three years
- Granted funds must be spent on low-income housing
- Granted funds must be held for investment, with only the resulting interest subject to expenditure

A *time requirement* specifies when resources can be used or when usage may begin. Time requirements impact when nonexchange transactions can be recognized. The proper accounting treatment depends on the type of nonexchange transaction, and so is addressed in several of the following sub-sections that deal with each of the transaction types.

A *purpose restriction* specifies the purposes for which resources are to be used. These restrictions do not impact the timing of recognition for any type of nonexchange transaction. Instead, these resources are classified as a restricted net position until they have been used as intended.

Reimbursements

A grant program may be based on expenditures, where the recipient cannot qualify for payment until having first incurring costs. This requirement is considered an *eligibility requirement*, which impacts the recognition timing. In essence, the resource provider has no liability and the recipient has no receivable until costs are incurred.

Derived Tax Revenues

When a government is gaining assets from derived tax revenues (which are taxes imposed on an exchange transaction), the assets are recognized in the earlier of the period when the underlying exchange transaction occurs or when the resources are received.

Revenues should be recognized in the same period as the related assets, though the amount of revenue recognized should be net of estimated refunds and uncollectible amounts. Also, revenues should only be recognized once the underlying exchange transaction has occurred – not in advance of it. If resources are received in advance of the exchange transaction, then they are reported as liabilities. Once the exchange transaction has occurred, the liability is reversed and revenue is recognized instead.

Imposed Nonexchange Revenues

When a government is gaining assets from imposed nonexchange revenues (such as property taxes and fines), the assets are recognized in the earlier of the period in which there is an enforceable legal claim to the assets or when the resources are received. The date of the enforceable claim for property taxes is stated in the enabling legislation.

Revenues should be recognized in the period for which the taxes are levied, net of estimated refunds and uncollectible amounts. For any other type of imposed nonexchange revenues, revenue recognition occurs in the same period in which the related assets are recognized, unless there are time requirements in the enabling legislation. If there are time requirements, recognize revenues in the period when the resources must be used or when use can begin.

In cases where imposed nonexchange revenue transactions are received prior to the period for which property taxes are levied or before there is a time requirement for usage, report the transactions as deferred inflows of resources.

Undisputed fines are recognized at the earlier of the payment date or when the statutory time allowed for dispute lapses. Disputed fines are recognized when there is a ruling that the fine is valid, though the recognition should be netted against an allowance for estimated refunds linked to rulings that are overturned on appeal.

Government-Mandated and Voluntary Nonexchange Transactions

When one government is providing resources to a government at a different level, it is quite common for eligibility requirements to be inserted into the grants. Until these requirements are met, the provider does not incur a liability and the recipient cannot recognize a receivable. This situation also arises for voluntary nonexchange transactions, where there is a grant or donation.

The types of eligibility requirements that can apply to these transactions may include any of the following:

- The recipient must have certain characteristics, such as being a school district.
- A time requirement must be met, within which or after the resources must be used.
- Costs have been incurred that the provider will then reimburse.

Another eligibility requirement that only applies to voluntary nonexchange transactions is when resources are only made available after the recipient has engaged in a specific action. For example, a grant is only issued after the recipient has raised a certain amount of matching funds.

EXAMPLE

Pensive Corporation has a policy of matching all employee gifts made to qualifying nonprofits and educational institutions. An employee makes a $1,000 gift to a nearby state university, and sends the matching gift form to the university. This situation is a voluntary nonexchange transaction, where the action requirement – sending in a gift – is the first action taken. The university recognizes $1,000 of cash and a $1,000 receivable from Pensive Corporation. $2,000 of revenue can be recognized as soon as the employee gift is received, since this is the qualifying event; submitting the matching gift form to Pensive is not considered an eligibility requirement.

When all necessary eligibility requirements have been met by a recipient, the provider of resources should recognize a liability and expense, while the recipient recognizes a receivable and revenue, net of any estimated uncollectible amounts. If resources were sent by the provider before the eligibility requirements were met, the provider continues to record them as assets, while the recipient records them as a liability.

When resources have been received or recognized as a receivable after meeting all eligibility requirements except the time requirement, the provider reports them as a deferred outflow of resources, while the recipient reports them as a deferred inflow of resources.

There may be cases where a provider issues resources with a stipulation that the resources cannot be sold or consumed for an extended period of time (if ever). For example, a permanent endowment is sent to the recipient. In this situation, the recipient can recognize revenue at the point of receipt, as long as it has met all eligibility requirements.

EXAMPLE

A wealthy alumnus gives a state university $2 million with the stipulation that the funds be used to establish an endowment that is kept intact in perpetuity. The investment income from the endowment is to be used to maintain the university's science building. The stipulation that the principal be maintained intact is a time restriction, which is being met as soon as the university receives the funds. The university should recognize assets and revenue when the gift is received.

Donations of Capital Assets

An outside party may donate a capital asset to a government, to be held for use in general government operations. Since the measurement focus of a governmental fund is on its current financial resources, no record is made in the governmental fund of any revenue or an asset. However, if the donated capital asset is held for sale, it is recorded at its acquisition value, which is set at the donation date. This change in accounting treatment occurs because the capital asset will be converted into cash through a sale transaction when the asset is sold to a third party.

Subsequent Breaching of Eligibility Requirements

A recipient of resources may initially meet all eligibility requirements, but later falls out of compliance. When this breach occurs, if it is probable that the resources will no longer be issued or must be returned, the recipient should record a decrease in its assets and an associated expense, while the provider recognizes an increase in its assets and revenue in the amount that is expected to be reclaimed.

Nonexchange Revenues Administered by another Government

A government may collect nonexchange revenues on behalf of another government. A common example is when a state government collects all forms of sales taxes from businesses and then remits the receipts to the applicable city and county governments. In this case, the receiving government should be able to estimate and accrue for the receipts that it will collect from the disbursing government.

There may also be cases where one government decides to share its own receipts with another government. For example, a state government may collect a gasoline tax and then choose to disburse a portion of it to local governments. These resource allocations are usually relatively predictable, since they are triggered by a continuing appropriation. If so, the receiving government should be able to estimate and accrue for the resources that it will eventually collect.

Revenue Recognition in Governmental Fund Statements

As noted earlier in the Basis of Accounting and Measurement Focus chapter, governmental fund financial statements use the modified accrual basis of accounting. When this basis is used, the revenues associated with nonexchange transactions should be recognized in the following manner:

Type of Nonexchange Transaction	Recipient Accounting Treatment
Derived tax revenues	Recognize revenue when the exchange transaction has occurred and the resources are available.
Imposed nonexchange revenues for property taxes	Recognize revenue in the fiscal period for which it was levied, as long as it has been collected or will be collected soon enough to pay liabilities in the current period.
Imposed nonexchange revenues other than property taxes	Recognize revenue when an enforceable claim has arisen and the resources are available.
Government-mandated nonexchange transactions and voluntary nonexchange transactions	Recognize revenue when all eligibility requirements have been met and the resources are available.

Pass-Through Grants

A government may receive a grant that is to be sent to or spent on behalf of another party. This type of grant is called a *pass-through grant*. A cash pass-through grant should be reported by a government as revenue and expenditure or expense in the funds of the primary government and in the government-wide financial statements. This treatment is appropriate if the government has some administrative or financial involvement in the program. Administrative involvement may involve monitoring the ultimate recipient for compliance with program requirements, determining the eligibility of recipients, or having some discretion in how funds are allocated. When there is no administrative or financial involvement, the pass-through grant is instead reported in an agency fund.

On-Behalf Payments

A government may make payments to a third-party recipient for the employees of an employer entity. These on-behalf payments may involve fringe benefits and compensation, including pension plan contributions, health insurance premiums, and stipends. For example, a county government pays into a pension plan for the volunteer firefighters employed within its boundaries.

The employer government should recognize both revenue and expenditures or expenses for these on-behalf payments for fringe benefits and compensation. The accounting varies based on the situation, but the general concept is to recognize revenue for the amounts received by the third-party recipients, and which are receivable by the end of the current fiscal year.

On-behalf payments may be made into a multi-employer defined benefit pension plan. If so, the payments should be allocated among the covered employers based upon a consistently-applied and rational allocation method, based on the ratio of an employer's covered payroll to the total covered payroll.

The employer government does not have to allocate on-behalf payments to any of its funds. If the decision is made to engage in such an allocation, it can be based on the related salaries and wages charged to those funds. Conversely, if only a single fund is used to report on-behalf payments, that fund is usually the general fund.

Disclosures

The few financial statement disclosures associated with nonexchange transactions are as follows:

- *Non-recognition.* When a nonexchange transaction is not recognized in the financial statements, it should still be disclosed in the accompanying notes.
- *On-behalf payments.* The amounts recognized for on-behalf payments for fringe benefits and compensation should be disclosed. If on-behalf payments are being contributed to a pension plan for which the employer government is not legally responsible, disclose the name of the plan and the name of the contributing entity.

Summary

A government entity may recognize revenue from a broad array of sources, each with its own unique accounting. When there are many accounting options, there is a good chance that the accounting staff will be at risk of applying an incorrect accounting treatment to a transaction. To reduce this risk, consider having each of the accounting staff specialize in just one or two nonexchange transactions, and funneling the appropriate transactions to each of them for processing. Another option is to design a separate procedure for each nonexchange transaction and conduct ongoing staff training based on each of these procedures, so that they can more readily recognize and deal with each transaction type.

Glossary

A

Accountability. The obligation of an individual to accept responsibility for actions taken and to disclose the results in a transparent manner.

Accounting change. A change in principle, estimate, or reporting entity.

Accrual basis of accounting. The occurrence of a business event triggers the recognition of most transactions, irrespective of the underlying movement of cash.

Acquisition value. The price that an entity would have paid to acquire an asset having similar service potential in an orderly market transaction at the acquisition date.

Appropriated budget. A budget that has been created by an appropriation bill and signed into law.

Assets. Resources controlled by a government.

B

Blending. When the balances and transactions of a component unit are reported in a manner similar to the balances and transactions of a primary government.

Budget. A financial plan that covers a specific period of time.

Budgetary accounting. A control technique that involves the initial inclusion of budgetary accounts in fund ledgers in order to provide better control over expenditures.

C

Capital asset. A higher-cost tangible or intangible item that is used in operations and which is expected to have a useful life longer than one reporting period.

Capitalization rate. The interest rate at which debt related to a capital asset acquisition is capitalized.

Capitalization threshold. An expenditure level below which expenditures are classified as expenses, rather than capital assets.

Cash basis of accounting. The receipt of cash triggers the recognition of revenue and expenses, while the disbursement of cash triggers the recognition of expenditures, expenses, and transfers out.

Cash equivalent. A short-term, highly liquid investment that is readily convertible into known amounts of cash, and which is so near its maturity that it presents an insignificant risk of changes in value due to changes in interest rates.

Component unit. A legally separate entity for which the elected officials of a primary government are financially accountable.

Composite depreciation. Any depreciation method that is applied to a group of assets.

Comprehensive annual financial report. A comprehensive reporting package issued by a government at the end of its fiscal year.

Construction in progress. Those costs accumulated to date against an unfinished construction project.

Contingency. An existing condition or situation that involves some degree of uncertainty in regard to a possible gain or loss, with resolution based on a future event.

Coverage ratio. A measure of the magnitude of the resources available to pay the interest and principal associated with debt that is backed by pledged revenues. It is calculated by dividing pledged revenues (or pledged revenues net of certain operating expenses) by the total amount of interest expenses and principal repayments.

Current assets. A group of line items on the statement of net position that are either cash already or which can be converted into cash, sold, or consumed within one year.

Current liability. An obligation that is expected to be settled with current assets or by the creation of new current liabilities.

D

Deferred inflow of resources. The acquisition of net assets that applies to a future reporting period.

Deferred outflow of resources. The consumption of net assets that applies to a future reporting period.

Direct debt. A government's outstanding long-term debt instruments, such as bonds, loans, and notes.

Direct rate. The amount applied to a unit of a revenue base.

Discrete presentation. The use of separate columns and rows in the government-wide statements to provide an overview of component unit financial data.

E

Effective tax rate. The average rate that is calculated by dividing either total revenue or total collections by the total revenue base for a reporting period.

Exchange transaction. When there is a reciprocal transfer between two parties that results in one of them acquiring assets or services or settling obligations by surrendering other assets or services or incurring other obligations.

Encumbrance. A commitment related to an unperformed contract for goods or services.

Executive budget. The budget submitted by the executive branch to the legislature.

Exit price. The price the seller of an asset would receive or the price the holder of a liability would pay in order to settle an obligation.

Expected usable landfill area. The area within a landfill that is expected to receive solid waste during the operating life of a landfill.

Expenditure. A decrease in net financial resources.

Extraordinary item. An event that is unusual in nature and infrequent in occurrence.

F

Fair value. The price that a government would receive if it were to sell an asset, or the amount it would pay to settle an obligation in an orderly transaction between market participants at the measurement date.

Final budget. The original budget after it has been adjusted for all reserves, transfers, allocations, supplemental appropriations, and other authorized legislative and executive changes.

Final cover. A multi-layered system of materials that is used to reduce the amount of storm water that will enter a landfill after closing.

Financial accountability. A condition that exists when a primary government appoints a voting majority of an entity's governing board and can impose its will on the entity, or the entity can provide financial benefits to the primary government or impose financial burdens on it.

Financial reporting entity. A primary government and those organizations for which the primary government is financially accountable.

Fixed budget. A budget that contains fixed dollar amounts for all stated line items.

Flexible budget. A budget that contains formulas that will alter the stated amount of a line item, depending on the related activity level.

Flows statement. Refers to the government-wide statement of activities and the proprietary fund statement of revenues, expenses, and changes in fund net position.

Fund. An accounting entity with a self-balancing set of accounts that are used to record financial resources and liabilities, which are segregated in order to carry on certain activities or attain targeted objectives.

G

GAAP. Generally accepted accounting principles.

H

Highest and best use. That use of a nonfinancial asset that would maximize the value of the asset.

I

Infrastructure asset. A stationary asset that typically has a substantially longer useful life than most types of capital assets.

Intangible asset. A capital asset that has no physical substance.

L

Leachate. The liquid that drains from a landfill.

Legal level of control. The lowest budgetary level at which management is not allowed to reassign resources without first gaining legislative approval.

Long-term obligation. An obligation that is expected to mature more than one year from the date of the current financial statements.

M

Management's discussion and analysis. A key part of the comprehensive annual financial report, which is used to provide an analysis of a government's financial activities.

Market participants. The parties engaged in a transaction, who are located in the most advantageous market for the asset or liability being sold or settled (respectively), and where the parties are independent of each other, are knowledgeable, and are willing and able to enter into a transaction.

Measurement date. The date on which the fair value of an asset or liability is determined.

Modified approach. A method for avoiding depreciation for certain types of infrastructure assets.

Modified accrual basis. The accrual basis of accounting as modified for governmental accounting.

Most advantageous market. That market in which a government would maximize the amount to be received from the sale of an asset, or which would minimize the amount paid to settle a liability, after factoring in transaction and transportation costs.

N

Net cost. The total expenses of a function or program, minus related revenues.

Net position. The difference between a government's assets and deferred outflows of resources, and its liabilities and deferred inflows of resources.

Network of assets. Those assets providing a type of service for a government, such as a power plant and transmission lines.

Non-appropriated budget. A budget that is not subject to appropriation, since it is authorized by a constitution, charter, or statute.

Glossary

Nonexchange transaction. When an entity gives value without receiving an equal value in exchange, or the reverse occurs.

O

Observable input. Fair value pricing that is developed using market data, such as publicly available market information about actual transactions.

Orderly transaction. A transaction that has had a sufficient amount of time for normal marketing activities to be completed.

Original budget. The first complete appropriated budget.

Overlapping debt. The outstanding long-term debt instruments of governments that overlap geographically with the territory of the government preparing statistical section information.

Overlapping rate. The amount applied to a unit of a revenue base by governments that overlap, in part or in full, with the entity preparing the statistical section information.

Own-source revenues. Those revenues generated by a government itself, such as by levying taxes or charging fees.

P

Pass-through grant. A grant that is to be sent to or spent on behalf of another party.

Principal market. That market having the greatest transaction volume for an asset or liability.

Primary government. A government with a separately-elected governing body, which is legally separate and fiscally independent of other governments.

Purpose restriction. A specification of the purposes for which resources are to be used.

R

Related organization. An entity for which a primary government is accountable due to the primary government's ability to appoint a majority of its board, but for which it is not financially accountable.

Reporting entity. The primary government and any organizations for which the primary government is financially accountable.

Resources. An item that can be drawn down to provide services to citizens.

S

Segment. An identifiable activity that is reported within an enterprise fund or similar entity that has one or more bonds or similar debt instruments outstanding, where some portion of its revenue stream is pledged to support repayment of the debt.

Service utility. The usable capacity that a capital asset was expected to provide when it was acquired.

Short-term obligation. An obligation that is expected to mature within one year of the date of the current financial statements.

Special item. An event that is within the control of management and is either unusual in nature or infrequent in occurrence.

Spendable form. A condition that exists when there is no expectation that an asset will be converted into cash.

Stabilization arrangement. When a government sets aside funds for use in emergency situations, or when there are budgetary imbalances.

Statement of activities. A financial statement that is structured to report the net expense or revenue associated with a government's individual functions.

Statement of financial position. A financial statement that is structured to report all assets, deferred outflows of resources, liabilities, deferred inflows of resources, and net position of the reporting entity.

Subsequent event. An event that occurs after the date of the financial statements (meaning the date of the statement of net position or similar report), but before the statements are issued.

Subsystem. The sum total of all assets that, as a group, make up a portion of a network.

T

Time requirement. A specification of when resources can be used or when usage may begin.

Total direct rate. The weighted average of every individual direct rate applied by a government.

Transaction costs. Those costs that are directly attributable to the sale of an asset or settlement of a liability, result directly from the transaction, and would not have been incurred in the absence of the transaction.

U

Unobservable input. Fair value pricing that is developed using the best information available in the absence of market data.

Useful life. The estimated lifespan of a capital asset.

Index

Made in the USA
Middletown, DE
21 October 2017